NOTES FOR COMMANDING OFFICERS

Issued to
STUDENTS AT THE SENIOR
OFFICERS' SCHOOL,
ALDERSHOT, 1918.

The Naval & Military Press Ltd

Published by

The Naval & Military Press Ltd
Unit 5 Riverside, Brambleside
Bellbrook Industrial Estate
Uckfield, East Sussex
TN22 1QQ England

Tel: +44 (0)1825 749494

www.naval-military-press.com
www.nmarchive.com

*In reprinting in facsimile from the original, any imperfections are inevitably reproduced
and the quality may fall short of modern type and cartographic standards.*

CONTENTS

	PAGE
CHAPTER I—THE TRAINING AND EMPLOYMENT OF PLATOONS, 1918	1
CHAPTER II—THEORY, DEMONSTRATION, AND PRACTICE SYSTEM OF TRAINING ADVOCATED AT THE SENIOR OFFICERS' SCHOOL	35
CHAPTER III—	
Part I—Training Programmes	46
,, II—Programme of Training and Recreation	49
CHAPTER IV—NOTES, PROGRAMMES, ETC., FOR TRAINING OF SCOUTS, PATROLS, AND SNIPERS	58
Part I—Duties and Uses of Scouts	58
,, II—(a)–Scheme for Training Scouts	59
,, III—(b)–Scheme for Training Patrols	62
,, IV—(c)–Scheme for Training Snipers	65
,, V—Organization	68
,, VI—Practices and Games	71
CHAPTER V—MUSKETRY—	
Part I—Lecture by Lieut.-Colonel R. M. LUCKOCK, D.S.O., on The Use of the Rifle	75
,, II—Lecture by Lieutenant J. YOUNG, on Musketry Training in France	83
CHAPTER VI—	
Part I—Drill	104
,, II—Games	164

CONTENTS

	PAGE
Chapter VII—The Attack in the Open	174
Part I—The "Flagged Attack"	174
" II—The "Ground Attack"	176
" III—The Attack in the Open	177
Chapter VIII—Marches—	
Part I—Notes on Marches and March Discipline	190
" II—A March Discipline Demonstration	195
Chapter IX—	
Part I—Outposts	202
" II—Advanced Guards	207
" III—Notes on Reconnaissance	211
" IV—Notes on Raids	214
Chapter X—Orders and Messages	217
Chapter XI—Tactical Exercises	232
Chapter XII—Miscellaneous Exercises	245
Part I—Peace March	247
" II—March to Trench and Reconnaissance	252
" III—Duties to be Undertaken when about to Come out of the Trenches	283
Chapter XIII—Field Engineering	
Part I—Introduction	294
" II—Précis of Lecture on Consolidation	311
" III—Working Parties	322
" IV—Compass Notes	324
Chapter XIV—	
Part I—Lecture by Lieut.-Colonel T. G. Dalby, D.S.O., on Battalion Organization	334
" II—Interior Economy and Administration	345
" III—Lecture by Lieutenant H. Naylor on the Duties of a Quartermaster	375
Chapter XV—Lecture by Major-General C. H. Harrington, C.B., D.S.O., on the Relations of the Staff to Commanding Officers, etc.	387

NOTES FOR COMMANDING OFFICERS.

The information contained in this book is simply a collection of some of the circulars which were issued from time to time at the Senior Officers' School, Aldershot.

It was brought to notice that this collection of typewritten circulars had become very bulky, and that it would be a great convenience if certain selected circulars might be re-issued in pamphlet form.

Accordingly, under the direction of Brigadier-General R. J. Kentish, D.S.O., the first Commandant of the School, this book was printed for the use of Officers who attended the Course. It is a " private " publication, and is issued only to subscribers.

Since its first publication various official pamphlets have been issued by the General Staff. This has necessitated certain amendments in the book, and the opportunity has been taken to revise some of the papers and bring them up to date in the light of the most recent experiences of the war.

SENIOR OFFICERS' SCHOOL,
ALDERSHOT,

28th February, 1918.

CONTENTS

	PAGE
CHAPTER XVI—SOME OF THE THINGS THAT PLEASE AN INFANTRY BRIGADIER	398
CHAPTER XVII—PRÉCIS OF A LECTURE BY MAJOR P. O. L. JORDAN, R.E., ON TRANSPORT (HORSE-MASTERSHIP)	403
CHAPTER XVIII—	
Part I—The Methods of Dealing with Offences in a Battalion	413
" II—Field-General Courts-Martial in France	423
CHAPTER XIX—AN ADDRESS ON THE RÔLE AND THE RESPONSIBILITIES OF THE COMMANDING OFFICER IN A BATTALION MESS	443
MESS RULES FOR THE SENIOR OFFICERS' SCHOOL AND INSTRUCTORS' SCHOOL. ALDERSHOT	456

NOTES FOR COMMANDING OFFICERS.

CHAPTER I.

THE TRAINING AND EMPLOYMENT OF PLATOONS, 1918.

Organization.

1. THE BATTALION AND ITS COMPANIES.

1. In order to ensure the necessary degree of uniformity of training and tactical method throughout the Armies, there must be uniformity of organization in all battalions.

Before the battalion can fight with success it must be trained; before it can be trained it must be organized. There are three conditions essential for efficient organization:—

(i) Suitability for the battlefield.

(ii) Elasticity, to enable the battalion to suffer casualties, absorb drafts, and provide for extra regimental employ without its machinery being thrown out of gear.

(iii) Economy of man power, to ensure that no man is employed on any Headquarters or on administrative duties except on services which are essential to the efficiency of the fighting machine.

2. **Battalion.**

The Battalion will consist of—
  (i) Battalion Headquarters;
  (ii) Four Companies, consisting of four platoons of four sections each. (*See* Section 2, para. 1.)

3. **Battalion Headquarters.**

In addition to the personnel shown in War Establishments as forming part of the Battalion Headquarters certain other personnel will be attached. This personnel, which is principally employed on administrative duties, will be temporarily detached from Companies whilst so employed, but will remain on the establishment of the Company for accounting purposes. A Headquarters Company as such will not be formed.

The personnel composing the Battalion Headquarters can conveniently be divided into two categories, namely, the fighting portion and the administrative portion. (*See* table in Appendix I, columns *a* and *b*.)

4. *Companies.*

Each Company will consist of—
  (*a*) Company Headquarters, and
  (*b*) Four Platoons.

Company Headquarters will be composed entirely of fighting troops. (*See* table in Appendix I, column *c*.)

5. *Platoons.*

The organization of a platoon is given in Section 2, and is designed to create a fighting unit composed solely of fighting ranks and distinct from the necessary administrative establishment.

6. The essence of this organization is—
  (*a*) That the platoon should constitute a unit for fighting and training, and should contain all the weapons with which the infantry is now armed.

(b) That men trained in such special duties, such as signallers, Lewis gunners, etc., should all be with their platoons and companies, except such as may be required at Battalion and Company Headquarters either for the purposes of fighting or for instructional duties.

(c) That every portion of the battalion, including the fighting portion of Battalion Headquarters and Company Headquarters, should consist of a certan number of definite units.

(d) That the rifle and bayonet is the principal weapon of every soldier, and the bomb an auxiliary in which every soldier is trained for use in special circumstances; and that 50 per cent. of men are trained in the rifle bomb, and 50 per cent. in the Lewis gun.

(e) That every man is available for working and carrying parties, irrespective of the weapon with which he is armed.

(f) That sixteen Lewis gun sections are maintained within the battalion. Normally, there will be one Lewis gun section in each platoon, but it may often be advisable in dealing with particular tactical situations to allot a second Lewis gun to a platoon, or to withdraw temporarily one, two, or more of these guns from platoons for special tactical employment under the orders of Company or Battalion Commanders. The normal organization is not to interfere with any such temporary special grouping or employment as circumstances may render desirable.

2. THE PLATOON AND ITS SECTIONS.

1. Before a Platoon Commander can command and train his platoon, he must understand thoroughly the numbers and principles upon which its organization is based.

A platoon is the smallest unit which comprises all the weapons with which the infantry soldier is armed—namely, rifle and bayonet, Lewis gun, rifle bomb, and bomb. It normally consists of four sections of one N.C.O. and five to nine other ranks, and a Headquarters of one Officer and three other ranks. Exclusive of its Headquarters, therefore, its minimum strength is twenty-four other ranks, and its maximum forty.

If a section falls below six or a platoon (exclusive of its Headquarters) below twenty-four, it ceases to be an effective and self-reliant fighting unit; amalgamation, however, lowers the *esprit de corps* of sections and platoons, and every effort should be made to avoid it. In all training previous to operations, sections and platoons should be kept as such ready to receive reinforcements. Where, however, it is obvious that they will not be brought up to establishment before operations, amalgamation must be resorted to as a *temporary* measure. But even in amalgamation the identity of sections and platoons should be preserved, as far as possible; amalgamation should not mean abolition.

Platoon Headquarters consists of the Platoon Commander, the Platoon Sergeant, who is the second in command, one runner, and one batman, who may also be used as a second runner.

2. In every platoon there will be three rifle sections and one Lewis gun section, each having as their minimum strength one N.C.O. and five other ranks, and as their maximum one N.C.O. and nine other ranks. Less than five men cannot be worked together efficiently as a section and more than nine men cannot be controlled efficiently in the conditions of modern battle by a junior N.C.O.

Except Nos. 1 and 2 of the Lewis gun section, every N.C.O. and man in the platoon is first and foremost a rifleman. All men are trained also in the use of the bomb, and at least 50 per cent. in the use of the rifle bomb. If opportunity allows, it is desirable that one of the rifle sections should be trained also to act as a bombing team.

Each section is responsible for its own local protection, and should include two men trained to act as scouts.

The Spirit of the Platoon.

3. THE OBJECT AND MEANING OF DISCIPLINE.

1. All Commanders are responsible for leading and training their commands. They must therefore never forgo their functions of guidance and control. At the same time, the development of initiative in subordinates is of vital importance. Initiative is the power shown by the soldier of whatever rank of acting with decision on his own responsibility in the face of an emergency, and true discipline should aim at the development and not the repression of the intelligence of the individual. Criticism of a fault-finding or discouraging nature tends to create an unwillingness to face responsibility, while criticism which is kindly and constructive is a sure means of developing initiative in subordinates. It is therefore the duty of Platoon Commanders to do all in their power to foster the spirit of initiative by encouraging and teaching those under them to act on their own responsibility at times when superior guidance is not at hand.

2. The first essential in a soldier is the fighting spirit, controlled by discipline. Discipline increases the self-respect of the individual, and is shown by a smart and soldierly-bearing, scrupulous cleanliness, good saluting, punctilious care of arms, and the habit of unhesitating obedience to command. Discipline confers on troops the power of rapid, corporate action and of movement in formed bodies of great strength without loss of cohesion, even in difficult country and under heavy fire.

3. One of the methods by which the soldier acquires discipline is close order drill. Discipline is inculcated by drill, and good drill is, itself, an example of the spirit of discipline. Only those troops drill really well

who not only feel the grip of discipline, but are proud to exhibit it. This is exemplified in every motion, for instance, of drill with arms. A party of men who are learning arms drill may be said roughly to pass through three stages of discipline :—

(i) In the first stage, the recruit who receives the command to slope his arms thinks only of his own rifle and himself. Every soldier in the squad obeys the command individually as best he can. The action of the squad is not a disciplined movement, because it is carried out by the individual soldiers in the squad as individuals in their own way and not by the squad in one way as one man.

(ii) In the second stage, as discipline develops, every soldier tries to obey the command as smartly as he can, but each is afraid that his comrades will be smarter than himself. The result is a smarter and more uniform movement than in the previous stage; but there is competition between the soldiers of the squad instead of mutual confidence, and an air of hurry in the movement as a whole.

(iii) The third and final stage is reached only when discipline is fully developed and every soldier obeys the command without anxiety or haste, because he knows that his comrades will obey it and time it exactly as he does himself. The result is a rapid and precise but unhurried movement, with deliberate pauses between each stage, which conveys the strongest possible impression of trained and controlled collective power. The emulation is now between units, no longer between individuals.

Drill at this stage is a perfect embodiment of all the qualities of soldierly discipline—prompt and methodical obedience, skill at arms, confidence in comrades, and pride in the unit to which the soldier belongs. It is the basis of all sound training for battle, and the surest method of drawing men together and giving them confidence in each other and themselves. Its steadying power in action has been proved in military history again and again.

4. Every Platoon Commander will therefore aim at bringing his platoon up to this standard of drill, and will see that through his Section Commanders the whole platoon understands the meaning of the standard which he has set. The method is to drill regularly for short periods every day, and to make the drill intelligible by having its purpose understood. During drill the men should not be kept at attention for more than ten minutes at a time. After every ten minutes there should be a pause of two or three minutes, during which the men are ordered to stand easy; no parade should continue for more than an hour without an interval in which the men are allowed to break away, or in which recreational games are played—and a shorter period than an hour is advisable. To drill men for long periods without rest is scarcely better than to do no drill at all. On the other hand, a platoon which cannot drill lacks the first essential of disciplined fighting power.

4. THE ORGANIZATION OF COMMAND.

1. Though discipline is the first essential of fighting power, even the best disciplined men are ineffective in war without organized command. An Army is therefore controlled by a carefully established chain of command, which begins, in the case of infantry, with the section, and is carried up thence by a regular series of links to the Commander-in-Chief. The section is the unit of command, because experience has proved it to be the largest party of men which can be directly controlled in action by one leader. Every other commander must learn to command through his subordinate commanders—the Platoon Commander through his Section Commanders, the Company Commander through his Platoon Commanders, and so on.

2. For the Platoon Commander two important consequences follow from this fact :—

  (i) He must realize that on the battlefield everything will depend upon the previous training of himself and of his Section Commanders and sections, because in many critical periods orders cannot be conveyed from the company or the platoon, and sections must therefore be able to keep together, maintain direction, and fight on their own initiative.
  (ii) He must learn to train and command his men through his N.C.Os., because N.C.Os. will never be able to lead their sections in action unless they are made to feel their responsibility at all times and trained to exercise command.

5. THE SPIRIT OF THE SECTION.

1. It is by fostering the spirit of the section that the spirit of the platoon can best be cultivated, and upon this spirit depends the efficiency of the platoon as a fighting unit. Every effort must be made to give men a pride and confidence in themselves, both as sections and as platoons : in this lies the foundation of the unity of companies and battalions and of that wider, greater pride in the regiment which was so powerful an inspiration to the old **Regular Army.**

It is inevitable that sections should undergo constant changes, and the spirit of the section cannot be as binding a force as the spirit of the platoon, but much may be done to foster the spirit even of sections, if appeal is made to the genius for discipline and comradeship which is inherent in the British race. In all the national games men of British race submit with enthusiasm to training and discipline for the sake of the side; they have an inborn instinct which makes them naturally work for the side and play the game. The spirit is easily evoked in military training by keeping the men of sections together, so that all the men know their Section Commander and the Section Commander knows all his men.

A Platoon Commander is responsible for creating the spirit of his sections and linking them together into the spirit of the platoon, making it in a real sense *his* platoon. He should know not only the names but also the general character of every man in his platoon, and should see that every Section Commander knows the names of his men, and that the men know the name of their Section Commander.

2. Sections and platoons should never be broken up, or men shifted from one section or platoon to another, unless absolute necessity exists. (See Section 2, para. 1.)

As a general principle, whatever men have to learn, they should learn as a section, the older soldiers helping the younger ones. Competitions between sections—in drill, in musketry, or in games—are easily arranged.

3. Sections will also be kept together in guards, in working parties, and in all other fatigues. The Company Sergeant-Major will keep his roster for duty by platoons, and the Platoon Sergeant a similar roster by sections. Section Commanders can then keep section rosters for themselves, and make up any inequalities as between their own men.

4. It is the Platoon Commander's duty to see that these things are done; but in all things that affect the men he must act through his N.C.Os. and endeavour to develop their power of initiative and make them realize their responsibilities.

6. THE TRAINING AND SELECTION OF N.C.Os.

1. Platoon Commanders should realize that the task of N.C.Os. in this war is particularly hard. The majority of N.C.Os. are of recent promotion from the rank and file. They have to learn to exert authority and exercise command while living entirely with their

men. It is essential, therefore, to support their authority, and to make them feel their responsibility, by every possible means.

2. At the same time a very definite responsibility rests upon both Platoon and Company Commanders to get the best men in their platoons and companies as N.C.Os. Officers must not only note men who have done well in action and bring their names forward for promotion; they must also note men who fail. There should be no hesitation either in recommending men who have proved themselves capable and courageous for command of sections, or in recommending men who have grown tired or shown themselves deficient in powers of command for removal from the commands they hold. The object to be kept steadily in view must be the efficiency of the section, platoon, and company. The test of efficiency must be the conduct of men in battle. Men's lives depend upon leadership.

3. The only method of training N.C.Os. to command is to make them actually command a party of men. A Section Commander will therefore be trained to take his section in close order drill and to develop a good word of command. The most important element, however, in the training of Section Commanders is extended order drill. This drill should be carried out by sections for short periods at least three times a week. No other system is so effective in teaching men to follow their Section Commander or in giving the Section Commander confidence in manœuvring his men.

4. In building up the authority of his N.C.Os. the Platoon Commander should bear in mind two things. Authority is rightly delegated only to those who use it well; and an Officer must see that a Section Commander deals fairly with his men. It is his duty therefore to investigate carefully every charge made by a N.C.O. against a man, and every complaint made by a man against a N.C.O. On the other hand an Officer must never undermine a N.C.O.'s authority by appearing to support the men against him. No charge

against a N.C.O. will be investigated in the presence of the men; if a man's evidence is required, he will be ordered to give it and then to fall out. In the same way an Officer will never, if he can help it, find fault with a N.C.O. before his men; and if he has to do so, he will address the N.C.O. as one of whom an example is expected, so as not to lower his standing in the eyes of the rank and file.

5. It is, in fact, essential to give all N.C.Os. an *esprit de corps* as the atmosphere of non-commissioned rank. Platoon Sergeants will therefore be made to see that off duty the N.C.Os. keep company together, and do not, except for special reason, keep company with the men. Platoon Sergeants are also responsible for seeing that when a private soldier addresses a N.C.O. he addresses him by his rank as "Sergeant" or "Corporal."

6. When training, Platoon Commanders should hold a conference with their N.C.Os. every evening on the work of the following day. Past work should be discussed, and the Section Commander should be made to feel that he is responsible for any failure on the part of his men. N.C.Os. should be encouraged to ask questions, and all Section Commanders should afterwards hold a conference with their men.

7. Finally, in order to keep up the supply of N.C.Os., Section Commanders will be made in every section to train an understudy, who, after a period of probation, will be given lance-rank. A Platoon Commander will see that this is really being done by falling out the Section Commander during training from time to time and ordering him to watch and criticise his section while the understudy carries on.

7. THE FIGHTING SPIRIT.

1. If the platoon is trained on the principles outlined in the preceding sections, it will have gained the

surest foundations for the development of the fighting spirit, which is the bedrock of success in war. All ranks will have learnt to have pride in themselves and confidence in their leaders. They must be trained also to have confidence in their weapons. They must be made to feel themselves, individually and collectively, better men than the enemy. The use of the rifle must become an instinct, and the aim and object of all ranks must be to come to close quarters with the enemy as quickly as possible.

Every Platoon Commander must realise that the repeated act of putting his platoon over the bayonet-fighting course, if carried out with energy, determination, and individual effort, has the direct effect of raising the fighting spirit of his command. In the Infantry the culminating point of all training is the assault. All musketry and bayonet practices, therefore, should be made as realistic as possible, and the spirit of competition should be introduced, so that the sporting instinct is aroused and every man stimulated to do his best for the honour of his section and platoon and, above all, his regiment. Practices must be made intelligible and interesting, and monotony avoided; men should be encouraged, and not driven.

2. Too much attention cannot be paid to the part played by games in fostering the fighting spirit. They afford the Platoon Commander an unrivalled opportunity, not only of teaching his men to play for their side and work together in the spirit of self-sacrifice, but of gaining an insight into their characters. He should not only personally and actively arrange for games and competitions for his men, but take part in them himself. If he induces his platoon to be determined to produce the best foolball team in the battalion, he will have done a great deal to make it the best platoon in every way.

8. ORDERS.

1. It is sometimes necessary for Commanders to give orders which put an almost intolerable strain upon

their troops. What tells most at such moments is confidence, bred by previous experience, that no order is given inconsiderately or without sufficient cause. It is a Platoon Commander's duty to establish this confidence in his N.C.Os. and men, and he will best do so by always bearing four rules in mind :—

    (i) He will think all orders out before he gives them in the ordinary routine of trench or billet life, and he will always make an exact picture in his mind of what the soldier or party executing them will have to do.

    (ii) He will make all orders absolutely clear, and he will let those who receive them know enough about their reason to carry them out with intelligence.

    (iii) He will make sure, before they are carried out, that they are properly understood.

    (iv) He will see that his N.C.Os. also are careful and considerate in the orders which they give.

The failure of subordinates is not seldom due to the looseness or inadequacy of orders received from their superiors; and it is a common fault in inexperienced N.C.Os. to blame their men for failing to understand an order which was not clearly or not correctly given. This reacts most seriously upon the discipline and spirit of troops, and it is the Platoon Commander's duty to guard against such failings constantly in training both his N.C.Os. and himself. If he bears in mind the four rules laid down above, he will find that confidence is soon established and that even a very exacting order is cheerfully obeyed.

9. THE LINE OF MARCH.

1. The object of march discipline is two-fold. It is essential, in the first place, in order to save fatigue and maintain *moral* in troops. The longer and more exhausting a march, the more important it is to keep fours closed up and in step, to prevent falling out and straggling, and to observe the proper distances and

halts. The observance of halts from ten minutes to every hour until the hour should be regarded as an invariable rule, even when a unit marches off at quarter to the hour, and must therefore halt at the end of fire minutes' marching, or when the halt comes due within a few minutes of the unit's destination. All marches are timed to include the clock-hour halts; and if any unit fails to observe them, it may interfere seriously with the distances and halts of other units in rear or in front upon the same line of march. March discipline, in the second place, is the necessary basis of calculation regarding the road space occupied and the time taken by troops upon the march. During big movements of troops, careless marching by one unit may cause blocks upon the road and other delays, which not only inflict needless fatigue on other troops, but may also prejudice operations at the front. It is, therefore, of the first importance that all Commanders should observe punctiliously both the standard rules of march discipline and also any special orders which local traffic may necessitate. The most essential of these, wherever there is heavy movement on the roads, is to keep well to the right, to observe the distances laid down, and to halt clear of cross roads. Every Officer on the march with a party of men will remember that he is only one element in a very complex organization, some part of which will inevitably suffer for the carelessness or bad discipline of another part.

2. Whenever possible, an Officer will reconnoitre his route in advance in order to ensure against mistakes and to save needless fatigue to his men. A Company Commander, being mounted, can do this upon the line of march. A Platoon Commander also can sometimes avert mistakes and delay by using the clock-hour halt in cases of uncertainty to go ahead of his men. Where personal reconnaissance is not possible, an Officer will endeavour to secure by other means the most precise information available about his route before he marches off. To march off in any uncertainty which it might have been possible to remove is to fail in duty both to his superior Officer and to his men.

3. Finally, on arrival at his destination, an Officer will always report the fact, and also the location of his Headquarters to the senior Officer available either of his own unit or, when detached, of the unit to which he has been detached. Small parties on the march are often exposed to needless fatigue and even to loss of rations because their Officers fail to report arrival at the end of their day's march, with the result that orders which should reach them at once either do not reach them at all or only reach them after long delay.

10. TRAINING THE PLATOON.

1. Training for action and leadership in action are dealt with in Chapter III and in the training and tactical instructions issued. Platoon Commanders should not only study these themselves, but should also communicate the fruits of their study to their N.C.Os., who in turn must instruct the men. The more intelligently training is carried out the greater will be the keenness and efficiency of both N.C.Os. and men.

2. In training for action there are two principles of paramount importance which every Platoon Commander should bear constantly in mind :—

    (i) The organization of the platoon must be constantly and scrupulously maintained in training, so that it may stand the shock and confusion of battle.

        Fire-effect, for instance, depends less upon individual marksmanship than upon fire direction and fire control. Unless men are made familiar with fire direction and fire control by sections when they train, the maximum fire-effect of their sections will never be developed in the excitement of battle.

    (ii) All ranks must be trained to re-organize on the first opportunity, when, as must sometimes happen, the organization of the platoon is broken up by casualties and the other accidents of battle.

A Platoon Commander is responsible that no party of his men is ever left without organized command; and he must train his N.C.Os. always to re-organize with the men nearest to them, whenever the organization of sections is broken up.

The necessity for organization and re-organization should therefore be ever present in every Platoon Commander's mind. No power of leadership in battle will compensate for neglect of these two principles in the daily life and training of the platoon.

3. The fighting efficiency of the platoon in action will depend almost entirely upon the quality of its training out of the line. The object of this training must therefore be to establish certain forms of action as a habit, the force of which will dominate N.C.Os. and men even in the stress of the hardest fight. This object is the aim of all military training simply because habit alone can give men in the mass an instinctive capacity for the right forms of combined action in whatever emergency they may be placed. The effective use of the rifle by the individual, the efficient control of fire by the Section Commander, the capacity for rapid re-organization in the unit, will all depend in action upon the force of habits formed by training in the ordinary daily life of the platoon. Commanders who do not understand this fact will fail in action, however well they may act themselves, because they have neglected to construct the essential framework of leadership while training their men.

11. THE CARE OF MEN.

Platoon Commanders are responsible for the fitness and sound equipment of their men. They should watch both constantly, working through the Section Commanders, and making the Section Commander responsible if a man in his section is deficient of anything he should possess. They should also see that their men get all possible rest, food and sleep both before and in the course of an action. The fitness of a reserve when called upon will often depend on whether or not the Platoon Commander has nursed and rested his men during the pauses in the approach march and at any other available time. He should think of himself in this connection as a trainer bringing a team on to the field for a decisive match, and make sure, as a good trainer does, that all the men under him are, so far as he can answer for it, at their best. The cause for which he is training, and the lives of the men he commands, will depend in no small degree upon the soldierly care which he bestows upon the clothing and equipment and the feeding and physical well-being of his platoon at all times and in all circumstances.

Tactics.

12. CHARACTERISTICS OF WEAPONS AND USE OF GROUND.

1. All infantry weapons are contained in the platoon, and in each section enough ammunition and bombs can be carried for immediate requirements. The equipment of the sections for battle will be decided by the Commanding Officer according to circumstances.

2. The following is given as a guide :—(i) In a trench-to-trench attack every man should carry 170 rounds of S.A.A., except signallers, scouts, runners, Lewis gunners, and carrying parties, who will only carry fifty rounds; the number of bombs and rifle bombs to be carried will be determined by the task to be carried out, the condition of the ground, and the general physique of the individual man. Flares must be distributed throughout sections.

The Lewis gun section carries a supply of magazines for the gun; for this purpose two forms of carrier are issued, namely, three sets of pouch equipment (holding four to eight magazines each) and canvas "collar-box" carriers for the remainder. Thirty magazines is the maximum likely to be required immediately with the gun in any operation, and for rapid movement or long distances this number must be reduced, if they are all to be carried by the section. Additional ammunition for refilling can be carried in bandoliers, if required.

Where a section is used as a bombing team, the bayonet men, throwers and leader, should carry seven bombs, and the carriers up to 14; where a section is used as a rifle bombing team, each man should carry seven rifle bombs, including a proportion of smoke bombs.

Any further requirements in S.A.A., bombs, etc., will be met by carrying parties from other platoons or companies specially detailed.

(ii) In open fighting it may be taken as a general guide that 170 rounds S.A.A. on every man, except the Nos. 1 and 2 of the Lewis gun, will usually be sufficient for all purposes; the number of rifle bombs and bombs carried will depend entirely on the nature of the objectives to be attacked.

Two 1-inch Véry light pistols should normally be carried with each Company Headquarters for signalling to the Artillery. It may, however, often be convenient to have one at least of these forward, for example, with a Lewis gun section.

3. (i) The rifle and bayonet is the weapon upon which every soldier must learn to rely both for attack and defence. Confidence in the bayonet carries men to the assault; confidence in the bullet beats off the counter-attack. These two are not separate, but one. The bullet supports the bayonet by covering fire; the bayonet completes what the bullet begins. This principle of the combined use of the rifle, namely, that the advance of any body of troops to the assault is covered by the fire of another body, lies at the root of all infantry tactics, and is known briefly as "fire covering movement." It applies also to the use of rifle bombs and light mortars as well as to rifle fire, machine gun and Lewis gun fire, and is, in addition, the basis of artillery support.

(ii) The bomb is the auxiliary in which every N.C.O. and man is trained, for use in killing or dislodging the enemy from behind cover or underground, and driving him into the open where the rifle, Lewis gun and machine gun can satisfactorily deal with him. The bomb is in no way a substitute for the rifle; its revival is the result of trench warfare, and the more open the warfare becomes, the fewer opportunities will occur for its useful employment. It would then find its chief value in clearing out cellars in village fighting or at close quarters in an attack upon a fortified point.

(iii) The rifle bomb may be regarded as the "howitzer" of the platoon, and is used to support the attack by dislodging the enemy from behind cover or by forcing him underground, and so enabling the attacking troops to establish superiority of fire and get to close quarters. Concentrations of rifle bombs can be used to put out of action machine guns or other points of resistance, or smoke bombs may be used for blinding them.

(iv) The Lewis gun provides a concentrated and intensified form of rifle fire, and supplies covering, enfilade and sweeping fire, both in attack and in defence. It is the weapon of opportunity; with its mobility and the small target it and its team present, it is peculiarly suited for working round an enemy's flank in attack or for guarding a flank in defence. Its power of applying heavy fire in any direction at a moment's notice makes it specially valuable in covering movement in attack, and enables men to be economized in defence, and with its small personnel it can be used to reinforce a firing line in cases where it is impossible to get forward an equivalent number of rifles.

4. Every Platoon Commander must understand thoroughly—

    (i) The characteristics of the platoon weapons and the principles of their employment.

    (ii) The use of ground.

These two subjects are interdependent, and until they have been individually mastered and their relation to one another appreciated, the Platoon Commander is not in a position to employ his command to the best advantage in battle.

The use of ground and the choice of cover in both trench and open warfare is of the utmost importance. If skilfully taken advantage of, a platoon can frequently be moved forward to the attack without loss, or so disposed in defence as to establish surprise and inflict heavy losses on the enemy. In the choice of cover, as a general rule, anything marked on a map or very well defined, such as a road or line of trees, should, if possible, be avoided, so as to obviate casualties from shell-fire.

5. The Platoon Commander should practise himself in the quick selection of fire positions, concealed as far as the nature of the ground allows, mutually supporting one another by their fire, and arranged to suit the strength and disposition of his sections. He should avoid committing himself and his command to positions without having first sent scouts forward to make good the intervening ground, and he should advance as far as possible direct from one fire position to another: that is to say, he should " reconnoitre before movement " and " advance by bounds."

13. PRINCIPLES OF ATTACK.

1. The platoon is the unit in battle, but, except in minor enterprises, such as raids, it is only one unit of many, and even in minor enterprises it will almost invariably be supported and its flanks protected by other units. The same principles of mutual support and co-operation which apply to sections apply also to platoons, companies, and battalions. The frontage of a battalion will range from 200 yards in an attack against a highly organized position to 600 yards or more against one less highly organized; and the covering fire of rifles, Lewis guns and rifle bombs, if limited solely to the support of their own platoon, will be used only within limits of, on an average, 100 yards. A Platoon Commander must be constantly alive, therefore, to the necessity of assisting other units by covering

fire, and must look to them for similar co-operation. It will often be possible for one platoon to provide flanking or enfilade fire in support of another, which will be more effective than any fire which the supported platoon could of itself bring to bear on the particular point of resistance. Enfilade fire, especially of Lewis guns, is the most annihilating form of fire, because the cone of the bullets sweeps along, rather than merely across, the target, and it can often only be secured by co-operation.

2. The conditions of a modern battle are so varied that it is only possible to lay down the principles on which the various formations successfully adopted in the past are based. Commanders should study these principles, and apply them to each particular case.

3. The task allotted to infantry in the attack is—
   (i) To capture a final objective;
   (ii) Completely to clear the enemy from the area between the position of assembly and final objective;
   (iii) To occupy the captured ground in such a manner that hostile counter-attacks will be successfully met or a further advance can be made.

An infantry battalion should therefore on the completion of its task be disposed in depth.

The battalion will normally be called upon to fulfil all three of the above tasks, and its dispositions will need to be made accordingly; it will require to be divided into assaulting troops, troops in close support, and troops in reserve. Similarly, the company, which may be called upon to fulfil more than one of the above tasks, will require to be disposed in depth so that a reserve is retained in the hand of the Company Commander.

The platoon, which is, as has been said in para. 1, the unit in battle, will be given any *one* of the above tasks. Whichever of these is allotted to it, the formation adopted will be governed primarily by the conditions of ground and fire; that is to say, the aim will be to adopt such a formation as shall provide the greatest amount of immunity from shell-fire, while enabling the platoon to bring fire to bear or to deploy for assault with the least possible delay. Two formations for a platoon advancing to attack are suggested in Plates IA and IB (see S.S. 143, official publication), but it cannot be too strongly emphasized that the responsibility for adopting formations suitable to the circumstances of the particular attack rests upon local commanders.

4. There are two systems by which the attack may be carried out :—

    (i) The leading troops going straight to the furthest objective, rear troops following them to nearer objectives in succession—that is, the " straight-through " system.

    (ii) The leading troops being given the near objective, and the rear troops passing through them to the further objective—that is, the " leap-frog " system.

Of these two, " leap-frogging " is the system which has been almost universally adopted during recent operations with limited objectives.

5. In the earlier attacks, in 1916 and 1917, on highly-organized lines of trenches, parties were specially detailed to follow the second line of a wave, and clear out dug-outs, snipers, etc., who had been passed over; they preceded the unit for which, in the phrase hitherto used, they " mopped up." But in the type of fighting now adopted by the enemy, when lines of trenches have changed more and more to shell-hole defences, arranged in depth chequerwise, it is necessary to clear whole areas rather than definite trenches and fortified positions. Ground can only be considered " held " when the whole area behind it has been entirely cleared of the enemy; and Commanders of every unit are responsible for seeing that their arrangements are suited to this end, according to the actual circumstances. The essential point is to give every unit in the attack, down to sections, a definite objective and task, and to ensure that every part of the

objective, including all known intermediate points of resistance, has a definite party detailed to deal with it. How these parties are best assembled and formed up must depend entirely upon the conditions of assembly, the nature of the objectives, and the movement of the barrage. Every position should be organized for defence after capture.

6. In trench-to-trench attacks it cannot be too rigidly insisted on that the secret of a successful assault rests upon the assumption that the assaulting troops conform their movements exactly to the timing of the barrage. When a shrapnel barrage is employed, the shells should be bursting just above the heads of the assaulting troops. Platoon and Company Commanders are responsible that their Section Commanders and, through them, their men, are told all that is possible about the halts and lifts of the artillery programme, and have it impressed upon them that they must keep close up to the barrage, so as to deliver their assault before the enemy have had time to pull themselves together again, and to bring machine guns into play. The ground over which the attack is to be made must be studied from maps, aeroplane photographs, and direct observation from this point of view, as well as from every other.

7. More attacks fail from loss of direction than from any other cause. Every Platoon Commander must understand the vital necessity of practising himself and his Section Commanders in the use of the compass, selecting points, such as a tree or other conspicuous object on which to advance, and reconnoitring before movement whenever possible. In a trench-to-trench attack it is of special importance that every section should be formed up square to its objective. The Platoon Commander must satisfy himself that every possible assistance for forming up for the attack in the way of tapes or flags or discs has been put out, and that his Section Commanders understand, and have made their men understand, exactly what they have to do and how they are to advance.

8. In either trench or more open warfare the tactics of the platoon in attack resolve themselves in the majority of cases into the method of attack of tactical points. A tactical point may be described as a locality, the possession of which is of the first importance locally to either side. It may take the form of any of the following :—A " strong point," whether an organized group of shell-holes or a " pill-box," a piece of ground furnishing an advantageous fire position or good observation, a bank, a hedge, a house, or any locality of limited dimensions.

The tactics to be employed may be summarised as follows :—

    (i) Push on to the objective with the fixed determination of getting in with the bayonet as soon as possible.

   (ii) If held up, open covering fire to assist a movement to envelop one or both flanks; always move rapidly under covering fire, especially under the cover of fire from rifle bombers, whose stock of bombs is limited. If possible, use the Lewis gun section to open flanking fire as soon as the best way of employing it has been decided by reconnaissance; if it is impossible to move the Lewis gun to a flank, try to advance under frontal covering fire, and be ready to rush forward directly the neighbouring platoon assists with covering fire from a flank.

  (iii) If reinforcing a platoon which is held up, remember that this does not necessarily mean thickening up the platoon supported; assistance may often be more effectively given from a flank. It is *always* the duty of a Commander to make himself acquainted with the situation by personal reconnaissance before committing his platoon or company to any line of action.

  (iv) Co-operate and keep in touch with platoons on either flank, and be on the look-out to assist them with flanking fire across their front. Co-operation means help, and the means to be employed must be decided by the circumstances of the moment. More may often be accomplished by reinforcing a platoon which is not held up than by directly supporting one which is; the surest means of helping a neighbour in battle is to push on. Touch can be maintained by means of a patrol of two men, and also by the use of signals.

(v) In trench warfare go direct *above ground* to the objective; if the conditions necessitate the employment of men as bombers, remember that a bombing attack unaccompanied by an attack above ground is seldom of any value.

9. The above principles apply equally to semi-open and open warfare, but owing to the more extended field of action the use of scouts and the personal reconnaissance of the Platoon Commander becomes of even greater importance. Greater opportunities also will occur to give mutual support from rifle or Lewis gun fire to the movement of neighbouring sections or platoons; the employment of covering fire generally and the selection of and occupation of fire positions are the governing factors of successful tactics.

14. PRINCIPLES OF DEFENCE.

1. A principle which underlies all defensive tactics is that positions should be organized in depth, arranged chequerwise, so as to bring as much mutually supporting fire to bear as possible.

This organization should have for its object the maximum development of fire over all ground which may be crossed by an enemy in the course of his attack. The fire of rifles and Lewis guns, controlled by Section Commanders, has been proved again and again to be a decisive factor; wherever possible, Lewis guns should be sited in flanking positions from which they can develop their maximum fire effect on the deep, dense target then presented by an attacking enemy.

2. Organizing a position for defence, or, in the term frequently used, " consolidating " a position, does not *necessarily* imply digging. Though the digging of a trench usually is a means of securing both fire positions and protection, positions may be, and in open warfare often are, organized to resist attack in a very few minutes. The first essentials are the occupation of mutually supporting tactical points, screened as far as possible from artillery fire, and the creation of fire positions. When possible, the wiring of these should always precede digging, and the wire should be sited in accordance with the fields of fire—that is to say, it should never be put out haphazard in front of the positions occupied, but should run along lines selected with a view to checking the enemy where he can be caught by flanking fire or caused to bunch at some spot commanded by rifles or Lewis guns. Practice in the siting of wire with regard to the positions occupied and in putting it out rapidly will never be wasted.

3. The occupation of a forward defensive position does not in the first instance demand a continuous line; it may be necessary at a later stage to link up the positions to facilitate command and communication, but as long as the element of surprise is present, short lengths of fire position arranged according to the lie of the ground, each accommodating a section and supporting one another by cross and converging fire, will be less conspicuous, and therefore less exposed to shell fire, and more effective in breaking up the hostile attack. Behind the barrier presented by these the main line of resistance can then be organized.

4. The soul of defence lies in offence; passive resistance—that is, resistance by fire alone, may check, but it cannot overthrow the enemy. Commanders must be ready to take the initiative, both to use the bayonet, when necessary, and to restore the fight if any part of the position is overwhelmed. Every situation must as far as possible be foreseen and arrangements made in advance so that it may be met *immediately*.

The ground over which immediate counter-attacks will be made must be reconnoitred beforehand, and every Section Commander given clearly to understand the rôle which his section may be called upon to fulfil. The unexpected is the rule in war, but if every Commander realizes that he is directly responsible for making in advance detailed plans for every likely event the unexpected may be turned to advantage, and confusion, loss of time and consequent failure avoided. It is frequently possible to practise counter-attacks over the actual ground on which they may have to be delivered : where this can be done, it is the best security that every man will know exactly where to go and what to do. A local counter-attack to be successful must be delivered immediately after the enemy's capture of a position. If he is given time to organize it for defence, it will ordinarily be necessary to arrange for a methodical counter-attack at a later date.

5. Every Commander must not only guard his flanks and keep in touch with neighbouring units, but be ready either to co-operate in a counter-attack or to throw back a defensive flank in the event of a neighbouring unit being driven from its position. He will never withdraw from a position without being ordered to do so; by holding on he may enable the whole position to be restored.

6. The above principles apply to defence as much in open as in trench warfare, but in open warfare still greater importance attaches to the personal reconnaissance of the Commander, the work of reconnoitring patrols, and the selection and organization of fire positions.

7. In all warfare, both in the attack and in the defence, in open and in trench warfare, Commanders must study their system of communications and keep their immediate superiors and neighbouring Commanders fully and frequently informed of the situation ; they must not refrain from sending back word because they have nothing particular to report; this very fact may be of the first importance. No possible means of

keeping up communications should be neglected. Tactical exercises will be carried out by Company, Platoon, and Section Commanders, in which the importance of rendering reports as to their position and the tactical situation should be emphasized.

15. WORKING AND CARRYING PARTIES.

1. Working and carrying parties should be found by detailing by complete sections, platoons or companies, as may be necessary, under their own Commanders. They should never be found by detailing a given number of men, lacking in cohesion and under leaders independently selected. When a platoon is detailed for a working party, the Platoon Commander and no one else is responsible to the Company Commander for the quality and quantity of work performed; he is himself a part of it, and cannot take too much interest in it. Similarly, if a company is detailed the Company Commander should go with it and personally direct the work.

2. When the work is being done under the direction of the engineers, it is the duty of the engineers to show the Commander of the party the work to be done, and of the Commander to see that it is done. The details of the work, distribution of the party, etc., should be arranged as far as possible beforehand, and, if necessary, the route reconnoitred. The amount of work to be done by each unit should also, whenever possible, be arranged beforehand. It is preferable to set a unit a definite task on the completion of which it can go rather than to set it to work for a fixed period of time. Where possible, the work itself should be reconnoitred.

The guiding principle in the mind of every Commander should be to spare his men all unnecessary fatigue or delays.

3. A platoon acting as a carrying party should move in file, the Platoon Sergeant at the head with the guide, the Platoon Commander bringing up the rear. The

pace at the head should be slow, and Section Commanders must pass up word if their men cannot keep up.

APPENDIX I.

The Organization of a Battalion.

Good organization is the basis of economy in manpower.

Organization must start from the top. Before starting to organize his Battalion, the Battalion Commander should decide upon the exact number of men required for the efficient carrying out of the necessary administrative services within his battalion; that is to say, he should decide on the most economical composition of Battalion Headquarters (fighting and administrative), Company Headquarters and Platoon Headquarters, before permitting sections to be made up within platoons. It is important that Divisions and Brigades should help in this matter by making early demands for any personnel that may be required from Battalions within these formations.

The following table has been compiled with the object of assisting a Battalion Commander in the organization of his Battalion. It should be pointed out that it is not possible to lay down an exact distribution of N.C.Os. and men amongst the Headquarters within the Battalion for all conditions. It is suggested, however, that the numbers given in the following table form a reasonable and economical distribution of duties within the Battalion to meet all ordinary circumstances of warfare :

Suggested Distribution of Warrant Officers, N.C.Os. and Men to Headquarters within the Battalion.

To be Studied with War Establishments, 1918.

		(x)		(a)		(b)		(c)		(d)	
		Total Nos.		Bn. H.Q.				Four Company Hdqrs.		Sixteen Platoon Hdqrs.	
				Fighting portion.		Adminis. portion.					
Serial No.	Personnel.	W.Os. or N.C.Os.	Ptes.	W.Os. or N.C.Os.	Ptes.	W.Os. or N.C.Os.	Ptes.	W.Os. or N.C.Os.	Ptes.	W.Os. or N.C.Os.	Ptes.
1	Sergt.-Major	1		1							
2	Qr.-Mr.-Sergt.	1				1					
3	Ord.-Room Clerks	1	2		1	1	1				
4	Coy. Sergt.-Majors	4						4			
5	Coy. Qr.-Mr.-Sergts.	4				4					
6	Platoons Sergts.	16								16	
7	Qr.-Mr. Storemen		6				6				
8	Pro. Sergt. and Police	1	4	1*	4*						
9	Scouts and Snipers	2	16	2					16		
10	Signallers	2	51	2	23				28		
11	Runners		28		4				8		16
12	Stretcher-Bearers	1	19	1	3				16		
13	Gas Personnel	1	4	1					4		
14	Pioneers	1	10	1*	10*						
15	Transport and Grooms	2	43			2	43				
16	Shoemakers	1	4			1	4				
17	Tailors	1	2			1	2				
18	Butcher		1				1				
19	Postman	1				1					
20	Batmen		30		7		3		4		16
21	Cooks	1	11			1	11				
22	Sanitation	1	10	1	1		1		8		
23	M.O.'s Orderly		1		1						
24	Officers' Mess	1				1					
25	Water Duties	1	4			1	4				
	Sergt. Instructors										
26	Musketry	1				1					
27	Lewis Gun	2				2					
28	P. & B.T.	1				1					
29	Bombing and R.B.	1				1					
		49	246	10	54	19	76	4	84	16	32
	Total	295		64		95		88		48	

* Interchangeable between Fighting portion and Administrative portion of Battalion Headquarters according to situation.

NOTES.

Column (x) shows approximate numbers of Warrant Officers, Non-commissioned officers and men on all Headquarters (Battalion Fighting and Administrative H.Q., Company H.Q., Platoon H.Q.), within the Battalion.
Column (a) shows distribution to Bn. Headquarters, Fighting portion.
Column (b) shows distribution to Bn. Headquarters, Administrative portion.
Column (c) shows distribution to Company Headquarters.
Column (d) shows distribution to Platoon Headquarters.

Serial No.	NOTES.
3	In fighting or administrative portion as required.
7	2 Quartermaster's permanent storemen; 4 Company storemen or Company clerks.
9	1 Sgt., 1 Cpl.
10	1 Sgt., 1 Cpl., 33% either at Divnl. classes or left out before operations.
11	Increased when necessary—*see* Note 20.
12	Requires increase during heavy fighting.
13	1 Cpl. or L./Cpl. per Company; 1 Sgt. at Battalion Headquarters.
14	Includes 1 saddler. Convenient if the following trades are found within the pioneers:—Signwriter, wheelwright, tinsmith, plumber, bricklayer, 4 carpenters. 1 pioneer should understand repair of bicycles; 1 should be understudy to Armourer Sgt.
15	Includes 2 coldshoers; also men on probation and under instruction. There should be 1 Sgt., 1 Cpl., and 4 L./Cpls.
20	A proportion act as runners. This number does not allow for seconds-in-command of 4 Companies.
21	Distributed according to the situation.
23	Corporal.
24	Caterer for Officers' Mess or Messes.
25	"B" men.
26 27 28 29	Instructors for Divisional, Brigade, and Battalion Classes.

APPENDIX II.

Recent Publications.

The following are the principal S.S. publications to which Infantry Commanders should turn for further information on the various branches of infantry tactics and organization. It must be remembered that the principles laid down in "Field Service Regulations," Part I, 1909 (reprinted with amendments, 1914), and in "Infantry Training, 1914," are still the basis of all sound knowledge.

S.S. No.

193. "Standing Orders for Defence against Gas." (October, 1917.)
> Every Infantry Officer in France should be in possession of a copy of these Orders and familiar with them.

620. "Box Respirator Drill and Inspection." (January, 1918.)
> Issued to every Officer and N.C.O. in France as a card, taking the place of S.S. 535, "Gas Defence Card."

182. "Instructions on Bombing." (Revised Edition, December, 1917.)
> Issued in two separate parts: Part I gives the technical description, with diagrams, of the principal British and German bombs in common use; Part II deals with the training and tactical employment of bombers.

195. "Scouting and Patrolling." (December, 1917.)
> Contains full hints as to the use of ground, the principles of scoutcraft and the employment of snipers, with chapters on night work, and also on observation and reporting.

137. "Recreational Training." (Revised Edition, October, 1917.)
> Contains details as to the "running" of games, athletics, boxing, and other competitions, together with notes on the obtaining of kit and prizes.

S.S. No.

185. "Assault Training." (September, 1917.)
Outlines the three stages in which the use of the rifle—that is, the combined use of the bullet and the bayonet—should be practised.

197. "Tactical Employment of Lewis Guns." (January, 1918.)
Describes the Lewis gun section, its composition and duties, the duties of Company Officers and the Lewis Gun Officer, and the handling of the Lewis gun in action.
(The mechanism of the gun is described in the "Handbook of the ·303 Lewis Gun, Marks I and II, 1917." (40/W.O./4279.)

196. "Trench Warfare Diagrams for Infantry Officers." (February, 1918.)
Contains a short introduction on the general principles of field defences and a large number of diagrams of the simpler field defences which Infantry Officers may be called on to construct.

202. "The Organization of Shellhole Defences." (December, 1917.)
Consists of a short explanation of the various methods of organization successfully adopted in different parts of the line in 1917, with diagrams.

177. "Instructions on Wiring." (August, 1917, Revised Edition, January, 1918.)
Gives the principal types of wire entanglements and the drills for erecting them rapidly, with diagrams.

191. "Inter-communication in the Field." (November, 1917.)
Includes S.S. 148, "Forward Communication in Battle," and treats generally of all signal work in the field.

135. "The Training and Employment of Divisions, 1918." (Revised Edition, January, 1918.)

S.S.
No.

> Gives details of the main principles to be observed, and the preparations necessary to be made before offensive action.
>
> ("The Division in Defence" (February, 1918) is issued as a supplement to S.S. 135.)

152. "Instructions for the Training of the British Armies in France." (Revised Edition, January, 1918.)

> Contains the principles on which training is to be carried out, and full details of all Schools (G.H.Q., Army and Corps) now established in France.

192. "The Employment of Machine Guns." (January, 1918.)

> Issued in two separate parts: Part I describes their tactical employment, and is intended primarily for the information for the higher Commands, Staffs, and machine gunners; Part II deals with the direction and organization of fire, for the use of the Machine Gun Corps.
>
> [The mechanism of the gun is described in the "Handbook for the ·303-inch Vickers Machine Gun, Mark IV." (40/W.O./4589.)]

NOTE.—The conditions for the rifle competition for prizes given by the Army Rifle Association are published in a pamphlet O.B. 1618D, "Platoon Competition."

[In France all the above are issued down to battalions, and copies can be obtained for reference from the Battalion Orderly-Room.]

CHAPTER II.

An Address delivered to the Senior Officers and to the Commandants of Army Schools and Cadet Battalions and other Instructors, By BRIGADIER-GENERAL R. J. KENTISH, D.S.O., on the THEORY, DEMONSTRATION, AND PRACTICE SYSTEM OF TRAINING ADVOCATED AT THE SENIOR OFFICERS' SCHOOL.

Introduction.

I was recently asked by a Corps Commander to send him the pamphlet on the system of training advocated at this school, and which he understood was issued to every officer attending, and I had to reply that no paper giving the system in detail was in existence, but I would prepare something and send it to him. What I am going to say to you now is simply the matter contained in the paper which I have recently written on this subject. I desire, however, to point out to you that in Chapter III, Part I, " Notes for Commanding Officers," the Theory, Demonstration, Practice System is explained in general terms, and in Part III of the same chapter the system is brought right into the sample programmes of training that are given as a guide to officers finding themselves suddenly placed in command of battalions without knowledge as to how to train them.

There is no doubt that in these days when, in the training of troops, time is of paramount importance, the system that can achieve the best results in the shortest possible time is a system that should be known and used universally throughout our Army, or, for the matter of fact, every other army. The system advocated here, and that has, I am glad to say, now been reproduced practically throughout every school in France and in many battalions in that country, is the system known as "The Theory, Demonstration, Practice System," and it is a system that ensures good, sound training on rapid lines, without the loss of a minute.

I can vouch for its soundness because I have personally put it to the test in every kind of infantry unit both before and during the war, and under every possible condition. I enunciate to you the following cases in point :—

 (a) In a Territorial Brigade during its annual training before the war, when in every single battalion the whole of the officers and non-commissioned officers were first taken daily together and shown a picture, then made to carry it out themselves, and afterwards turned on to their men, the whole preceded by a short address on the movement or manœuvre to be carried out.
 (b) In a company before and during the war in France.
 (c) In two battalions during the war in France.
 (d) In an Infantry Brigade during the war in France.
 (e) In all the schools I have been connected with.

And in each particular case the system has, so to speak, made good, and excellent results have been obtained. I think that the system was really seen for the first time in France, and its soundness appreciated, when it was shown to the Commanding Officers attending the Commanding Officer's conference—the first of its kind ever held—at the Third Army Infantry School. At any rate, dating from about that time, e.g., November, 1915, it appears to have gradually been adopted throughout the rest of the Schools in France, and with the results that are already known to many of you here.

The Necessity For and Reasons Why This System Should be at Once Adopted.

The System in question not only saves time, but it also ensures that the training of our officers and men is carried out on practical and sound lines, and in such a way as to ensure the highest degree of efficiency in the field. It is without doubt a sure antidote to the hopeless situations so often met with in the training, both collective and individual, of our armies—both home and Overseas—to-day. Let me illustrate what I mean by taking a particular subject, which the Commander-in-Chief of our Armies in the Field has drawn the attention of his Army Commanders to as one requiring the closest attention of their subordinate commanders. The subject I take as an illustration is " Steady Close Order Drill and the necessity of every Battalion Commander devoting the most particular attention to it when training out of the line." This, perhaps, reaches the Battalion Commander in the form of a minute from the Divisional Commander, forwarded with a covering minute by the Brigade Commander to the following effect :—

76TH INFANTRY BRIGADE.

" The Divisional Commander wishes to draw the
" attention of his Brigade Commanders to the supreme
" importance and value of close order drill and the part
" it plays in all training of the infantry soldier. He
" therefore wishes Brigade Commanders to ensure that
" in the coming training a certain part of every day's
" programme is set apart for drill of a steady, close
" order and ceremonial nature."

(Sd.) A. J. BYNG, *Lt.-Col.*,
General Staff,
3rd Division.

In the Field,
14th October, 1917.

The 8th King's Own Regiment.

"The Brigade Commander wishes you to carry out
"the wishes of the Divisional Commander in this
"respect, and to devote part of your day's programme
"every day to close order drill. The Brigade Com-
"mander is in entire agreement as to its importance."

(Sd.) M. J. Playfair, *Capt.*,
Brigade Major,
76th Infantry Brigade.

In the Field,
15th October, 1917.

Now let us see what steps the Commanding Officer takes to carry out the wishes of his Divisional Commander. If he knows how to train, all is well; and if he does not, the following picture is revealed :—

(1) He issues a programme of training to his Company Commanders, which includes half an hour's steady platoon or company drill daily, either at the beginning or the end of the day's work.
(2) He sees all his Company Commanders and impresses on them its importance.
(3) He leaves them to carry on.

Now, how do they carry on? Let us see. If the Company Commanders know how to carry on, all is well; if they do not, another picture is revealed :—

(1) They issue their orders regarding the training of their companies, and include in the programme every morning a quarter of an hour's steady platoon drill, followed by a quarter of an hour's steady company drill.
(2) They see their four Platoon Commanders and impress on them its importance.
(3) They leave them to carry on.

Now, how do they carry on? Again, if they know how to train, all is well; if they do not, this is what we can see on any training ground at home or Overseas :—

(1) The Platoon Commanders proceed to drill their platoons, giving the men one word of command after another in an improper manner, and permitting the movements to be carried out in an equally improper manner.

(2) The men are permitted to do exactly as they like, the Platoon Commanders neither knowing how to give a word of command correctly or how to correct any false or wrong movement.

(3) The men know that their officers do not know their job; they intensely dislike being badly drilled or, as they call it, being " messed about "—this is putting it very mild—and they lose all respect for and confidence in their officers.

(4) The indirect result of this is that the men, knowing that they can do practically as they wish on parade with certain officers, gradually usurp the place of those officers, and really become, so to speak, their leaders.

(5) The direct result is bad training, a weakening of discipline all round, and loss of Moral.

An exactly similar state of things is revealed in the case of the Company Commanders and also of the Battalion Commander, should they attempt steady close order drill without knowledge of how to ensure it being carried out in a correct and proper manner.

The degree of harm done, however, in both these cases is intensified, because of the rank and position of these officers and the number of men, compared with the Platoon Commander, their incompetency affects.

Whilst the scene above depicted is being enacted, the Brigade Commander arrives, is met by the Battalion Commander, and together they proceed to have a look at the training. Now, the Brigade Commander, like the Battalion Commander, does not know how to train men, and not knowing how to train he is ignorant of the first principles which form the basis of a good drill system. Consequently he is unable to detect the hopelessness of the situation as revealed by the Platoon Commander struggling with his platoon, and being unable to do so he merely expresses himself as being perfectly satisfied with the situation, and rides off with that self-satisfied air that denotes that " all is well with me to-day."

As a matter of fact, the whole of the time devoted to this vitally important subject has been before and is at the actual moment of inspection by the Brigade Commander in the presence of the Battalion Commander being wasted, and neither of them probably knows it.

Both may belong to other arms of the Service, and they have never been brought up to the traditions of the infantry, and so cannot appreciate the situation from the infantry point of view, or, irrespective of the branch to which they belong, they have never been shown or taught how to train, their knowledge beginning and ending, as it so often does, with the issue of memoranda on training and all kindred subjects, and leaving their subordinates to carry on. How well they carry on in a good many cases is described above. It may safely be said that they do not carry on, and with the training of their men in the state depicted their commands march to the fight, and fight and sometimes fail, and the reasons attributed to the failure are generally every reason except the right and true one, viz., the absence of a really sound, practical system of training men quickly and sensibly under every condition without overtraining them and weakening their Moral.

I now turn to the other side of the picture, where the Divisional Commander, himself a trainer of men, imparts his system to his Brigadiers and Battalion Commanders, and so, from the very commencement of the training, ensures throughout his division uniformity and soundness of method.

The System Explained in Detail.

The Divisional Commander, knowing how to train, assembles his Brigade Commanders and their Brigade Majors, and his Battalion Commanders and their Adjutants, and explains in detail to them the Theory, Demonstration, Practice System of Training.

After expounding to them the theory of the system, he gives, with the aid of a company of one of his battalions, a series of demonstrations, and having done so he leaves them to carry on and to put the same into practice in the brigades. He thus ensures from the start that the leaders, so to speak, know exactly how to carry on, and all that remains for him to do is to visit the units at training and encourage them in their work. And there is in my opinion little doubt that the Divisional Commander will find his battalions being well and sensibly trained when he does visit them.

Now, with regard to the demonstrations the Divisional Commander gives to his Brigadiers and Battalion Commanders, I desire to point out at once that he cannot in the time—perhaps a morning—at his disposal expect to give them a demonstration of every form of movement in training, but he can, at any rate, show them sufficient to give them an idea of the system and of its sound, practical nature. The following are some of those suggested :—

(i) STEADY CLOSE ORDER DRILL.

(a) An officer's attitude on parade.
(b) An officer saluting and returning a salute.
(c) An officer giving a word of command.
(d) A soldier standing to attention.
(e) A soldier standing at ease.
(f) A soldier standing easy.
(g) A soldier marching.
(h) A soldier marking time.
(i) A platoon standing to attention, standing at ease, standing easy, marching, marking time, and halting.
(j) A company doing exactly the same.

(k) A platoon or a company marching past in line, column of route, column of platoons.

(ii) Field Work.

(a) A section extending.
(b) A section closing.
(c) A platoon as a vanguard, as a piquet, or in the attack.
(d) A company as an advanced guard, flank guard, and rear guard.
(e) A company in the attack.

(iii) Ceremonial.

(a) A regimental or company guard mounting, turning out, and dismissing.
(b) A platoon or company marching past in line or column of route, or a company in column of platoons, etc.

These are some of the many demonstrations that can be given in this way.

The Brigade Commanders order their Battalion Commanders to give their own officers and non-commissioned officers the same demonstrations, forming the non-commissioned officers into a company or platoon, as the case may be, whilst the officers stand by and watch.

The Company Commanders, before they start their morning's work, assemble all their Platoon Commanders and their non-commissioned officers and give them a demonstration of whatever they propose to do previous to doing it.

The Platoon Commanders will do likewise, if they consider it necessary, with their Section Commanders.

The Other Side of the Picture.

Now let us look at this picture, and what do we find when we do? The morning's work is, perhaps, platoon training, and the actual subject " The platoon disposed as (a) a vanguard, and (b) a piquet," preceded by the platoon at steady close order drill for half an hour. We see the following state of things going on everywhere we go on the training area :—

(1) The Company Commander, speaking to his Platoon Commanders and non-commissioned officers on steady close order drill, explaining to them what is meant by steady close order drill, and then giving them a practical demonstration with one of his platoons, the other three looking on. He then tells his Platoon Commanders to carry on, and they really do carry on, because they know how to.

(2) The Company Commander adopts the same methods later on in the morning, with the platoon as a vanguard and as a piquet, with the same excellent results.

(3) The whole battalion, the whole brigade, and the whole division is training on the same sound, sensible lines, with every individual knowing what to do and how to do it.

Further, the Divisional Brigade or Battalion Commanders, knowing that their commands are training on sound lines, are relieved of much anxiety regarding this most important side of the matter.

This is the Theory, Demonstration, and Practice System put into practice, and is the quickest method of training known. The amount of valuable time saved as compared with the " Carry on " system, when the platoon, Company, and Battalion Commanders commit their units to a movement such as a company or battalion in the attack, which scatters them, perhaps, over a wide area, without having first explained and shown them the movement in miniature, is inconceivable. I would, however, point out that this system can only be introduced into a division provided the Divisional Commander knows the system and how to act as the showman to his Brigade Commanders.

As a Brigade Commander I applied this system to my own Brigade previous to going to the Somme, for a brief period out of the line during the Somme, and on going north to Loos, and out of the line again, to train for further offensive action. On the latter occasion I was met on the training area by my Divisional Commander, who had only recently taken over the division. He had been looking at my Battalions training on the lines here suggested, and he had seen a picture which, as he told me at the time, had very much impressed him. His words were, as far as I can recollect: " You have an excellent system of training in your brigade. I have just been looking at all four battalions, all of which are carrying out their work on the same lines." And he added: " The —th Battalion (mentioning a service battalion in the brigade) might easily have been a regular battalion training before the war."

I do not refer to this for the sake of telling you what my brigade or what I myself was able to accomplish; I refer to it merely to emphasise the soundness and practical nature of this system, and because I know that the system paid every single time. And especially was this the case when my Battalions, depleted in officers and men after severe fighting, were refilled with officers and men of different arms and branches of the service, and who, therefore, required the most careful handling. The amount of time that could have been wasted with a bad system and was not because of our good system cannot be overestimated.

Conclusion.

I have referred above to the action of the Divisional Commander and the necessity of him knowing this system if he wishes to introduce it into his division. This will always be the case, but at the same time, as long as he ensures that his Brigade Commanders know the system, he can, of course, leave the demonstration, etc., to them, and if each Brigadier will assemble all his officers and non-commissioned officers, and, forming a company of the latter, will give a similar series of demonstrations before the actual training commences, exactly the same results will be achieved. I have nothing further to add except to ask you to introduce this system into every form of training you and those whom you are instructing are employed on, and I assure you that this can be applied to every form of training in every kind of unit belonging to either our home or Overseas armies, whether that unit be a Cadet or a Training Reserve Battalion, or one of our Command Schools or Military Colleges. If you do, you will, I feel convinced, very quickly see and appreciate the excellent results.

CHAPTER III.
By BRIGADIER-GENERAL R. J. KENTISH, D.S.O.
PART I.
TRAINING PROGRAMMES.

(In this connection, see S.S. 152, " Instructions for the Training of British Armies in France.")

The following principles are suggested for the Training of Battalions when resting out of the Line :—

1. **The Moral Side of Training when in Billets.**
    - (a) The aim and object of every Officer should be to create Moral.
    - (b) Moral will most assuredly be destroyed if the men, after having undergone a very severe period in the trenches, are overtrained.
    - (c) The men will be overtrained if the hours of training laid down are either excessive or ill-chosen.
    - (d) Except when a Battalion is operating away from billets for the day, five hours per diem in the case of the Officers, and four in the case of the men, should be sufficient.
    - (e) The hours of training will be ill-chosen if they commence before breakfast in the morning, when the men have nothing in their stomachs, or if they go on after dinners when the men, after a full morning's work, are not really in the mood to take in instruction.

2. The Physical Side of Training when in Billets.

  (a) Drill and smartness as a means to an end, the end being to obtain the highest form of efficiency in the field.
  (b) The attack from trench to trench and in the open.
  (c) The Battalion on the march.
  (d) Operations by night.
  (e) Field Engineering.
  (f) Bayonet.
  (g) Bomb.
  (h) Musketry.
  (i) Lewis Guns.
  (j) Gas Duties.

3. The weak point in some systems of training is the omission of any individual instruction of the Instructor before he is turned on to instruct his men. We sometimes see Officers and non-commissioned officers sadly in want of instruction themselves before they are fit to stand up and instruct their men.

Your system of instruction should therefore be based on a preliminary period being devoted to the instruction of Instructors before they are permitted to handle men. For instance, Colonel Snooks orders his Company Commanders to practise the "Attack in the open" on Monday morning. The Officers and non-commissioned officers first of all listen to a lecture on the "Attack in the open," and then they fall in at 9 a.m. as a company themselves, and carry out the attack under Colonel Snooks.

At 10 a.m. the men fall in on parade, when they carry out the attack, under their own Officers and non-commissioned officers, who have just been instructed in this manœuvre. And so with every other subject let it be :—(a) Theory, Demonstration, and Practice by the Instructors, followed by (b) Practice by the men under those Instructors,

4. The Light Side of Training.

The light side may be best catered for by concentrating on a certain number of miscellaneous forms of amusement, etc., which will give pleasure to the men, and incidentally raise their Moral. The following are suggested :—

(a) A well-thought-out series of Brigade, Battalion, and Company Competitions in every manly form of exercise.

(b) A well-arranged series of Concerts by either the Division or Brigade or Battalion Troupes of Artists.

(c) A well-thought-out series of Lectures given :—

    (i.) To the Officers alone.

    (ii.) To the Non-commissioned officers alone.

    (iii.) To the whole Battalion.

The subjects of these lectures should be varied, and should embrace matters not only affecting training, but also subjects which go to create Moral, i.e., Leadership, the Ethics of the War, the Psychological side of the War, History of the Regiment, etc.

5. General Notes.

If, in addition to the above, attention is also paid to March Discipline and Interior Economy, it will be found that a Battalion is bound to benefit from its period of rest when out of the trenches.

A golden rule is: If you overtrain men they will not be in the mood to respond willingly and eagerly when they are called upon for an effort. On the contrary, they will be in the wrong mood and in the wrong temper, and, as such, will be a danger to their own side.

PART II.

A suggested programme of training and recreation for a Battalion resting out of the trenches for a week. This programme has been considered both from the moral as well as from the physical point of view.

FIRST DAY.

The Battalion, after a very wet and hard week in the trenches, reaches its billets at about 12 midnight, the Officers and men wet and caked in mud from head to foot.

Réveillé not before 8 a.m. and Breakfasts at 8.30 a.m.

9.30 a.m. (i.) "A" and "B" Companies proceed to the Divisional Baths for hot bath and change of underclothing.

(ii.) "C" and "D" Companies clean up clothing, arms, equipment, etc., ready for Company or Platoon Inspection at 12 noon.

12 noon. "C" and "D" Companies' inspection by Company or Platoon Commander.

12.30 p.m. (i.) "C" and "D" Companies are paid.

(ii.) "A" and "B" Companies have returned from the Baths, and are paid at the same time. If they have not, *vide* below.

1 p.m.	Dinners. All Company Officers visit their men's dinners. The Commanding Officer visits "A" and "B" Companies.
2 p.m.	(i.) "A" and "B" Companies clean up clothing, arms, equipment, ready for Company or Platoon Inspection at 4 p.m.
	(ii.) Headquarters and "C" and "D" Companies proceed to Divisional Baths for hot bath and change of underclothing.
4 p.m.	"A" and "B" Companies' inspection by Company or Platoon Commander, and if not already paid (*vide* above), they are paid immediately afterwards.
5 p.m.	(i.) Teas for the Battalion.
	(ii.) The Commanding Officer has meeting of all Officers, including Medical Officer, Quartermaster, Transport Officer, and Padre, and speaks to them regarding the Training Programme he intends to carry out during the week.
6 p.m.	The Battalion attend concert arranged by the Officer Commanding Amusements.

SECOND DAY.

9—10 a.m. (i.) The Officers (less the Adjutant) and the non-commissioned officers (less the Regimental Sergeant-Major and Company Sergeant-Majors), together, under the Commanding Officer, in the work it is proposed the Companies should carry out between the hours of 10.15 a.m.—12.30 p.m., viz. :

(a) Words of command.
(b) Position of Officers and non-commissioned officers giving the word of command.
(c) Saluting with and without arms.
(d) Inspection and telling off of a Platoon.
(e) Platoon and Company Drill.

The whole of the non-commissioned officers are formed into a Company for the purposes of Demonstration, whilst the Officers look on. Only certain movements in Drill are carried out, these being decided on beforehand.

(ii.) The rest of the Battalion, under the Adjutant, is disposed as follows:—

"A" Company.—Gas Helmet inspection and lecture on gas by the Medical Officer.

"B," "C" and "D" Companies.—10 minutes' Arms Drill, 10 minutes' Musketry Exercises, 10 minutes' Bayonet Exercises, 10 minutes' Bomb Throwing Exercises, 10 minutes' Games.

10—10.30 a.m.
Fall out for half an hour and smoke.

10.30 a.m.–12.30 p.m.
The Officers carry out with their Platoons and Companies exactly, and no more, than they have been instructed in during the first hour.

12.30—1 p.m.
The whole Battalion forms for a Ceremonial March Past if the ground permits, and then marches back to billets. At a point just short of the billets the Commanding Officer takes up his position and the Battalion salute him as they pass.

1 p.m.	Dinner.
2 p.m.—	(i.) " A " Company on the Range.
3 p.m.	(ii.) All Subaltern Officers and non-commissioned officers, " B," " C," and " D " Companies, under the Adjutant or Regimental Sergeant-Major, in Communication Drill and Guard Duties.
3 p.m.	Sports and Games on well-thought-out lines, e.g., an Inter-Platoon Knockout, 15 minutes each way, Competition (Football).
5 p.m.	Teas.
6 p.m.	Lecture to the whole Battalion, if accommodation is available, by the Commanding Officer on the Progress of the War, and a word on the work of the following day.

THIRD DAY.

9—10 a.m. (i.) The Officers and non-commissioned officers, formed as for the Second Day, together are instructed in Battle Drill, e.g., Extended Order, etc. (*vide* I.T., Chap. V.).

(ii.) The rest of the Battalion, formed as for the Second Day, is disposed as follows :—

" B " Company.—Gas Helmet inspection, followed by a lecture on Gas, etc., by the Medical Officer.

" A," " C," and " D " Companies.—As for Second Day.

10—10.30 a.m. The whole fall out and smoke, etc.

10.30 a.m.–12.30 p.m.	As for Second Day.
12.30–1 p.m.	

2—3 p.m. (i.) " B " Company on the Range.
(ii.) As for Second Day.
5 p.m. Teas.
6 p.m. Battalion Boxing and Wrestling Tournament, arranged by Battalion Amusements Committee. (N.B.: A suitable day for the Divisional Band.)

FOURTH DAY.

9–10 a.m. (i.) The Officers and non-commissioned officers, formed as for the Second Day, together, and instructed in the Company in the Attack in the Open.
(ii.) The rest of the Battalion formed for the Second Day is disposed as follows:
" C " Company.—Gas Helmet inspection, followed by a lecture by the Medical Officer.
" A," " B," and " D " Companies.—As for Second Day.

10—10.30 a.m. The whole fall out for half an hour.

10.30 a m.–12.30 p.m.	As for Second Day.
12.30–1 p.m.	

2—3 p.m. (i.) " C " Company on the Range.
(ii.) As for Second Day.
3 p.m. As for Second Day.
5 p.m. Teas.
6 p.m. Lantern Lecture on the Royal Navy, by the Special Lecturer (*vide* note attached).

FIFTH DAY.

9—10 a.m.	(i.) The Officers and non-commissioned officers, formed as for the Second Day together, are instructed in :— (a) March Discipline. (b) Battalion in the Attack.
	(ii.) The rest of the Battalion, formed as for the Second Day, is disposed as follows :— "D" Company.—Gas Helmet inspection, followed by a lecture by the Medical Officer. "A," "B" and "C" Companies.—As for Second Day.
10—10.15 a.m.	The whole fall out for a quarter of an hour.
10.15 a.m.- 1 p.m.	The Battalion in a combined march, and simple attack scheme.
2—3 p.m.	(i.) "D" Company on the Range. (ii.) As for Second Day.
3 p.m.	As for Second Day.
5 p.m.	Teas.
6 p.m.	Company Concerts in billets.
7.30 p.m.	Brigadier and Staff dine with the Officers, and Divisional Band plays at Mess, and, if possible, where the men can hear it as well.

SIXTH DAY.

Reveille not before 7 a.m.

10 a.m.	The Commanding Officer holds conference of all Officers and non-commissioned officers, and discusses all papers received during the week which affect the Battalion going into the trenches that evening.

11.30 a.m.	The Company Commanders hold conferences of all their Officers and non-commissioned officers.
12 o noon.	The Company Commanders see their men on parade, and speak to them on any subject necessary.
1 p.m.	Dinners.
2.30 p.m.	Final of the Knock-out Competition.
4.30 p.m.	Teas.
5.30 p.m.	**The whole Battalion returns to the Trenches in good heart, the men ready for any effort their Officers may call on them to make.**

II. SPECIAL NOTES ON THIS PROGRAMME.

1. The first hour every morning is invariably spent in the preliminary instruction of the Officers and non-commissioned officers previous to the latter actually handling their men, and instructing them in the subject which is laid down as the subject for the day.

2. Special attention is directed to the fact that by the evening of the first day the whole Battalion has been—

(a) Bathed.
(b) Given clean underclothing.
(c) Paid.

The men are consequently clean; they have money in their pockets, and consequently they are cheerful and in good heart; in other words, their MORAL is strong, and they are in a fit mood and ready to commence their training the following day. Contrast their state and MORAL with the men of another Battalion, who, at the end of the first day, have neither been bathed, given clean underclothing or their pay; on the contrary, in an unclean and dirty state they have been pulled out of their beds at

7 a.m. to commence a long day's training on no system, and at the hands of young Officers, many of whom are quite unqualified to instruct.

3. In this system all Specialists fall in and carry out the first hour's instruction with their respective groups, viz., the Officers and non-commissioned officers with the rest of the Officers and non-commissioned officers of the Battalion and the men with their companies. For the rest of the morning they train on a well-thought-out system under their own Officers, and every morning they finish their work with a quarter of an hour's Arms Drill, finally marching past their Officer and saluting him on the return to their billets. In the afternoon, from 2 p.m. to 3 p.m., the Officers and non-commissioned officers under instruction attend the Adjutant's and Regimental Sergeant-Major's parade.

4. At an hour to be selected, and if possible on the first day, the Commanding Officer sees every Officer, non-commissioned officer and private who has joined the Battalion since it was last in billets, and gives them an Address of Welcome to his Battalion.

N.B.—**Even should the numbers only total 5, the Commanding Officer will carry out this duty. He will also see the officers separately and make their acquaintance; he will find out all the particulars he can regarding their attainments, record of service, and then give them clear direction as to what he expects of them, etc.**

5. The Special Lecturer referred to is an Officer, or a specially gifted civilian dressed like an Officer, who is attached to either Army or Corps Headquarters for the purpose of interesting and so raising the MORAL of their FIGHTING Units who are resting behind the front line. His express duty is to tour each Army area, and to deliver, either with or without

a lantern, a series of well prepared lectures to the Officers, non-commissioned officers and men.

6. The attached programme provides for an interesting, and at the same time instructive, week's work. If the Battalion has 14 days at its disposal, then the same system should be employed with the following variation, viz., the preliminary days—perhaps 4—should be devoted to the ground work of Open Warfare; by this is meant, the work should partake of constant Platoon and Company Close and Extended Order Drill, all leading up to the point when the Battalion Commander is satisfied that his companies can intelligently carry out the Attack. He then proceeds to instruct the Battalion as a whole in the Attack. The Instruction of the Companies and of the Battalion is carried out on the lines indicated in the Chapter entitled " The Attack in the Open."

CHAPTER IV.

NOTES, PROGRAMMES, Etc., FOR TRAINING OF SCOUTS, PATROLS, AND SNIPERS,

By MAJOR F. M. CRUM, K.R.R.C.

(*In this connection see S.S. 195.*)

PART I.

DUTIES AND USES OF SCOUTS.

Finished Scouts should have been trained in the following duties :—

(1) SCOUTING
  - (a) for protection.
  - (b) as ground scouts.

(2) RECONNAISSANCE for information about
  - (a) the enemy.
  - (b) the ground.

OBSERVATION
  - (a) for Intelligence.
  - (b) for Artillery and Trench Mortars.
  - (c) during an engagement.

(3) REPORTING.

(4) AS RELIABLE
  - *Guides.*
  - *Messengers.*

(5) AS A SEPARATE BODY for special purposes.
  - Patrolling.
  - Covering a rear guard.
  - Seizing important points.

(6) NIGHT WORK
  - Reconnaissance.
  - Patrols.
  - Guides.
  - Connecting files.

(7) SNIPING.

It would be a valuable asset to a Battalion, wherever it went, to have a body of men trained in the above duties.

When time is available, say one month, it will be found best to train men under three distinct heads :—

        (a) Scouting.
        (b) Patrolling.
        (c) Sniping.

A suggested syllabus for each is given, the time allotted to each subject and the order in which they are taken will depend on circumstances.

More often, however, time is limited, say to six days. In this case the C.O. should send for his Scout Officer, explain what he specially wishes his Scouts to do when they return to the front, and arrange with him some suitable scheme of training.

It might be well to train the Scouts all together in such subjects as Scout-craft, Map and Aeroplane-photo Reading and Reporting; while certain of them specialised, e.g., in patrolling, or sniping, or observing.

The ideal should be to have men well trained under all three heads, who were qualified to perform all the duties of Scouts.

PART II.

(a) **SCHEME FOR TRAINING SCOUTS.**

One Week (with trained men).

FIRST DAY.

Organise and tell off Leaders, pairs, groups, issue note-books and maps, explain use of them.

Lectures.

Uses and duties of Scouts.

Organisation and system.

Scouts for protection and ground Scouts.

Scouts for information. A branch of the Intelligence Department.

Tactics. Ground. Scout-craft. Observation. " Day and Night should be alike to the Scout."

Reporting.

Kind of man required; privileges.

Discipline. Smartness. Esprit de Corps.

Practice.

Various formations. ⎫ In daylight
Signals. Keeping touch. ⎬ and
Reporting and Messages verbally. ⎭ dark.

Second Day.
Lecture.

Scouting for information about ground and enemy. Knowledge of tactics. Eye for ground. How to get there and how to get back. Crawling. Visibility. Stillness. Skirmishing.

Practice.

Crawling and Stalking. Use of ground and cover. Right and wrong ways. Demonstration of visibility and protective colouring. Study of ground from some high point. Skirmishing.

Third Day.
Lectures.

What to observe and how to report it.
Map reading.
Training in eyesight and use of glasses.
Reports, written.

Practice.

Reconnaissance and Report.

Fourth Day.
Lecture.

Scout-craft and Cunning. Baden-Powell's "Aids to Scouting." Study of Nature. Tracking and deduction. Finding the way and keeping direction. Compass, etc. Care of self.

Practice.

Stalking and disguises. Tracking. Ruses.

Fifth Day.

Night Work.

Lecture.

Advantages and disadvantages of working by night. Superiority of the man accustomed to dark over untrained man. Difficulties and how to overcome them. Need for practice. Confidence. Not being seen or heard. The senses of hearing and smell. False alarms and panics. Noises. Wind. Dogs. Finding the way. Landmarks. Distances. Stars, etc. Examples of operations at night. Signals and signs of recognition. Use of luminous paper and compass. Read " Scouting at Night," by G. Cooke. (Gale and Polden.)

Practice.

Go over the ground by day, pointing out probable difficulties at night, noting landmarks and distances, bearings and direction. Practise listening, signals, moving quietly, whispering and keeping touch. Reconnoitre a position; this may be lightly held and the capture of a lamp in rear be the objective.

Sixth Day.

Recapitulation. Examination, with Note-books.

Or, if Course lasts longer, Last Day.

Inspection. Display. Allotment of Badges. Good men brought to notice of C.O. and mentioned in Battalion orders.

Note.—It will be seen from the above that there is far more than a beginner could learn in one week. At least three weeks would be required.

In addition to the above, Drill, Physical Culture, Map-reading and Sketching, Cooking, and any training which goes to make a man handy require attention, and should be fitted in, the services of any experts available being secured.

PART III.

(b) SCHEME FOR TRAINING PATROLS.

1. Probably 75 per cent. of casualties to Officers, non-commissioned officers and men sent on patrol were due to lack of system and insufficient training and practice.

It takes many months of practice to make Scouts really efficient in patrol work. Scouts should, however, never be sent on patrol in No Man's Land until they have undergone at least a week's continuous training.

During the training, reconnoitring and fighting patrols should, as far as possible, be kept distinct.

A Suggested Syllabus for a One Week's Course.

FIRST DAY.

Tell off leaders, pairs and groups; issue note-books, maps, compasses, boiler suits, etc.

Lecture.

Patrols (General). Importance of patrolling in trench warfare and semi-open fighting. Objects: How to avoid casualties. Study of maps and aeroplane photographs. Careful and constant study of ground, both before and after patrolling it. Importance of all knowing objective and plan. Conferences. Reports. Study of reports of previous patrols. Protection, always one listening while others move. Informing all concerned. Recognition. Signals. Picked men. Moral. Privileges. Use of Arms. Ju-jitsu, the "Osaka" method (as taught by Sergeant Nuthall, S.A.I.) will be found invaluable, and can be taught easily and quickly.

Practice.

(With and without dark glasses (see Note 1), also at night.) Walking quietly, put your brain in the sole of your boot. Crawling hands and knees, elbow and knees, hands and toes. Crawling backwards. Turning round. Use of cover. Whispering. Listening. Concentrate the mind, and don't try to see sounds.

Second Day.

Lecture.

Reconnoitring Patrols. Object: information without detection. Importance of knowing "No Man's Land." Size of Patrols, smaller the better. Useful kind of information, reliefs, working parties, gaps in wire, machine guns, etc. Definite objectives. Where to go, what to do, when to come back. Touch. Reconnaissance of definite point, e.g., with view to a raid. Instances of success or failure. Need of caution when returning. Formations. Arms should seldom be used. Osaka method invaluable for reconnoitring patrols. Absolute silence. Enemy ruses and our own. Equipment. Reporting.

Practice.

(With or without dark glasses, also at night with Véry lights.) Formations: Observe ground from a distance by day, and point out objectives, features, etc., with the aid of maps. Reconnoitre same ground by night, e.g., stalk and locate a sentry. Reports both while on the spot and afterwards. Finding gaps in wire entanglements. Locating sentry posts by the flash of a rifle at night.

Third Day.

Lecture.

Fighting Patrols. Object: kill, capture, or knock out the enemy. Size of patrols largely depends on numbers used by the enemy. Formations. Bombing sentry posts, etc. Waiting for enemy patrols. Fighting to get information or bring it back. Co-operation with Lewis guns and bombers. Arms. Equipment.

Practice.

(With and without dark glasses, also at night with Véry lights.) Formations. Bombing sentry posts. Waiting for patrols. Manœuvring.

Fourth Day.
Lecture.

Inspire the Fighting Spirit. Uses of revolver, rifle, knob-kerrie and bombs. How to capture and kill, Osaka method for preference. How to bring a wounded or captured man back. Wire-cutting.

Practice.

(With and without dark glasses, also at night.) Shooting. Killing. Capturing. Bomb-throwing. Wire-cutting.

In most Battalions some good gymnast, wrestler, or ju-jitsu expert will be available. The Osaka methods are now being taught at the Aldershot Command Sniping School, and it is hoped in time to train sufficient instructors to spread this method throughout the Army.

Fifth Day.
Lecture.

Raids. Need for careful thought and preparation of details. Need for rehearsing and training in model trenches. Originality and imagination should be encouraged, and suggestions invited. Men should know each other and their leaders. Need for previous reconnaissance by all concerned, and these to be given every possible assistance and information. Great importance of secrecy and surprise. What to do, if the enemy is not surprised, or in any and all possible eventualities. Uses of Scouts as guides. Covering parties. Keeping touch. Reconnaissance. Dress. Arms. Formations. Signs for recognition. Signals for withdrawal.

Practice.

(With and without dark glasses, also at night with Véry lights.) Forming up in "No Man's Land." Finding the way about model trenches, etc., etc.

SIXTH DAY.

Recapitulation. Discussion and suggestions on the training. Discuss and practise best methods to adopt when unexpected situations arise.

SEVENTH DAY.

Inspection and demonstration of work carried out during the Course. Everything to be carried out as near the real thing as possible.

GENERAL NOTES.

1. Black glasses have been found most useful in training. While the scout is in the dark and is practically working under night conditions, the instructor can see and correct mistakes, and other Scouts looking on can learn from noting the work done. Suitable glasses for this purpose are being prepared by the Munitions Department. It is hoped that before long these may be issued for the training of Scouts.

2. It has been found that when patrols are out, Company Officers sometimes think they can relax their arrangements for the vigilance of sentries. It must be understood that patrols in no way release sentries from their responsibilities.

PART IV.

(c) SCHEME FOR TRAINING SNIPERS.

One Week (with selected men previously trained in musketry and scouting).

FIRST DAY.

Organize and tell off pairs and groups. Issue note-books, etc.

Lecture.

Sniping and observing. Trench warfare. System. Uses and duties of Snipers. System of training on Sniper's Range with German and British trenches. See "Scouts and Sniping in Trench Warfare."

Practice.

Testing rifles. While not firing, use of telescopes, glasses, compass, range-finder, and judging distances. Visit to Sniper's Range and explanation.

Second Day.

Loopholes and O.P.'s.

Lecture and practice in putting in by day and night. Practice with periscopes and telescopes.

Third Day.

Observation. Telescopic Rifles.

Lecture and practice. Telescopic rifles tested. Sniperscope.

Fourth Day.

Reports and Observation.

Lecture and practice.

Fifth Day.

Lecture.

Fixed Rifles.—Selection of points. Visibility of points. Direct and indirect fire.

Practice.

Sighting and putting in by day and night.

Sixth Day.

Selection of O.P.'s and Sniping Posts; invisibility and cunning. Observing from O.P. Observation for, Reporting to, and Co-operation with R.A. and T.M. Officers. Use of Telephone. Taking over Trenches. Allotment of Duties. Lectures and practice.

Note.—If more time available, repeat as found most needed. Bring on any talent in sketching and map and aeroplane photo reading. Bring on instructors. Give individual instruction. Competitions and prizes. Allot badges. Inspection and encouragement by C.O. and Coy. Commanders. Make use of any drill, gymnastic, bayonet and musketry experts. Ask Artillery and Flying Corps Officers to speak on co-operation. Give display to the Battalion, illustrating common mistakes of sentries, etc.

GENERAL NOTES.

(1) Have a syllabus or general scheme for each course.
(2) Previous preparation by instructors.
(3) Interest the men and get them keen.
(4) Use a blackboard and lecture first, then demonstrate, then carry out each practice. A magic lantern helps.
(5) Encourage taking notes.
(6) When questioning or recapitulating allow men to refer to their note-books.
(7) Give as much individual instruction as you can to men who get behind in any subject.
(8) Make them think for themselves and encourage sensible questions.
(9) Encourage originality and ingenuity.
(10) Bring on any talent (e.g., sketching, handy men).
(11) Bring on instructors, and give responsibility. Let men make their mistakes and then see the error of their ways.
(12) In lecturing select a place where all can hear and see, and where there is no distraction.
(13) During demonstrations unemployed men may look on and criticise.
(14) Men learn and remember better by acting.
(15) It is not enough to throw out a suggestion. You must see it carried out.

Interesting the Commanding Officer and Company Officers.

It is well to interest Commanding Officers and Company Officers and get them to encourage the Scouts. Often they do not realise their value or know how to use them as—

    Scouts.
    Orderlies and Messengers.
    Observers.
    Keeping Touch.
    Instructing others.
    Passing on keenness and intelligence.
    An intelligence department.

Young Officers should do a course of Scouting.

PART V.

ORGANIZATION.

(S.S. 195.)

General Principles and Organization.

1. The present circumstances do not allow of sufficient time to enable all soldiers to be trained in reconnoitring, observing, and reporting the result of their observations, but the principles laid down in "Infantry Training, 1914," Section 110, hold good, and as many men as possible should receive instruction in these important duties. Every unit is responsible for its own protection, and is not relieved of this responsibility by the selection of the men most fitted by physique and previous experience for further special training as scouts or snipers.

The object of this publication is to assist Scout Officers and N.C.Os. as well as Platoon Commanders in this further training.

2. At the Army Scouting, Observation and Sniping Schools it is not possible in the time available to give a complete training. Only an outline of what to teach and how to teach it can be given, and the general

principles of a uniform system laid down. The training should be continued in the unit, both in and out of the line.

Conditions and requirements will always vary. Originality, inventiveness, and adaptability are essential to success in scouting and sniping. It is, therefore, not desirable to lay down any hard and fast lines on which scouting should be carried out, and the manual is intended to act as a guide and enable all concerned to adapt its principles to any given situation.

3. The distinction between scouting and sniping is clear : the primary object of a scout is to obtain information ; of a sniper, to kill.

Sniping is essentially the outcome of stationary trench warfare, and its importance has been increased by the introduction of the telescopic-sighted rifle. But during offensive operations snipers can be employed usefully only in the intervals between the actual infantry assaults, and then only if they are skilled in the use of ground. A sniper is in practice no other than an expert rifleman, who makes use of ground in order to bring him into a position from which he can fire his rifle effectively ; and the use of ground is one of the principal qualifications of a scout. Men employed as snipers in these circumstances, therefore, should be drawn from the scouts, who should receive instruction in the use of telescopic-sighted rifles, so that they may also be qualified to carry out the duties of snipers in trench warfare.

In addition, in trench warfare the scouts should carry out the duties of observers for which their training makes them specially fitted.

Section Scouts.

4. Every section of the Platoon should, if possible, maintain a pair of men who have received further training in scouting, observing, and sniping.

Company Scouts.

Each Company of the Battalion should maintain four specially trained scouts, who will normally be grouped with Company Headquarters, but may temporarily be employed collectively under the Scout Officer for special tasks as the Battalion Commander may direct. (" Infantry Training," Section 110, para. 2.)

When the Battalion is out of the line, these sixteen Company scouts, after receiving such training as the instructions of the Battalion Commander demand and time allows, should be allotted to their Companies and Platoons to assist in training as many men as possible. Their employment in action will depend on the nature of the fighting.

The Battalion Scout Officer.

Each Battalion should have a Scout Officer who is responsible to the Battalion Commander for scouting, sniping, and intelligence duties. He is responsible for the training of the sixteen Company scouts, and should assist Company and Platoon Commanders in the training of Platoon scouts. When necessary, he should hold, or assist at, the Brigade Classes laid down in S.S. 152 (revised edition), Section 5, para. 9.

The duties of the Battalion Scout Officer are important and arduous, and he should devote the whole of his time to them. He should be one of the additional Officers of a Battalion, not an Officer from a Company. He should live at Battalion Headquarters and attend all Battalion conferences.

The Scout Sergeant and Corporal.

These N.C.Os. are appointed to assist the Scout Officers, and the N.C.Os. should have attended an instructors' course at an Army Scouting, Observation, and Sniping School.

5. Scouts should be picked men selected for their character, physique, intelligence, and education. They should have good sight and hearing, and be expert shots.

Scouts should be men who volunteer for the work, which is often hard and dangerous. They should, therefore, receive encouragement, being excused other duties when possible, and helped in the matter of changing clothes, and obtaining hot coffee or rum or something extra on return from a hard night's work. The fact of a man being a scout should never stand in the way of his promotion; rather, it should help him towards promotion.

PART VI.

PRACTICES AND GAMES.

The following are given as a few suggestions, which can be varied and improved upon. Scout Officers should also see "Aids to Scouting," Baden-Powell, pp. 167-182.

Protection.

Move along a road or across country with a flag to represent any sized party to be covered. Scouts practise formations. Keeping touch and direction, signals, messages, and reporting. It can be done with or without an enemy. Any ruses by enemy or Scouts can be practised.

Scouting for Information.

(1) Demonstrations in visibility and crawling; badly done and well done. Use of ground. Keeping direction. One man stalking a rabbit or a bird while the rest look on is good practice.

(2) Occupy some position so lightly that it is possible for a good man to get through. Mark the flanks with flags and place a flag, or lamp at night, to represent the support. Send Scouts—
    (a) To locate and report on position.
    (b) To engage the party holding the position while Scouts sent to endeavour to get through and bring back support flag.

A whole day may be spent on this practice. It should not be hurried.

(3) Reconnaissance of positions, villages, rivers, woods, etc., and reports, in own country first, then in enemy country.

(4) Scouts v. Snipers. Snipers take up positions and see how many shots they can get in without being seen. Scouts try to locate snipers without being shot at.

Observation and Memory.

After marching to any point ask questions as to the route taken. Landmarks, distances, direction, points of compass, wind, animals, etc.

Observation of animals and birds should be encouraged.

" Kim's Game " (see Baden-Powell's " Scouting for Boys "). This can also be carried out with a telescope at a distance.

With imitation German trench, give, say, 10 minutes to memorise. Scouts look the other way while alterations are made, and then report on the changes they notice, e.g., a loophole sandbagged up, new wire, a gap in the wire, a hurdle removed, etc.

Ground.

(1) Skirmish a line of men over any ground. When whistle sounds, each man halts, with his feet at the place where his head would be to get the best cover within reach.

(2) Demonstrate movement of Scouts, Patrols, etc., with stones on any suitable ground, showing features on small scale.

(3) Construct raised maps, showing contours.

(4) Take men to commanding ground. Study ground. Imagine a flood rising and ask where the water levels would reach. Look for covered lines of approach, good positions, etc. Let the men shut their eyes and then describe the ground. Estimate distances and points of the compass.

Eyesight.

Teach the men where to look and what to look for Practise them pointing out objects seen to each other quickly. At the same time the use of telescopes and glasses may be taught. You will find some men have exceptionally good sight.

Finding the way.

Take the men by train or in closed lorry; take them into a thick wood. Send them home in pairs. Arrange a "Treasure Hunt."

Messages.

Extend men, say, at 20 yards' interval, down each of four cross-roads. Start a verbal message from the end of each line simultaneously. Scouts pass the message up to you. One non-commissioned officer should go along each line to note where and how mistakes occur. This can also be done as in a relay race.

Hearing and Moving Quietly.

(1) Prepare a difficult bit of ground with tins, bricks, twigs, trip-wires, etc., and teach Scouts to pick their way, by day or night, and whisper some message to you.

(2) Stand a man blindfolded representing a German sentry listening.

(3) Blindfold one man and stand him, say, in a wood with twigs and dry leaves on the ground. Extend men round him in a circle. At a given signal they close in on him. He points in any direction from which he hears a noise. The man who gets closest without being heard wins.

(4) Take them out at night practice hearing sounds, e.g., man talking, coughing, stamping his feet or moving in various ways, noises of spades, picks, transport, cries of birds, etc., etc. Read to them "Scouting by Night," Cooke (Gale & Polden): an excellent book.

Night Patrols.

Imitation German and British trench. Reconnoitre by day. Give definite object. Practise by day with dark glasses on. Practise by night.

Send out patrols from each side, arranging for them to meet at various points and distances from their own wire. Practise with flare lights. Place dummies at unknown points. Men not engaged watch from both trenches and note visibility.

Sniping.

Imitation German and British trench. Any movement seen in real trench warfare can be reproduced e.g., opening loopholes, exposure of figures, periscopes. telescopes, etc. These can be observed and fired at from loopholes or from natural cover and concealment, or with sniperscopes.

CHAPTER V.

MUSKETRY.

PART I.

Lecture by
LIEUT.-COLONEL R. M. LUCKOCK, D.S.O.,
on
THE USE OF THE RIFLE.

For a great many centuries the fire-arm has been the chief weapon of the infantry soldier. The method in which it has been employed has varied from time to time, according to the efficiency of the weapon itself. It has been recognised all along that, in addition to the fire-arm, a weapon for hand-to-hand fighting has always been required—the arrow and the hatchet; the musket and the pike. In later days it was found possible to combine the two, and we now have only one weapon in two parts, the rifle and the bayonet, the function of the bayonet being for killing at close quarters, that of the bullet for killing beyond hand-to-hand distance. Owing to various circumstances, the value of the fire-arm portion during the present war has wrongly depreciated, whilst the value of the rifle as a handle to carry a bayonet has received its due importance.

In the 18th century Frederick the Great realized the importance of the intimate connection between fire and movement. He gradually built up an army which became almost invincible, the foundation of which was great precision of drill and manœuvre, combined with fire effect. In the early years of the Napoleonic wars the French Army, by employing similar tactics, was also invincible, but gradually the practice died away until, in the Peninsular War, Wellington realized the principle himself and used it as an effective counter. The essence of Wellington's minor tactics was the fire effect of the thin red line against the French columns and skirmishers. After firing two or three volleys from the line into the French columns the line advanced to get in with the bayonet. After Wellington had gone our Army again gradually forgot the lesson, and, during the last twenty years of the 19th century, the value of the rifle was hardly appreciated at all. The study of tactics hardly concerned itself with its use—all attention was paid to obtaining advantage in battle by manœuvre alone and without the aid of fire. Musketry was looked upon by the troops as a necessary evil, which had to be got through once every year; it was looked upon as something quite apart from all other methods of training, and was, in consequence, quite divorced from manœuvre when troops were being trained in the field.

The Boer War revived the importance of rifle shooting, and, on its conclusion, a revival set in. The Boers were moderately good natural shots, and had attained a measure of efficiency owing to the constant use of the rifle for sporting purposes, and as their means of obtaining food. As a race they were not expert shots, but, having used it for practical purposes in peace, they realized its value for war. We, on the other hand, had not realized its full value during peace, and, in consequence, our Army went to war untrained in its use, and suffered accordingly. Our efforts were chiefly concentrated on training a small band of experts, the best of which constituted the Battalion "eight," and the Battalion depended for its reputation on their prowess at the various rifle meetings held both in Commands and at Bisley. The results obtained by these experts in no way reflected the musketry efficiency of the units, and no efforts were made to get a general level of efficiency throughout the unit.

In 1903, however, a small number of determined Officers set about to try and remedy this state of affairs, and, after several years of very hard work with nearly everyone's hand against them, gradually won the day, and by 1908 the Army was fully alive to the necessity of altering our training. When once that necessity was realized musketry never looked back; the standard all through units improved in leaps and bounds until, in the summer of 1914, our Regular Army at home, which formed the Expeditionary Force which went out to France, was superior in every form of musketry to the armies of the other nations engaged in the Great War.

Let us compare this standard with what we have to-day. Comparisons may be odious, but they often result in good fruit being borne. The most astounding feature of the musketry of the old Army was the standard attained in rapid fire. That standard was attained after a good many years of toil, a good many heartburnings as regards proficiency pay, but—whether individuals were badly treated or not—as a nation we have a lot to thank for it. We set a high standard, the standard ensured that our troops were efficient in the use of the rifle. It was our rapid fire, combined with a high standard of drill and manœuvre, which enabled our Expeditionary Force in 1914 to accomplish the retreat, to turn round and face the enemy on the Marne, to fight the critical battle of the first Ypres. Efficiency in the use of the weapon gives confidence, confidence begets Moral, and it was the Moral of the individual soldier which then saved the day.

During the first three years of war the standard of the individual soldier gradually decreased. This is due chiefly to the length of time available for training before the soldier is required to take his place in the fighting line. Other causes are lack of instructors, the introduction of new weapons, and our characteristic habit of blowing hot and cold, and in not being able to keep a just balance. With the new organisation of recruit training at home now in force, the standard is steadily improving. In the spring of last year matters had come to such a pitch that practically no soldier in the field ever let off his rifle at all; if he ever did it was doubtful if he aimed; if he aimed it was a hundred to one he aimed at the wrong target. Let me give you a few examples. During the Boche retirement in April last year our troops in the neighbourhood of Havrincourt Wood saw a German field gun limbering up 500 yards away, a target which our old Army would have prayed for. The troops of 1917 threw a bomb at it. The gun is not in our possession. Again, in May last year I was watching the training of a Battalion of the Guards Division, which was the first Battalion in the British Army to take up modern musketry in 1908. The scheme was a simple one for a Company, and designed to emphasise the importance of coverng fire. The Lewis gun section of the Platoon covering the advance was sent out to the right flank. It used ground well, and took up a position in a heap of old rubble from which it had a good field of fire on to the objective of the Company. In company with the Divisional General I watched the section. This was what I saw: The Lewis gun was firing at the wrong target, one rifleman was firing at the right target, one at the wrong target, three were firing into the opposite side of the rubble, and could see nothing, and in the centre was the section leader firing at the right target with his revolver at 600 yards range!

Last June a revival of musketry was started. It caught on, and the standard has since improved by leaps and bounds. Every battle that has taken place since then has shown indisputably the value of the bullet. The failure of the enemy's counter-attacks in the fighting in Flanders during August and September was largely attributed to the fact that, almost for the first time since 1914, our men used their rifles and did not depend on artillery alone to hold the captured ground. No finer results have ever been attained than were those in the fighting near Cambrai, when the enemy, by force of numbers, attempted to break our line on November 30th. A more magnificent tribute to the value of the bullet could not have been written than the report of the Second Division in those operations.

Time after time the Division was attacked by three Divisions at once; an equal number of times were the enemy repulsed. By the end of the day the Second Division line was practically intact, with the exception of one or two points, at which advanced posts had been driven in, and one in which a small advanced salient on the canal had been cut off. Let me read you a few extracts from the report :—

"The men had marked confidence in their rifles, and hundreds of men actually killed Germans, and in future it will not be difficult to encourage musketry. There are instances of one man cleaning and loading a rifle for a comrade who was picking off Germans. It was noticeable that when an attack had been beaten off men on their own initiative cleaned their rifles and collected S.A.A. and got ready for the next attack.

"Great stress had been laid during the training on the constant practice of rapid fire. This was well repaid.

"It would be beneficial to have opportunities of practice at longer ranges than are usually available. A 400 yards range is not often met with.

"The bayonet was used on many occasions, and had a discouraging effect on a very determined enemy."

"South of the Sunken Road in E.17.d. their attack was driven off with heavy loss by machine gun, Lewis gun, and rifle fire, but north of this road the enemy forced back the 140th Infantry Brigade, who were then much thinned out, and captured our three extreme right posts, the garrisons of which fell fighting to the last, and there was such a heap of German dead in and around these posts that after the line had been restored (2nd December) it was impossible to find the bodies of our men.

"They met attack after attack of the enemy, who were always in vastly superior numbers, and who came on right up to them time after time, only to be mowed down and retire in disorder."

These are good reading. I doubt if anyone would dispute me if I said that it was the magnificent Moral engendered by their confidence in the power of the rifle which kept that line intact that day.

In this revival the most important factor has been the introduction of Bullet and Bayonet Training. The scheme is still in process of evolution. Some of us may not like all the detail, but the principle that the rifle and the bayonet are two parts of the same weapon and should be taught together is right, and is now generally recognised.

Before the war the system on which we taught musketry was the Hythe system, and a very fine system it must have been when one sees the results attained. There we taught our instructors to teach the raw recruit; to begin at the very beginning and to leave out no details. It was a slow and sure method.

The situation in France is difficult; a unit comes out of the line, it knows not for how long—it is impossible for it to know or be told. The men are not raw recruits, they are partially trained men—they have all done musketry, some more, some less—it is hopeless to start with them all over from the beginning; if you do you never get beyond the Introduction. What is wanted is *practice* combined with instruction, and this is our present modified system in France in a nutshell.

The only fault in our musketry teaching is that it is apt to be too academical. It is rather like the old bayonet exercise we taught before the war, namely, a series of stereotyped actions, which had to be done correctly and exactly without any thought of being face to face with the enemy. There is no fighting *spirit* in trigger-pressing or in taking a careful aim—neither of these are fighting acts. We must make our musketry teaching "Live," we must give the impression to the soldier that trigger-pressing and aiming are acts which must be carried out during fighting. In battle, knifing and shooting are alternate, either may have to be done at any moment. It is chiefly a question of nerve control; we have got to try to imitate battle conditions in peace. In the later stages of musketry training we should do our shooting with as many distracting elements as possible. What situation can be less like the modern battlefield than a classification or prize meeting range with the atmosphere of " sh-h-h !"

How much more practical and realistic it would be if, after we had finished the elementary stage of musketry, we had to shoot with bands playing, rattles rattling, crackers cracking, lumps of mud being thrown at the firer, etc., etc. The action of rifle shooting and knifing must become second nature. Loading, aiming, and trigger-pressing must become automatic. The perfect fighting man must be capable of accurate and rapid shooting, even after movement, hand-to-hand fight, and during nerve exhaustion and strain.

What is the psychology, the feelings of the man who first goes into battle and knows he is coming up against a Boche? If he knows nothing of hand-to-hand fighting, he has no fighting spirit, and does not want to get there. If he has no skill with the rifle it will not be conducive to his getting there or to helping his side in the varied circumstances of the modern battle. What are his feelings when he sees a Boche running away, a Boche shooting at him, a Boche a few yards away coming for him with a bayonet and a determined face? It is the spirit of the bayonet fortified with discipline and confidence in the weapon which makes him want to get there. It is skill with the bullet which gets him there. It is skill with the rifle as a whole which enables him to dispatch his enemy when he gets there. The two parts of the rifle cannot be divorced. This doctrine finds its expression in a minor degree in the modern assault course and in the new A.R.A. platoon competition—the approach—the hand-to-hand fight—the pursuit by fire or the repulse of the counter-attack. And so with the recruit. It is submitted that this doctrine can be carried out in the elementary stages just as easily as it can be in the advanced stages, only in a modified degree. From the day the recruit first handles a rifle he must be impressed with the idea that the rifle is a means of winning a battle. Whether he uses the bayonet or the bullet, he must be made to realize that it is for one purpose, and for one purpose only, namely, to make him useful in battle. At the same time, no single detail of the technique of shooting or knifing must be slurred over or neglected. The recruit must be made as nearly technically perfect as is possible whilst imbuing him the whole time with the fighting spirit.

Finally, it is Moral that has made us successful in the past, it is Moral that is going to see us through this war, and Moral is only a synonym for true fighting spirit.

PART II.

Lecture by

LIEUTENANT J. YOUNG, 2/8th Royal Scots, Musketry Officer, Seventh Corps,

on

MUSKETRY TRAINING IN FRANCE.

The commencement of trench warfare marked the start of the decline in musketry efficiency. The danger of this decline was felt generally, and has resulted lately in a revival of musketry training. The difficulties entailed in carrying out this training will now be considered :—

(1) Time was short.
(2) The normal system of musketry training was suitable chiefly for recruits, and was very elaborate.
(3) The appliances necessary for musketry training are not usually at hand.

The result of the above difficulties was that progress in making up lost ground was slow, the results gained were not proportionate to the time spent. A system of musketry training was therefore devised which was suitable to the conditions in the field, and which produced good results in a short space of time.

The new system is based on the following requirements :—

(1) That the man is made to realize that the rifle is his first and last weapon, and that it is there to kill with.

(2) That all orders are implicitly obeyed, and at once.

(3) That the enemy is shot at at sight.

The system itself is simple and adapted from the Hythe system, with the addition of a few new elements, the reason for these additions being the three difficulties already mentioned above, *i.e.*, shortage of time—the fact that men are *semi-trained* and shortage of apparatus.

The fact that the men in France are semi-trained gives a foundation on which to work. There has been a tendency in the past to keep on laying the foundation instead of getting on to build the structure which will produce results, *i.e.*, Practice.

As often as not the whole of the time devoted to musketry, especially elementary musketry, has been spent on one subject only, such as the "standing position." Again, three-quarters of the time is often devoted by the instructor in explaining, while the men become more and more bored, and very often cold—men had to stand around doing nothing, making the best show of listening they could whilst their thoughts were far away.

In the second place, the time, which is all-important, is short, so that, even although one had a mind to proceed along the old lines, little can be accomplished. (See Appendix B for Intensive Training.)

In the third place, apparatus for such training is not available. The constant movements of divisions makes it impossible to keep up the supply. (See Appendix C for improvisations for out of the line training.)

Think, again, of the system of training at home, and compare it with the system being followed in France.

At home, the system followed is—

> **1st, Teach.**
> **2nd, Practise.**
> **3rd, Test.**

This is right for recruits, but **in France,** where we have trained or semi-trained men, the following order is required :—

> **1st, Test.**
> **2nd, Practise.**
> **3rd, Teach, but only where necessary.**

To find out what the men know must be a necessary preliminary to all musketry training out of the line.

Coming to details, work by Q. and A., or give an order and have it carried out without explanations. If it is seen that the men know or can do what is wanted, don't waste time in going into long explanations on points improperly understood.

Do not go into detail; think of the time spent on that. Recall instruction in Positions, and see how much time was occupied by the Instructor in talking on details, even although at the first glance he could see that his section had more than a reasonable grip of the subject. Cut all that out with your semi-trained men, except in the case of backward men, and then only give what is necessary to rectify the particular fault.

The keynote of everything is **Spirit and Simplicity.**

By the former, discipline is maintained, and a man is taught as it were instinctively to engage every target which presents itself.

By the latter, time is saved and boredom is removed by the eradication of less important and more intricate points.

Throughout all Musketry training now, Spirit—the fighting spirit—must be developed.

The rifle and bayonet have gone into partnership. They have started business as the " Bullet and Bayonet Combine." In their Articles of Association they give as their first object Blood (Boche blood) on the Bullet, Blood on the Bayonet.

They came to recognise that the one was essential to the other. The Bayonet recognised that it could wound, the Bullet that it could kill. The Bayonet saw that, while it could take a position, it was the Bullet that held it, and the outcome has been a working agreement.

So in the training they go hand in hand. The Spirit of the Bullet is being developed as has been the Spirit of the Bayonet.

Everyone has realized that the former system of musketry training for present conditions has been of too milk and water a variety. There was nothing in it to inculcate the fighting spirit. Sir Douglas Haig is quoted as having said that 80 per cent. of our best endeavours in training must be to produce that fighting spirit. In musketry it cannot be neglected.

The Bayonet has stipulated that it has to be present on all musketry training, and that it will always be fixed. It argued that its bloodthirsty look must, by its constant association, imbue the Bullet with the same Spirit.

What is wanted is that the man will realize in musketry training what he realizes in bayonet training, that its object is to kill. To the inculcation of this spirit many of the bayonet fighting methods are being introduced.

Games and quickening exercises are as much a part of musketry training as they are of bayonet training. Throughout the whole of musketry training the fighting spirit will predominate, at the same time remembering how accuracy is got. The aversion in the past to use the rifle at all at good targets of Boche has to be overcome. Therefore train for aggressiveness.

In the past it is recognised that there has been too much artificiality. Aiming discs, black bull's-eyes stuck up or painted on walls all around the parade ground, have, especially in these rapid training days, tended to obscure the real aim of musketry training, which is to kill.

The bayonet fighter soon swept away the idea of pointing and withdrawing to music. He soon brought in targets that meant something, and made the men even in training grind their teeth to get at them. So now with the Musketry man. The targets at which he gets his men to aim and fire represent Boche.

      Boche Bull's-eye.
      Boche Figure.
      Boche Silhouette.

They look offensive. They give the desire to kill. Targets that move, take cover and attack are all brought in. The Training in Musketry should be brisk. (See Appendix D.)

Throughout it all a degree of confidence must be inspired. Encouragement, not denunciation, is wanted. Don't cast aside a man and make him think he is useless. It makes a rifle less, it reduces fire effect. Make a man realize that if he cannot do everything, his best is not negligible.

Strive for automatic use of the rifle. To that end Training should be as continuous as possible. Bullet Fighting, as Bayonet Fighting, requires special muscles and unless the use of those muscles in a correct manner is a matter of habit, other muscles not so well developed will take charge of the weapon under excitement and faults will predominate.

Make the Training simple in nature, at least so far as consistent with efficiency. Remember, if exercises are simple men can help themselves. Think of the Tests of Elementary Training and the effect which their simplicity had. For this purpose introduce simple exercises which will bring out points in Elementary Training. (See Appendix E.)

Discipline.

Again, in the past there has been a tendency to slackness in musketry training. It is realized now that " go as you please " methods do not suit the conditions of " out of the Line Training." After a spell in the line there is a tendency to slackness which musketry, as taught in the old way, accentuated to a degree inconsistent with general efficiency. Now musketry is to a great extent taught as a drill. (See Appendix F on Positions.)

Commands are given, time is saved, and the fighting spirit developed.

Battalion Commanders are encouraged to engender the spirit of competition both on and off the range. (See Appendix G.)

The Instructor.—The essentials of an instructor are :—

(1) Powers of command—no sloppiness or carry on in your own time. Do much—talk little.

(2) Quick eye to detect faults. Jump on them at once, and let all hear the corrections.

(3) Ability to carry out himself the commands given, and assume the correct positions.

(4) Discretion in dealing with the different natures and builds of his men.

(5) Spirit, life, energy.

The question arises from the above as to how far it can apply to training at home, and the following should be kept in view :—

(1) That the fighting spirit is capable of early development. A man is not long a recruit in these days.

(2) That there are thousands of returned Expeditionary Force men at home undergoing further training for further service to whom the system can be applied.

THE WAR SHOT IN

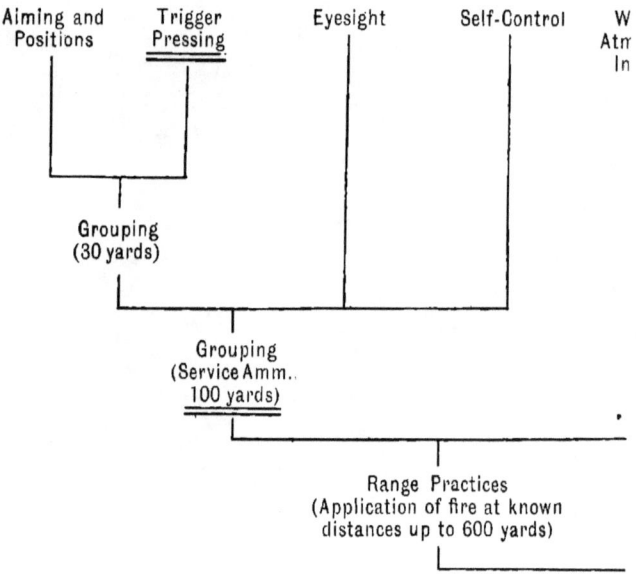

NOTE.—Subjects underlined should be kept particularly in view when time for more cannot be had; and add Cultivation of Fighting Spirit.

THE MAKING.

APPENDIX A

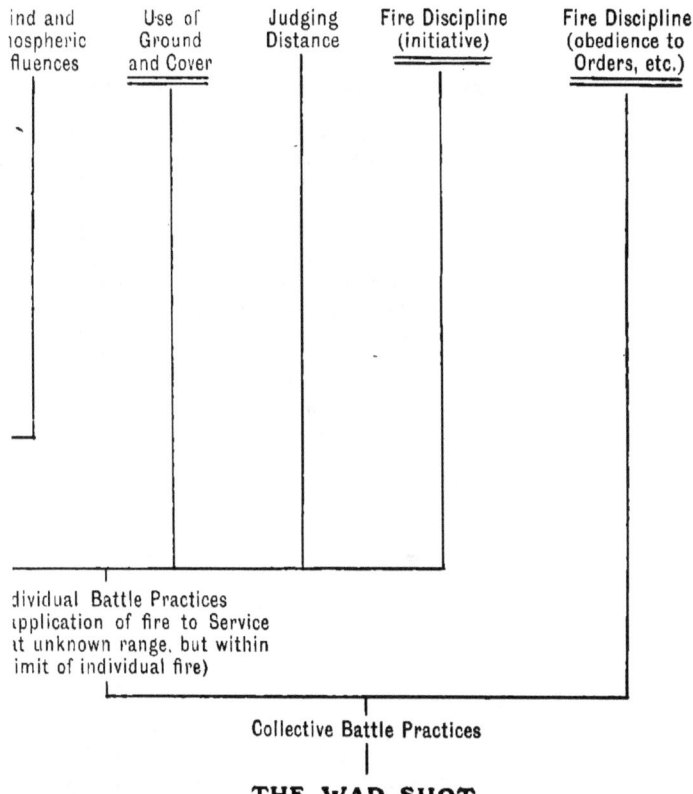

THE WAR SHOT.

APPENDIX B.

Intensive Training.

1. It is not usually possible to devote more than six hours in one week's training to musketry; the following is a suggested programme of training during such a period.

2. Elementary training, 2 hours; tests of elementary training, 1 hour; range practices, 3 hours.

3. The detail of each of the above can be as follows :—

   (a) *Elementary Training.*—The men should be squadded in their usual sections, and taught primarily exercises which will assist them to pass the tests of elementary training mentioned below. The usual subjects of elementary musketry training can also be included. The more important are as follows :—

   Hard Subjects.—All Firing Positions. Bolt Drill and Muscle Exercises. Bayonet—Attack and Defence. Rapid Loading—Fire Discipline. Rapid Fire. Assault Training.

   Easy Subjects.—Care of Arms. Trigger-Pressing. Fire Orders and Recognition. Judging Distance. Visual Training. General Theoretical Knowledge. Elementary Aiming

   (b) *Tests of Elementary Training.*—The tests for rapidity of aim, loading, and firing, as laid down in Musketry Regulations (para. 299, VIII, IX, X). Also the grouping test in para. XI. It is essential that a definite method of testing is laid down and known by instructors, so that no time is wasted, one of the most important points being the list of articles required to enable instructors to carry out the tests.

(c) *Range Practices.*—A simple qualifying standard form of practice should be made out, based on the practices in Musketry Regulations, and adapted to the appliances and ranges at hand. This can be called a qualifying practice, the most suitable form being—Five rounds grouping at 100 yards; five rounds application at 300 yards, followed by fifteen rounds rapid.

It is essential that details not actually firing are carrying out some form of musketry training behind the firing point.

4. One of the essentials to getting the full value out of the allotted time is to have N.C.Os. waiting with the required appliances both on the range and on the elementary training ground, so that sections or other units going to these places do not waste time.

APPENDIX C.

Notes :—To assist Platoon Officers and N.C.Os. in improvising simple appliances so that Musketry Training will not suffer in back areas.

Necessity for Improvisations.

(a) During offensive operations Back Areas constantly change and the usual means of supply (i.e., R.E. and Ordnance) cannot be maintained, and

(b) Because Musketry Training is of paramount importance, and must not be allowed to suffer through lack of initiative to improvise appliances.

Appliances Necessary and How they may be Improvised.

Subject.	Appliances Necessary.	How Improvised.
Aiming Instruction	(a) Aiming rests	(a) Two filled sandbags, trench, folded greatcoat.
Firing Instruction	(b) Targets	(b) Pioneer Sergeant ; paint Boche head on ration box (see 30 yards range below).
Tests of Elementary Training.		
Trigger-Pressing Regulation Aim Rapid Aim Rapid Fire	(c) Eye disc	(c) Inky cork will make bull's-eye on Field Service postcard : perforate with pin.
Rapid Loading Rapid Firing	(d) Dummies	(d) A few may be made by sandpapering empty cases, and inserting wooden plugs similar in shape to bullet ; plug should be long enough to reach base of cartridge. For rapid loading practice, use ball ammunition on 30 yards' range. For rapid loading practice with ball off the range, insert three ball cartridges behind the trigger. Needs very strict supervision.
Aiming off for Wind or Movement.	(e) Fatiguemen	(e) Men of section.

Subject.	Appliances Necessary.	How Improvised.
Judging Distance	(a) Natural objects	(a) No improvisation necessary; use tree-stumps, etc., for unit of measure.
	(b) Fatiguemen	(b) Men of section. (Appearance at various distances.)
	(c) Rangefinder	(c) On regimental charge.
	(d) Large scale map	
Visual Training	(a) Silhouettes	(a) Pioneer Sergeant can make from ration boxes.
	(b) Fatiguemen	(b) Men of section. If blank needed, extract bullets from ball cartridges.
Indication and Recognition	(a) Landscape target	(a) Double-page picture from *Graphic*, etc.: railway posters.
	(b) Open country	
Fire Orders	Aiming rest	Trench or sandbags.
Fire Discipline Training	(a) Targets	(a) Screens made of empty sandbags.
	(b) Fatiguemen	(b) Men of section.
30 yards Range	(a) Stop butt	(a) 1. Sunken road or suitable hillside. 2. Quarry. 3. Ruins sandbagged or banked up with earth.
	(b) Targets	(b) 1. R.E.'s supply. 2. Pictures from periodicals; newspapers with suitable aiming marks improvised. 3. Tiles, bricks, jam-tins, empty cartridge cases. 4. Ground landscape, cardboard and paper cuttings. For targets and reference objects.
	(c) Supports for targets	(c) 1. Cleft sticks. 2. 9" strip of canvas, with 1" at bottom turned up to form pocket; wire clip to hold top of target. 3. Tin frames supported on wire.
	(d) Grouping rings	(d) Pioneer Sergeant will make from wire or cardboard

APPENDIX D.

The following simple practices are devised to bring together the Bayonet and the Bullet :—

First Practice.

Object.
> To develop quickness and determination.

How carried out.
> Inspect rifles, etc.
> For assault training—" open out."
> Section " Load " (prone)—this brings the ranks about 4 feet apart.
> Odd or even numbers " Rest."
> At the right eye (of the man in front), five rounds, fire.
> Instructor checks faults during firing.
> " Rest."
> Target rank criticise arms, etc.
> Change over and carry on.

Second Practice.

Object.
> To develop quickness in changing point of aim, etc.
> Ranks 50 yards apart and extended four paces.
> " Load " or position. One rank " Rest."
> At the right Boche or left Boche, etc., " Fire."
> Instructor again checks faults and looks for—
>> (1) Quickness in changing position.
>> (2) Spirit and determination.
> Change over and carry on.

Third Practice.

How carried out.
> To develop words of command of section.
> One taken out and given commands for Practice 2, as above.

Fourth Practice.

Object.
To develop initiative, control, etc.

How carried out.
Scabbards " on."
Half-Section " out " in front.
Half-Section behind cover.
On given signal men of " Out " Half - Section expose themselves and fire. Half-Section behind cover take advantage and fire.
" Out " Half-Section next advance at high port.
Other Half-Section open appropriate fire (rapid).
Rapid fire insufficient to stop them.
Half-Section then come out from behind cover to meet charge.
Ranks pass through and assume new positions.
Close. During firing, etc., instructor checks faults.

Fifth Practice.

Object.
On assault course, combining bayonet work, control, etc. Not necessary to have regular gallows. Bayonet sacks in two lines on ground sufficient.

How carried out.
Section under instructor, who acts as Section Commander behind cover, say 25 yards behind first row of sacks. One man detailed as sentry, and he alone should be looking over top. "Stand-to" on targets appearing (on signal). Section Commander gives fire order. Targets disappear. Section over takes two rows of sacks and final objective. This taken, section consolidates. Sentry posted. Counter-attack. Fire order. No undue excitement. " Close." Criticism.

APPENDIX E.

Example of Simple Section or Platoon Exercises,

Combining—
  1. Snapshooting.
  2. Aiming off for movement.
  3. Rapid fire.

How carried out.

Fatiguemen (three or four) out in front under cover about 300 yards each with silhouette target of some sort.

Section or Platoon drawn up, and Section or Platoon Commander explains exercise.

Order given to load in required position.

Part I. Snapshooting.

Section or Platoon ordered to watch front; Signal given and targets appear at different places exposed for five seconds working down to three.

On appearance of a target Section or Platoon without further orders fire and declare hit or otherwise.

Meanwhile Section Commander keeps his eye on Section for faults, and insists on—
  (a) Watching front.
  (b) Quickness in coming to aim.
  (c) Quickness in reloading, etc., etc.

Part II. Aiming-off, etc.

Fatigueman as called up walks or doubles across front, comes towards or goes away. Section or Platoon calculates how much to aim off, aim, and fire.

Commander watches for—
  (a) Positions.
  (b) Quick manipulation of rifle.
  (c) Proper calculation (questions put).
  (d) Trigger pressed on swing, etc., etc.

Faults checked.

Part III. Rapid Fire.

All targets up for one minute while men rapid fire. Commander—

(1) Sees that firing is done properly.
(2) Sees that faults are checked.
(3) Ascertains number of rounds fired with a view to checking progress.

NOTE.—Suitable and practical Section and Platoon exercises can be arranged for—

(1) Aiming at ground. See Musketry Regulations
(2) Fire direction. See Musketry Regulations.
(3) Fire Orders.

BOLT DRILL (Supplementary to Muscle Exercises).

How carried out.

1st Practice.

Position—any.
" Load."
" Safety catches forward."
" Reload." Men open and close bolt properly. Return hand to small of butt and take first pressure.

2nd Practice at aim.

" Take aim."
" Reload," as above.

APPENDIX F.

NOTE.—*This appendix is not exhaustive, but is merely notes and examples to show how explanation and detail can be cut down in practising musketry with semi-trained men out of the line.*

Elementary Instruction in Use of the Rifle.

Firing Instruction.

The following method and words of command should be used in *practising* positions :—

- (a) Inspect arms and pouches.
- (b) " Fix Bayonets " (as in drill or as a quickening exercise).
- (c) " To the Right (or Left) to two Paces—Extend."
- (d) Targets pointed out. (Boche figures where possible.)
- (e) Caution. Going to practise the standing (or other) position.
- (f) " Load." (Men assume loading position and load.)
- (g) " Rest." Check faults, demonstrating with rifle.
- (h) " Position." Men return to loading position.
- (i) " 300 yards " (or other elevation).
- (j) " Rest." Check faults and, if necessary, demonstrate.
- (k) Position. Men return to loading position. " Five Rounds—Fire." Men put safety catches forward on number of rounds being named. Instructor moves about smartly to check faults while firing.
- (l) " Rest," if faults are very bad and require lengthy correction.

(m) "Fire." To complete number of rounds.
(n) "Unload." Men unload and order arms. Instructor demonstrates and checks faults.

Note.—The instructor must know the points to note for all positions as given at the foot of Plates XIX to XXIX, M.R. These constitute his detail in tabulated form, and do away with long explanations. Other branches of Firing Instruction to be practised (M.R., Section 45).

APPENDIX C.

Competitions off the Range.

1. Bolt Drill—(*a*) Loading position.
   (*b*) Aiming position.
2. Rapid Loading—Cartridges or cork to lock the trigger when ball is used.
3. Quickest man to fix his bayonet, assume prone position, and fire first shot.
4. Assault course.
5. Individual bullet and bayonet (direction test).

Competitions 1 to 4 should be carried out collectively by sections.

Best of sections then compete for best in Platoon.

Suggested Competitions on the Range.

Competition.	Range.	Conditions and Scoring.
1. GROUPING	25 yds.	Bayonet fixed. 1, 2, and 3 inch : 25 points.
	100 yds.	From cover, 4, 8, and 12 inch : 20 and 15 points.
		(No wide shots allowed.)
2. APPLICATION	25 yds.	Bayonet fixed.
	200-500 yds.	Targets and scoring as in M.R., Part I—*i.e.*, 4, 3, 2, 1.
3. RAPID	25 yds.	15 rounds issued : 5 rounds magazine, 5 rounds left pouch, 5 rounds right pouch. Time, 1 minute. Scoring, 3, 2, 1 ; two points deducted for each pouch left unfastened.
4. INDIVIDUAL ADVANCE	400-200 yds.	10 rounds. Fig. 3. Targets (1 per firer) exposed for 10 seconds at 400 yds., then disappears for 25 seconds, during which the firers advance 50 yds. Exposures and intervals to be same throughout. Competitors to fire 2 rounds each at 400, 350, 300, 250, and 200 yards respectively. Scoring, 3 points per hit.

Competition	Range	Conditions and Scoring
5. PATROLS (Teams of 4)	Unknown range (up to 350 yds.)	(a) Tiles, falling plates, or bottles, worked on the "knock-out" principle—*i.e.*, as a target is struck, opposing firer ceases fire. Smart umpires required. Or— (b) "Knock-out" principle *by Patrols*, not individuals—*i.e.*, two Patrols. Best Patrol the one which knocks down *all* targets first. One umpire only required.
6. THE PILL BOX (3rd Army Musketry School)		*Object.*—To practise men in applying fire at a pill box. *Number.*—1 N.C.O. and 6-8 men. *Method of Conducting.*—The section, extended to 1 pace, lies down 50 yds. from the firing point, rifles loaded with 5 rounds, bayonets fixed. When ready, the Section Commander gives the order "Advance," and leads his men at the double to the firing point. He orders fire to be opened at the pill box. One minute after the order "Advance" the superintending Officer will give the order "Cease fire." *Target.*—4 by 4 feet (2nd Class figure target), coloured grey or white, with a black band 8 inches wide across the target, the top of the band being 1 foot from the top of the target. *Range.*—200 yds. *Rounds.*—15 per man. *Marking.*—1 point per hit on the black band. *Deduct* 3 points if fire is opened before the Section Commander gives the order "Fire." Deduct 1 point for each shot fired after the order "Cease fire."
7. THE ELUSIVE HUN (3rd Army Musketry School)		*Object.*—To practise men in quick alteration of their point of aim, and to demonstrate the importance of watching the front, and of recharging magazine at the first favourable opportunity. *Numbers.*—1 N.C.O. and 6-8 men. *Method of Conducting.*—The section assumes a firing position on the firing point. The use of cover is optional to the firers. The superintending Officer gives the caution, "Watch your

Competition.	Range.	Conditions and Scoring.
		front," and signals to the butts. A target will be exposed five times, each time in a different place for 6 seconds; 8 seconds' interval between exposures. Unlimited rounds may be fired at each exposure. *Target.*—A figure 3 or 4 (silhouette). *Range.*—200 yds. *Rounds.*—15 per man. *Marking.*—1 point per hit.
8. SUPERIORITY OF FIRE		*Object.*—To emphasise the importance of reaching the objective quickly, and of obtaining superiority of fire when counter-attacked. *Numbers.*—1 N.C.O. and 8-10 men. *Method of Conducting.*—The section will be extended to 2 paces, 20 yds. in rear of the firing point, where there will be a sack filled with straw representing a Boche opposite each man. Rifles to be loaded with 5 rounds and held at high port. Bayonets fixed. When ready, the Section Commander will give the order " Advance " ; 8-10 figure 3 silhouette targets (according to the number of firers) will appear at the butts. The section will open fire by order of the Commander. Ten seconds after the first targets appear 2 more will come up, and similarly after every 10 seconds 2 additional targets will appear. Targets will disappear when hit. If at any time the number of targets exceeds the number of firers, the order " Cease fire " will be given. *Time Limit.*—One minute from the first appearance of the targets. The section which has the fewest targets up at the end of the minute wins. *Range and Target.*—200 yds. Figure 4, or 300 yds. Figure 3. *Rounds.*—Ten per firer.
9. THE BOCHE PATROL (1 N.C.O. and 6 men)		*Object.*—To train men to watch the front and develop tactical sense. *Range.*—250-350 yds. (for gallery range). *Rounds.*—Five per man. *Targets.*—Six figure 3 on poles. *Method of Conducting.*—Section Commander is informed that a Boche

Competition.	Range.	Conditions and Scoring.
		patrol of six men has been seen collecting behind a wall (represented by a brown screen erected on butt gallery). His orders are to watch for them and try to bag the lot. When the section takes up a fire position, the following exposures of targets are made :— (1) A figure slowly looks out from behind the screen for 6 seconds, and withdraws. (2) A figure looks out from the opposite side for a similar period. (3) Three targets look out for 6 seconds—one on either side, and one over the top of the screen. If fire is opened, no further exposures take place, and the practice is finished. If no shots are fired, the whole Boche patrol—six figures—move out from cover, and proceed at a walk along the gallery, traversing a distance of 30 yds. to a second screen representing cover. *Scoring.*—Two points per hit ; 5 points extra if all targets are hit.
10. THE DISABLED BOCHE MACHINE-GUN (1 N.C.O. and 6 men)		*Object.*—To train men to watch for, and prevent, removal of enemy guns. *Range.*—250-300 yds. *Rounds.*—Ten per man. *Targets.*—Screen 4 by 3 feet to represent machine-gun ; four figure 3 targets. *Method of Conducting.*—Section Commander is informed that the screen represents a Boche machine-gun out of action, and his orders are to prevent it being taken away by the enemy. Twenty seconds after the section has taken up position two figure 3 targets will stealthily appear (one on each side of the screen), and will slowly move gun to a flank. Figure 3 targets will disappear if hit, and movement of gun ceases for five seconds, after which four casualties will be replaced in a similar manner and the gun movement resumed. The practice ceases one minute after the firing of the first shot. *Marking.*—Hits on the figure 3 targets only to count. Scoring : 2 points per hit.

CHAPTER VI.

PART I.

DRILL.

By MAJOR S. J. HEATH, M.C.,
East Lancashire Regiment.
Drill Adjutant, Senior Officers' School.

FOREWORD.

" Drill " in close order is of first importance in producing Discipline, Cohesion, and the habits of absolute and instant obedience to the order of a superior. ("Infantry Training," Section 1, para. 6.)

Too much stress cannot be laid upon the importance of drill, and an Officer cannot expect to aspire to the command of a Battalion unless he has knowledge of what is right and wrong in this respect. He can never attain this knowledge unless he has first studied the fundamental principle of section drill.

Drill for the sole purpose of practising movements is *not* what is required. Little knowledge of drill movements is actually required in the field, but the power of command, powers of observation, *and the habits of absolute and instant obedience to the orders of a superior,* and many other valuable assets which are acquired by the Officer, N.C.O. and man at drill, are of absolute necessity.

Avoid at all costs drill of the type sometimes met with, *e.g.:* A Section or a Platoon Commander is ordered to take his unit for half an hour's drill. In the first place his knowledge is lacking, he has a bad word of command, his appearance and bearing on parade is bad. He runs through a number of movements, all of which are performed incorrectly; no faults are checked. Result: men lose confidence in their leader, they are disgusted with their half an hour's drill, or, as they describe it, "being messed about," half an hour wasted, and discipline, instead of being tightened up, has depreciated.

Keep in mind the *spirit of drill*, which calls for from the *Commander*—

- (i) Knowledge.
- (ii) Correct attitude and bearing.
- (iii) Good words of command.
- (iv) *Command* your men, and don't let them command you.
- (v) Never let mistakes go unchecked.
- (vi) Faults are ever present, *observe* them.
- (vii) Strive for the object of drill, *absolute and instant obedience*.
- (viii) *Confidence*.

FROM THE MEN—

- (i) *Confidence* in their leader.
- (ii) Instinctive and unquestioning *obedience*.

In Appendix I will be found a forty minutes Drill Training Programme for a Section, Platoon, Company, and Battalion.

The object in view in submitting this programme is to get the maximum value out of drill during the forty minutes which it is assumed is all the time that is allowed for drill in the Training Programme.

It is suggested that before sending off Platoon or Section Commanders to exercise their commands in drill that the Officers or N.C.Os. should parade about fifteen minutes in advance of the men, and that they receive instruction under the Company Commander or Company Sergeant-Major in those movements which it is proposed to carry out.

BATTALION DRILL.

GENERAL NOTES.

(*a*) The Battalion Commander, when drilling, will place himself where he can best exercise supervision. Normally this is in front of the centre of the Battalion.

(*b*) Use the caution, " The Battalion will retire" for the purpose it is intended, *e.g.*, to fall back for a short distance only, before resuming the original direction, when ranks will not be changed. (Section 40, I.T.)

(*c*) When the command " About Turn " is given, ranks are changed, but Companies will not re-number. (Sect. 40, I.T.) [Section 82, I.T. (amended by A.O. 275/16).]

(*d*) The RIGHT of a Battalion is the right of the *leading platoon* of right Company. The LEFT of a Battalion is the left of the *rear platoon* of left Company. [Section 84, 2, I.T. (as amended by A.O. 275/16).]

(*e*) Normally, the Battalion will move off in column of fours or route, from the RIGHT of the Battalion [see (*d*)] or LEFT of Battalion [see (*d*)]. [Section 84, I.T. (as amended by A.O. 275/16).]

The Battalion may be moved off from any Company other than the above, and in any order by giving caution accordingly, *e.g.*:—

" Advance in column of route, in following order : —Nos. 3, 2, 1, and 4 Companies."

(*f*) The senior Major will normally be beside the guide of directing platoon, except when ranks are changed, as in Battalion in mass, turned about (not retiring), when he will be on outer flank.

(*g*) The normal directing flanks are as follows :—

Movement.	Directing Flank.
Advancing	Right.
Retiring	Left.
Column of route (at home)	Left (Section 77, 4, I.T., as amended by A.O. 479/15).
Column of route (France)	Right.
Column of fours (from right).	Left (Section 77, 4, I.T., as amended by A.O. 275/16).
Column of fours (from left)	Right.
Wheeling (or changing direction, as in column of platoons)	The flank to which the Battalion is being wheeled.
Deploying	The flank opposite to that of deployment.

(*h*) Where the flank is normal, *do not* name the flank. It is incorrect to give " The Battalion will advance, *by the right*—Quick—March."

(*i*) In deployments, send your Adjutant to mark the outer flank.

(*j*) The normal position of the Regimental Sergeant-Major is on the outer flank, except when the ranks are changed, as in Battalion in mass, turned about (not retiring), when he will be beside the guide of the directing platoon.

(*k*) For drill purposes it is preferable to move in " column of fours " than " column of route "; the

Commanders and supernumeraries are then in positions relative to line.

(*l*) " Column of fours " is distinct from " column of route," the former being used for drill purposes, the latter when it is intended to move on the road.

(*m*) In the following examples there are movements, the executive command of which could obviously be given by the Battalion Commander. Purposely, these examples are given to exercise the control of the subordinate Commanders.

(*n*) The question of dressing requires special attention, but if the principle laid down in Section 28, I.T., is observed, there ought to be little difficulty. There it states that—" *Commencing with the man nearest the flank by which the dressing is made, he will move up or back to his place successively.*" Platoons and Companies ought to apply this principle.

(*o*) In executing movements which entail waiting by the last Company for three or four minutes before moving, such as moving off in column of route, it is suggested that the whole Battalion be *not* brought to the slope, but that all except the leading Company " stand easy " until such time as they are required to move.

(*p*) A common fault is for Officers Commanding Companies to keep to their normal positions at all times. When Companies are moving on the executive word of the Battalion Commander, Company Commanders must keep their normal positions. At other times see they place themselves where they can best supervise the movement, *e.g.*: When a Company Commander gives to his platoon, which is in close column of platoons, " Order Arms," the best position is to the flank of the Company, and not six paces in front of the Company.

A FEW DON'TS.

Don't turn the horse's head away from the Battalion and shout over your shoulder. Keep horse's head towards the Battalion.

Don't get too close to the Battalion.

Don't carry out a movement until the preceding one has been correctly executed.

Don't treat the saddle as an arm-chair.

Don't, when the Battalion is marching, give commands until they are in step.

Don't allow the Sergeant-Major to call out the step unless you tell him to do so.

Don't finish up parades without a " march past."

Don't attempt to drill a Battalion when riding a restive horse; far better to dismount.

KEY.

⊕ Battalion Commander.

⊕ Company Commander.

○ Platoon Commander.

1. Telling Off and Proving a Battalion.

⊕ " Battalion, Order — Arms." " Tell off by Companies."

⊕ " No. 1 Company," " No. 2," " No. 3," " No. 4 Company," or " A," " B," " C," " D," according to their lettering or numbering in the Battalion, not as they stand on parade.

"Nos. 1 and 2 Right Half Battalion, Nos. 3 and 4 Left Half Battalion."

"Nos. 1 and 3 Right Companies, Nos. 2 and 4 Left Companies."

"Right Half Battalion, Slope—Arms." "Left Half Battalion, Slope—Arms."

"Right Companies, Order—Arms." "Left Companies, Order—Arms."

Important Points.

    (a) Insist on *absolute steadiness* in the execution of these movements. Even if only these movements are carried out correctly, good value is obtained.

    (b) The telling off has no bearing on future movements, *e.g.*, if No. 3 Company is the leading or Right Company they are still No. 3, *not* No. 1. (See Section 82 (2), "Infantry Training," as amended by A.O. 275, 1916.)

    (c) If Companies are lettered, substitute letters for numbers.

2. A Mass Advancing and Retiring.

"The Battalion will Advance, Quick—March." (The right will direct. The flanks will *not* be named.)

"The Battalion will Retire, About—Turn." (In retiring the left will direct.)

"The Battalion will Advance, About—Turn."

"Battalion—Halt."

Note.—The Second-in-Command will be beside the guide on directing flank, *e.g.*, when advancing, beside the right guide of leading Platoon of right Company. When retiring, beside left guide of leading Platoon of left Company. When the Battalion is turned about, but not retiring, he will not change over to new directing flank. The Regimental Sergeant-Major will in this case give direction to the guide.

Important Points.
- (*a*) Words of command given on proper foot, VERY IMPORTANT.
- (*b*) See that men do not look down or swing arm about when turning about.
- (*c*) Allow no one but yourself to talk on parade unless you tell them, *i.e.*, "Sergeant-Major, call out the step."

3. A Mass Moving Off in Column of Route.

"Advance in Column of Route, A Company Leading." (Or No. 1 Company, or, normally, whatever Company is on right.)

"A Company—'Shun." "Slope—Arms." "Form —Fours." "Right."

"1, 2, 3, 4, Left Wheel, Quick—March." (In time to follow preceding Platoon.)

"B, C, D, Stand—Easy."

"B, C, D Companies—'Shun." "Slope—Arms." "Form—Fours." "Right." (In time to follow A Company.)

"5 to 16, Quick—March." (In time to follow preceding Platoon.)

Important Points.
- (*a*) Do *not* bring Battalion to Slope before moving off. The Company Commanders will do so before they march off.
- (*b*) See the Platoon Commanders march off in step.
- (*c*) See that Officers and N.C.Os. take posts in Column of Route positions after giving words of command to get unit moving, and that correct distances are observed between Companies.

4. A Column of Route Forming Mass, Facing in the Same Direction.

"At the Halt, on the Left, Form—Mass."

"1 to 16, at the Halt, on the Left, Form—Platoon." (No. 1 immediately, the remainder as they arrive in their positions in Mass.)

"A, B, C, D (when Companies are steady), Order—Arms." "Stand at—Ease."

Important Points.
    (a) See that Platoon Commanders commence giving words of command in sufficient time to halt their Platoon at correct distance.
    (b) Company Commanders lose no time in bringing Companies to Order, "Stand at—Ease" on completion.
    (c) If required to stand easy on completion, order the Company Commander to carry this out.

5. A Mass Moving Off in Column of Fours.

"*Advance in Column of Fours, A Company (or No. 1 Company, or, normally, whatever Company is on the right) Leading.*"

"A Company—'Shun." "Slope—Arms." "Form—Fours." "Right."

"1, 2, 3, 4, Left Wheel, Quick—March." (In time to follow preceding Platoon.)

"B, C, D, Stand—Easy."

"B, C, D Companies—'Shun." "Slope—Arms." "Form—Fours." "Right." (In time to follow A Company.)

"5 to 16, Quick—March." (In time to follow preceding Platoon.)

(Company, Platoon, and Section Commanders will retain the relative positions they occupied before fours were formed, see Section 77, 3, "Infantry Training.")

Important Points.

- (a) Same as 3.
- (b) Commanders and Supernumeraries occupy positions relative to line.
- (c) No distances between Companies.

6. A Column of Fours Forming Mass, Facing a Flank.

"At the Halt, Facing Left, Form—Mass."

"1 to 16—Halt." "Left—Turn."

"1 to 4, Order—Arms." "Stand at—Ease." (Given when Companies are steady.)

Important Points.

Same as 4.

7. A Battalion in Mass Wheeling.

"Change Direction Right, Right—Wheel."

"Quick—March."

"Forward," "Mark—Time," or "Halt" (given when wheeled to required angle).

Important Points.

- (a) Before "Quick March" is given, see that the leading Platoons look to their right, and that the remainder of the Battalion make a partial turn to the left.
- (b) Apply the principles of a Company in Close Column Wheeling.

(c) Senior Major carries out the duties assigned to C.S.M. in Company movement. The R.S.M. carries out the duties assigned to Second-in-Command in Company movement.
(d) Although RIGHT Wheel is given, the Battalion will continue wheeling until "Mark Time," "Forward," or "Halt" is given.
(e) In the left wheel the positions of Senior Major and R.S.M. are the same, but their duties are reversed.
(f) A Battalion moving to right or left in fours wheeling, the Senior Major and R.S.M. will retain their positions and act on the inner or outer flank, as the case may be. The Adjutant will move to the opposite flank.

8. A Mass Moving Off in Line of Platoons in Fours.

"Move to the Right in Fours, Form Fours—Right."
"Quick—March."

Important Points.

(a) Company Commanders will take posts three paces in front of centre of their Companies, *i.e.*, a point midway between 2nd and 3rd Platoons.
(b) Platoon Commanders will take posts two paces in front of centre of their Platoons.
(c) Platoon Sergeants will take posts two paces in rear of the centre of their Platoons.
(d) *The left will direct unless otherwise ordered.*
(e) The Senior Major and R.S.M. will be in position relative to mass.

9. A Mass Retiring in Column of Route.

"Retire in Column of Route, D Company, or No. 4 Company, leading (or, normally, whatever Company is on the left).

"No. 4 Company — 'Shun." "Slope — Arms."
"Form—Fours." "Left."

"16, 15, 14, and 13, Left—Wheel." "Quick—March." (15, 14, and 13 in time to gain positions in column of route.)

"1, 2, 3, Stand—Easy." "'Shun." "Slope—Arms." "Form—Fours." "Left." (Given in time to gain position in column of route.)

"12 to 1, Quick—March." (Given in time to gain position in column of route.)

Important Points.

    (a) Company Commanders give their commands *in time* to gain their positions.

    (b) Platoon Commanders give command "Quick—March" on proper foot.

    (c) Left of rear Platoon of each Company to lead

    (d) Correct distance between Companies.

10. A Mass Retiring in Column of Route, Forming Mass, Facing in Same Direction.

"At the Halt, on the Right, Form—Mass."

"16, at the Halt, on the Right, Form—Platoon." (Given immediately.)

"15 to 1, at the Halt, on the Right, Form—Platoon." (Given when on their positions in Mass.)

"4, 3, 2, 1, Order—Arms." "Stand at—Ease." (Given when Companies are steady.)

Important Points.

    (a) 3, 2, and 1 Companies deploying to Mass interval immediately following Battalion Commander's command.

    (b) Platoon Commanders giving word of command in sufficient time.

(c) If "On the Left" is given it changes the ranks. Commanders and supernumeraries take post accordingly.

11. A Battalion in Mass Forming Open Mass.

"Form Open—Mass." "The remainder will Retire, About Turn, Quick—March." (On which 1, 5, 9, and 13 (or leading Platoons) Stand Fast; remainder turn about and step off.)

$$\left.\begin{array}{c} 2, \ 3, \ 4 \\ 6, \ 7, \ 8 \\ 10, \ 11, \ 12 \\ 14, \ 15, \ 16 \end{array}\right\}$$ "Halt. About—Turn."

(or succeeding Platoons).

Note.—This movement may be carried out from rear Platoons, when command would be "Form Open Mass, the remainder Quick—March."

Important Points.

(a) Platoon Commanders will not give "About —Turn" until guides have turned about and obtained their covering and distance from right guides of leading Platoons.

(b) Open Mass is a line of Companies in Column of Platoons. Therefore Platoons will not necessarily be in line with each other except 1, 5, 9, and 13 (or leading Platoons), or, in the case of forming from the rear, the rear Platoons.

12. A Battalion in Open Mass Advancing in Column of Platoons.

"Advance in Column of Platoons, A Company (or No. 1 Company, or any named Company, normally the Right Company) leading.

"1—'Shun." "Slope—Arms." "Company will advance. Quick—March."

"2, 3, 4—'Shun." "Slope—Arms." "Move to Right in Fours. Form Fours—Right. Quick—March." (Given in time to clear rear of preceding Company.)

"Left In—cline." (Given when leading guide is in line with centre of preceding Company.)

"Left In—cline." (Given when in rear of position in column.)

Important Point.

Company Commanders moving off their Companies in sufficient time so that leading guides just clear left of rear rank of preceding Company.

13. A Battalion in Column of Platoons Advancing in Same Direction in Column of Fours.

"Advance in Column of Fours from the Right."
"Form Fours—Right. Platoons, Left—Wheel."

Important Point.

Commanders and Supernumeraries occupy positions relative to line.

14. A Battalion in Mass Advancing in Line of Companies in Fours.

"Advance in Fours from the Right of Companies, Form—Fours. Right."

1, 5, 9, and 13 (or leading Platoons). "Left—Wheel. Quick—March." (Given immediately.)

2, 3, 4
6, 7, 8
10, 11, 12
14, 15, 16
} "Left — Wheel. Quick — March." (In time to follow preceding Platoon.)

(or succeeding Platoons).

Important Points.

(a) Officers and N.C.Os. take posts as for Column of Route.

(b) Battalion Commander will give the Company of direction, *i.e.*, "The Company on the right will direct," or, "The Company on the left will direct."

15. A Battalion in Line of Companies in Fours Forming Mass, Facing in the Same Direction and Halting.

"At the Halt, on the Left, Form—Mass."

1, 5, 9, and 13 (or leading Platoons). "At the Halt, on the Left, Form—Platoons." (Given immediately.)

2, 3, 4   "At the Halt, on the Left, Form—
6, 7, 8   Platoons." (Given when leading
10, 11, 12   guide is 7 paces from front rank of
14, 15, 16   preceding Platoon.)

(or succeeding Platoons).

Note.—This movement is more successful if open mass is formed first on the executive command of Battalion Commander "At the Halt, on the Left, Form—Platoon," then form mass in the usual manner.

Important Point.

Platoon Commanders give words of command in sufficient time so as not to get their Platoons over the alignment.

16. A Battalion in Mass Opening to Deploying Interval.

Note.—A Battalion may deploy direct from Mass on Battalion Commander's command, "On the Left (or Right), Form—Line. The remainder, Form—Fours,

Left. Quick—March." This method does not make for so accurate an alignment as the following :—

"To the left (or right, or from a named Company), open to deploying interval. The remainder (*i.e.,* Companies other than the Company of formation), Form—Fours, Left (Right or Outwards). Quick—March."

2, 3, 4 (or Companies other than Company of formation). "Halt." (Given when Companies are at deploying interval.)

"Right (or Left)—Turn." (Given when right [or left] guides are steady.)

Important Points.

(a) In deploying to the right, the left will be named as the directing flank.

(b) After deploying outwards, the directing flank will be named, but Companies will be aligned with the Company of formation.

(c) Good judgment on part of Company Commanders necessary. Deploying interval is interval equal to frontage of Company in line. In above movement the intervals will, of course, be equivalent to frontage of preceding Companies.

(d) In deploying it is usual for the Adjutant to mark the outer flank.

17. A Battalion at Deploying Interval Deploying into Line.

"On the Left, Form—Line. The remainder (*i.e.,* all except 1, 5, 9, and 13 Platoons, or leading), Form Fours—Left. Quick—March."

2, 3, 4
6, 7, 8
10, 11, 12
14, 15, 16
} "Halt. Right—Turn." (Right turn to be given when Platoon on right is steady.)

Important Point.

If on completion of the movement there are intervals between Companies (due to bad judgment of Company Commanders), Company Commanders will be ordered to close their Companies on the right, which will be done in succession, Companies waiting until Company on right is steady.

18. A Battalion in Line Forming Mass, Facing in the Same Direction on the Right (or Left).

"On the Right, Form Mass, the remainder (*i.e.*, all except No. 1 [or leading Platoon of right Company] Platoon), Form Fours—Right. Quick—March."

2—16, "Halt. Left—Turn." (Left turn given when right guide is steady.)

Important Point.

If the Battalion Commander desires companies to Stand at Ease and Stand Easy on completion of the movement, he will inform Company Commanders accordingly.

19. A Battalion in Mass Advancing in Double Column of Platoons.

Note.—This movement is more suitable if carried out from open mass.

"Advance in Double Column of Platoons, Nos. 1 and 3 Companies leading."

1 and 3, " 'Shun. Slope—Arms. Advance in Column."

1, 2, 3, 4
9, 10, 11, 12
"Platoon will advance, Quick—March." 1 and 9 immediately, remainder when at column distance.

2 and 4, " 'Shun. Slope—Arms. Move to right in Fours. Form Fours—Right. Quick—March." (Given in time to just clear preceding Company.)

" Left In—cline." (Given when right guide is in rear of centre of preceding Company.)

" Left In—cline." (When in rear of position in column.)

" Halt. Advance in Column."

5, 6, 7, 8 } " Platoon will advance. Quick—
13, 14, 15, 16 }   March."

Important Points.

(a) 1 and 3 Companies advancing simultaneously.

(b) Leading Platoons of 2 and 4 Companies stepping off without loss of time and stepping out to correct distance.

20.—A Battalion Advancing in Double Column of Platoons, Forming Open Mass, and Halting.

" At the halt, on the left, form open Mass, the remainder (*i.e.*, 2 and 4 Companies), Left In—cline."

1 and 3. " Halt. Right—Dress. Order—Arms. Stand at—Ease."

2 and 4, " Right In—cline." (Given when five paces from left of strongest Platoon of Company on right.)

" Halt. Right—Dress. Order—Arms. Stand at—Ease."

Important Point.

Platoons, except Nos. 1, 5, 9, and 13 (or leading Platoon), will not necessarily be in line with the Platoon of Company on right. They will be at column distance from the leading Platoon of their Company.

21. A Battalion in Mass Moving Off in Line of Platoons in Fours.

" Move to the Right in Fours. Form—Fours, Right."

" Battalion, Stand at—Ease."

"Advance in four lines of Platoons in fours, by the left (or right, or any named Platoon), at —— paces interval, at —— paces distance—Move."

⊟ 1—2—3, "At the Double, Ad—vance."

From the left (or right, or any named Platoon) open to —— paces interval (on which Nos. 2—3—4, 6—7—8, 10—11—12 Platoons will be led by their Platoon Commanders to the required interval).

⊟ 1—2—3, Signal "Quick Time" (given when their Companies are at the required distance from the Company in their immediate rear).

⊟ 4, "Ad—vance. From the left (or right, or any named Platoon) open to —— paces interval, the remainder Double—March" (when 14—15—16 Platoons will be led by their Platoon Commanders to the required interval).

○ 14—15—16, "Quick Time" *signal* when at required interval.

Important Points.

(a) Words of command of the Company Commander given at once to move immediately from the shelled area.

(b) Men will move at the *Trail*.

(c) When at increased interval and distance Battalion and Company Commanders will exercise only those means of control which would be possible in the field.

(d) Words of command to be reduced to a minimum.

(e) Take care to give directing flank.

Note.—It would, of course, not be sound to move any unit in quick time. But to show the movement clearly it is done in this example with the rear Company.

22. Battalion in Line of Platoons in Fours Halting.

Signal, "Halt!"

1—16, Signal, "Halt!"

Important Points.

- (a) Platoon Commanders repeat Battalion Commander's signal; men to act on their Platoon Commander's signal.
- (b) Men to Stand at Ease and Stand Easy on signal, "Halt!"
- (c) Not too much use of whistle.

23. A Battalion in Line of Platoons in Fours at Intervals, etc., Advancing.

Signal, "Advance."

1—16, repeat signal (on which men act).

24. A Battalion in Line of Platoons in Fours, Closing to Mass Interval and Distance, i.e., Formation from which Battalion was Opened Out.

Signal, "Close" (indicating on which platoon the Battalion is to close, normally No. 1).

1—16, signal "Advance" (on which Platoons will be led by Platoon Commanders to position from which they opened out).

Important Points.

Same as 2.

Positions of Officers, W.Os., N.C.Os., and Supernumeraries in Mass.

Battalion Commander—10 paces in front of centre of Battalion.

Second-in-Command—2 paces from right of Battalion in line with right guide.

Adjutant—A horse's length to right rear of Battalion Commander.

Battalion Sergeant-Major—2 paces from left of Battalion, in line with left guide.

Company Commanders—6 paces in front of centre of leading Platoon of their Companies.

Seconds-in-Command of Companies—1 pace from left of the second Platoon of their Companies, in line with the leading rank.

Platoon Commanders—2 paces in front of centre of their Platoons.

Company Sergeant-Majors—1 pace from the right of the second Platoon of their Companies, in line with the leading rank.

Company Quartermaster-Sergeants—1 pace from the right of the third Platoon of their Companies, in line with the leading rank.

Platoon Sergeants—2 paces in rear of the centre of their Platoons.

Section Commanders—On the outer flanks of their Sections, in line with leading rank.

Drummer (when with Company)—2 paces in rear of third file from right of Platoon.

Positions of Commanders and Supernumeraries in Battalion in Line (if Ceremonial).

If not, Company and Platoon Commanders and Supernumeraries occupy positions as for Company in Line.

Battalion Commander—15 paces in front of centre of Battalion.

Senior Major—10 paces in front of right guide of Battalion.

Adjutant—10 paces in front of left guide of Battalion.

Company Commander—10 paces in front of centre of Companies.

Platoon Commander—3 paces in front of centre of Platoon.

Regimental-Sergeant-Major—4 paces in rear of centre of Battalion.

Company Sergeant-Major—Right guide of Company.

Company Quartermaster-Sergeant—Left guide of Company.

Platoon Sergeants—Divide supernumerary rank between them at two paces from rear rank.

DEMONSTRATIONS.

1. Battalion Demonstration.

1. The Battalion is drawn up in mass.

2. The rôle of the Second-in-Command, viz.: He calls the Battalion to "Attention," slopes arms, and reports "All present," or otherwise, to the Commanding Officer as the latter comes on to parade.

3. The rôle of the Commanding Officer, who at a glance should be able to see how the Battalion is carrying itself, and the training, cleanliness, and general appearance of the men.

4. The importance of letting Officers, N.C.Os. and men know what is going to be carried out.

5. How to do it :—(a) Commanding Officer speaks himself.
   (b) Company Officer speaks to the Platoon Commanders.
   (c) Good news to men.

6. Demonstration of the importance of one movement being correctly carried out before the next is attempted.

7. Demonstrate :—(a) The Battalion being brought to the " Stand-at-Ease " position.
   (b) Then to the position of " Attention."
   (c) Then to the " Slope."
   (d) Then to the " Quick — March."
   (e) Then to the " Halt."
   (f) Advancing and Retiring.
   (g) Moving Battalion to flank in fours, halting, and turning to front.

8. Demonstrate the Battalion changing direction to the right, and show the first movement correctly carried out, and then the second.

9. Demonstrate the Battalion advancing in Column of Route, and show the whole Battalion being brought to the " Slope " by the Commanding Officer for no reason.

10. Demonstrate the Battalion on the march, then, facing left, forming close column of Corps.

11. Demonstrate the importance of telling the men how they have done during the morning's work, making use of one of the methods of forming them up, and then demonstrate the Battalion in the March Past in Column of Route on their return to barracks or billets.

2. Guards.

No system of duties mounting is shown in any official publication; in consequence, a different system exists in practically every Regiment.

It is suggested that duties mounting ought to be conducted with a certain amount of ceremony—that the band, drums, or pipes be present and play during the inspection.

The Adjutant to take special interest in this parade.

It is not a bad plan, when practicable, to turn out the Battalion during rest to see the " duties mounting."

A suitable time for " duties mounting " is two hours after training is finished, say 4 p.m. This hour is suggested because then only the old guard is missing training. The new guard would carry out their training with their Companies and mount afterwards.

In some Regiments, N.C.Os. and men for " waiting guard " are detailed—say, one Corporal or Lance-Corporal and two men. This is very sound, for in the event of a N.C.O. or man for some reason or other not being present, or being present not being allowed to mount, there are men present to take their places.

Again, it is customary in some Regiments to detail the best turned out man for duty as Commanding Officer's orderly for the day, and replace him by a man who is waiting guard. Remember, the state of discipline which exists in a Battalion can generally be gauged by the manner in which it carries out its guard duties.

After mounting, the commander of the guard should, with the guard, go very carefully into such detail as sentry-go, challenging, duties on guard, dress, compliments, etc.; in fact, on a quiet guard he should practise them in turning out, and in arm drill. This is rather important, having regard to the lack of knowledge on the subject generally of the young soldier. The Regimental Sergeant-Major ought frequently to visit all guards and see that the N.C.Os. in charge are doing their job.

The following is a system taught at this School. It is hoped that where no system exists, or where the system is a bad one, it will prove of value :—

KEY.

- Adjutant or Orderly Officer.
- Regimental Sergeant-Major.
- Battalion Orderly-Sergeant.
- Company Orderly-Sergeants.
- Sergeant, or Senior N.C.O.
- Corporal.
- Privates, Front Rank.
- Privates, Rear Rank.
- Drummer.

PLAN OF DUTIES MOUNTING PARADE.

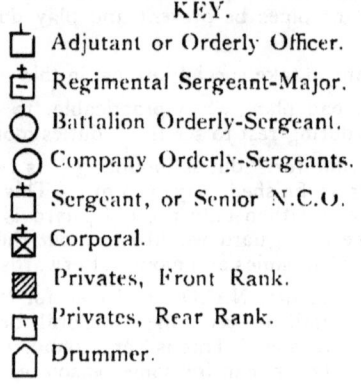

1. Duties will fall in in line, in two ranks if the Guard comprises five or more men. Quarter-Guard on the right; Billet Guards on the left. Commanders on the right of their Guards; Seconds-in-Command of Guards, if N.C.Os., on the left of their Guards.

2. The Adjutant or Orderly Officer, or both, will be present at Duties Mounting Parade.

3. The Regimental Sergeant-Major will be eighteen paces from the centre of the Duties, and will, until such time as the parade falls in, walk smartly up and down from one end of the Duties to the other.

The Drummer will be formed up facing the centre of the Duties and twenty-two paces from them.

The Orderly-Sergeants will form up eighteen paces in front of and facing the Duties, and two paces to the right. The Battalion Orderly-Sergeant will be two paces to the right of the duties.

The Guard Drummer will be immediately on the right of the Guard Commander.

4. FALLING IN OF THE PARADE :—

"*Duties, Fall In.*" (On which the drummer will beat a double flam; Commanders of Guards will come to attention, take one and a half paces forward, turn to the right, and cover.)

Covers the Guard Commanders, and gives the word "*Steady,*" on which they will turn to the front.

After a pause of four seconds will beat a flam, on which the Duties will come to attention. After a further pause of four seconds he will beat a roll, on which the Duties will take one pace forward, count a slight pause, and then take up their dressing by short, quick steps, gaining the remaining half-pace. When the drummer sees the Duties are steady he will end the roll, concluding with a sharp tap, on which the Duties will turn their head and eyes smartly to the front.

"*Duties, Stand at—Ease.*" "*Tell Off.*" (On the command "Tell Off" Commanders of Guards will come to attention, slope arms, march ten paces to the front, halt, turn about, and then proceed to tell off as follows):—

Quarter Guard

"*Quarter-Guard—'Shun.*" "*Rear Rank, one pace step back—March.*"

"*Guard—Size.*" (On the command "Size" the Guard will slope arms and move to the place where they size.)

"*Close ranks—March.*" "*Order arms.*"

"*Guard—Number.*" "*Right Files, Stand at—Ease.*" "*Left Files, Stand at—Ease.*"

A B C D Billet Guards

"*Guard—'Shun.*" "*Guard—Size.*" (On the command "Size" the Guard will slope arms and move to the place where they size.)

"*Order — Arms.*" "*Number.*" "*Right Files, Stand at—Ease.*" "*Left Files, Stand at—Ease.*"

"*Guard Commanders, Fall in.*" (On which Commanders will take ten paces forward, halt in line with the right of their Guards, turn about, order arms, and stand at ease.)

"*Duties — 'Shun.*" "*Are you present, Quarter-Guard?*" "*A Company Billet Guard?*" "*B Company?*" "*C Company?*" "*D Company?*" (On which Commanders will answer "Present, Sir," or otherwise.)

"*Duties, Right—Dress.*"

"*Duties, Eyes—Front.*"

"*Fix—Bayonets.*" "*Rear rank, one pace step back—March.*" "*Rear Rank, Right—Dress.*"

"*Rear Rank, Eyes—Front.*"

"*Slope — Arms.*" (Regimental Sergeant-Major then reports "Duties present" to the Adjutant, and places himself two paces to the right of the Battalion Orderly-Sergeant.)

" Order—Arms." (He then carries out the inspection, accompanied by the Regimental Sergeant-Major and the Battalion Orderly-Sergeant, who both salute as he arrives at right of Duties.)

" Unfix — Bayonets." " For inspection, Port—Arms."

" Duties — 'Shun." " Close ranks — March." " Duties, Right—Dress."

" Duties, Eyes—Front."

" Duties, Fix—Bayonets. " Slope—Arms."

" Non-Commissioned Officers, Take Posts." (On which Commanders of Guards turn about, march in quick time, and will halt and turn to their front at a point two paces in rear of the centre of their Guards. The Corporal of the Quarter-Guard will take the position vacated by the Sergeant.)

" Quarter-Guard to the Front, Remainder, Left—Form." (Assuming that rendezvous of Billet Guards lie in that direction.)

" To your Guards, Quick—March." (On which Guards will march direct to their posts, Commanders of Billet Guards giving the command *" Forward "* when their Guards are correctly formed to the left.

" Eyes—Right (or *" Eyes—Left "*) to the Adjutant or Orderly Officer as they march off.

Approaches the Adjutant or Orderly Officer and asks permission to dismiss the Orderly-Sergeants.

Waits on parade until the Old Guard is dismissed.

RELIEF OF GUARDS.

New *"Guard—Halt."* (When Guard is fifteen paces from front of Old Guard, or, when the ground does not admit of this, six paces from the left of the Old Guard.)

"Right—Dress." (On which Corporal will take post on left of Guard.)

"Eyes—Front." "Rear rank, one pace step back—March."

"Rear rank, Right—Dress." "Rear rank, Eyes—Front."

PLAN OF QUARTER-GUARD FORMED UP FOR RELIEF. (PLAN 2.)

(Other Guards relieve in similar manner.)

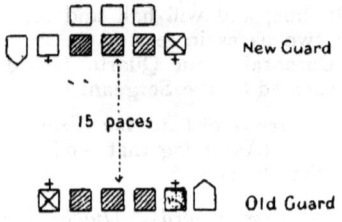

Old *"Old Guard, Present—Arms."*

Old Sounds "General Salute."

New *"New Guard, Present—Arms."*

New Sounds "General Salute."

Old Gives over detail of his Guard, *i.e.*, *"One sentry by day, two sentries by night."*

"*Old Guard, Slope—Arms.*"

New "*New Guard, Slope—Arms.*"

Old "*Old Guard, Order—Arms.*"

New "*New Guard, Order—Arms.*"

Old "*Old Guard, Stand at—Ease.*"

New "*New Guard, Stand at—Ease.*"

Now proceeds to tell off his Guard in reliefs, first of all calling them to attention, then giving the following commands :—

"*Corporal of Guard, first and last numbers, Slope—Arms.*" "*Quick—March.*" "*Halt*" (given when six paces in front of Guard). "*Form up.*" (On which the last number will proceed to the Guard-room and assist in taking over. The relief will form up as shown in Plan 3.)

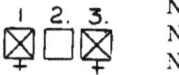

No. 1.—Corporal, New Guard.
No. 2.—First Relief.
No. 3.—Corporal, Old Guard.

Old Takes his post in the relief on the command "Form up."

New "*Relief, Right—Dress.*" "*Relief, Eyes—Front.*" "*Left Turn*" (given after inspection). "*To your posts, Quick—March.*"

After the command "Left—Turn" the relief will be as in Plan 4 :—

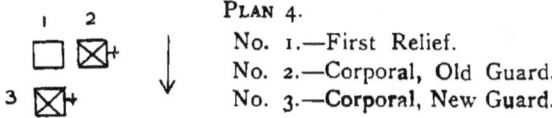

PLAN 4.
No. 1.—First Relief.
No. 2.—Corporal, Old Guard.
No. 3.—Corporal, New Guard.

"*Relief—Halt.*" (Given when about two paces from the sentry. On the approach of the relief the sentry, with rifle at the slope, will place himself in front of the sentry box. On the word "Halt" being given by the Corporal of the New Guard, the new sentry will move out from the relief and fall in on the left of the old sentry, facing in the same direction; the old sentry will then give over his orders, the Corporal seeing that they are correctly given and understood.)

Plan 5 shows position of Corporals and Sentries at this stage (before word "Pass" is given):—

PLAN 5.

No. 1.—Corporal, Old Guard.
No. 2.—Sentry, Old Guard.
No. 3.—Sentry, New Guard.
No. 4.—Corporal, New Guard.

"*Sentries—Pass.*" (The old sentry will move to his place in the relief, and the new sentry will close two paces to his right.)

Plan 6 shows position of Corporals and sentries after word "Pass" is given, and the old sentry has joined the relief.

PLAN 6.

No. 1.—New Sentry.
No. 2.—Old Sentry.
No. 3.—Corporal, Old Guard.
No. 4.—Corporal, New Guard.

"*Quick—March.*" (When relief will march to a point two paces in front of the Old Guard.) "*Halt.*" "*Right—Turn.*"

"*Right—Dress.*" "*Eyes—Front.*"

Now reports to Commander of the Old Guard *" Relief dismounted; correct, Sergeant,"* on which the Sergeant proceeds to inspect the relief.

Old *" Relief—Dismiss."*

New Reports to his Guard Commander *" Sentry posted; all correct, Sergeant."*

Note.—During the time that the sentry is being relieved the Sergeant of the New Guard will be taking over the Guard-room, etc., assisted by the "last number," who has already proceeded to the Guard-room. Before leaving his Guard he will detail a man to take charge in his absence.

Old Now prepares his Guard for marching off in the following manner :—

" Old Guard—'Shun." *" Right—Dress."* *" Eyes —Front."*

" Close ranks—March." *" Stand at—Ease."*

The Sergeant then places himself on the right of his Guard.

Old *" Old Guard—'Shun."*

New *" New Guard—'Shun."*

Old *" Old Guard, Slope—Arms."* *" N.C.Os., take Posts."*

New *" New Guard, Slope—Arms."*

Old *" Old Guard, Right—Form. Quick—March."*

New *" New Guard, Present—Arms."*

New Sounds " General Salute."

" Eyes—Left." *" Eyes—Front."*

Old Guard now proceeds to parade ground and is there inspected and dismissed by the Adjutant or Orderly Officer.

"*Guard, Slope—Arms.*"   "*Close Ranks—March.*"
"*Into File, Right—Turn.*"   "*Left Wheel, Quick—March.*"   "*Left—Wheel.*"   "*Halt.*"   "*Left—Turn.*"   "*Right—Dress.*"   "*Eyes—Front.*"

"*Rear Rank, one pace step back—March.*"   "*Rear Rank, Right—Dress.*"   "*Rear Rank, Eyes—Front.*"   "*Order—Arms.*"   "*Stand at—Ease.*"

(The New Guard should now be on the ground vacated by the Old Guard.)

The following very important points will now be noted :—

- (a) General Orders will be read and explained to the Guard.
- (b) Place of parade pointed out to the Guard.
- (c) Guard practised in turning out and turning in.
- (d) Guard shown how to turn out under various circumstances, such as to Commanding Officer, General Officers, etc.
- (e) Guard shown how to do sentry-go.
- (f) Guard shown how to challenge.

The following should be read in conjunction with the above :—

"King's Regulations," paras. 941 to 954, 1797 to 1804, and footnote on page 350.
"Ceremonial, 1912," paras. 127 to 131.
"Infantry Training," Section 74.

FAULTS IN DUTIES MOUNTING, GUARDS AND SENTRIES.

1. DUTIES MOUNTING.

No system, and lack of ceremony.

2. RELIEF OF GUARD.
      (i) No dressing.
      (ii) Ranks not opened.
      (iii) Old and New Guards both giving commands simultaneously.
      (iv) Corporal of Old Guard not accompanying the relief.
      (v) Orders not given over correctly.
      (vi) Relief marching off slovenly.
      (vii) Guard not correctly taken over.
      (viii) A man not detailed to take charge of Guard while Commanders are taking over.
      (ix) Bad marching off.
      (x) Dismissal from the parade ground without being inspected and dismissed by the Orderly Officer.

3. AFTER MOUNTING.
      (i) Taking off equipment whilst on Guard.
      (ii) Slow in turning out.
      (iii) Dirty in turning out.
      (iv) Commander not dressing his Guard when turning out.
      (v) Commander not reporting his Guard when visited by Orderly Officer.
      (vi) Commander not knowing General Orders of the Guard.
      (vii) Commander not frequently visiting his sentry.
      (viii) Commander and sentry not knowing distinguishing marks for Commanders' motor-cars.
      (ix) Failure to double to their posts on "Guard turn out."
      (x) Failure of N.C.O. to dismiss correctly.

(xi) Failure on the part of many N.C.Os. in charge of Guards to realise the importance of being on duty outside the Guard-room in order to watch the sentry and help him to perform his duties in a soldierly manner. Invariably N.C.Os., even where there are two on Guard, remain inside their barns or tents, and make no attempt to supervise their Guards.

4. **SENTRIES.**
    (i) Generally slovenly.
    (ii) Not knowing their orders.
    (iii) Not paying proper compliments.
    (iv) Speaking to people whilst on sentry.
    (v) Bad challenging.
    (vi) When at the end of their beat not turning to the front.
    (vii) Saluting whilst marching.
    (viii) Not knowing the names of Officers.
    (ix) Slack in turning out the Guard.

A SYSTEM OF CLOSING UNITS QUICKLY FOR PURPOSES OF GIVING INSTRUCTIONS, GIVING OUT ORDERS, PRELIMINARY INSTRUCTIONS BEFORE ATTACK, etc.

EXAMPLE 1.

A Battalion in Mass closing in to enable the C.O. to speak to the Battalion so that all are in a position to hear.

Position 1. Mass.

```
    D             C     ↑     B             A
...........   ———————       ———————   ·  · ·
...........   ———————       ———————   · · · · · · ·
...........   ———————       ———————   ············
...........   ———————       ———————   ············
...........   ———————       ———————   ············
···········   ———————       ———————   ············
...........   ———————       ———————   ············
...........   ———————       ———————   ············
```

Position 2. Mass closed in, occupying frontage and depth of two Companies.

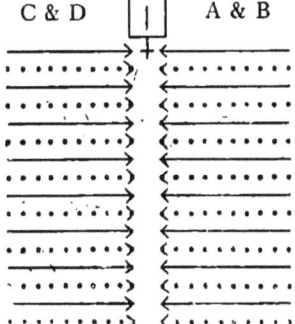

Words of Command to bring Battalion from Position 1 to 2.	╷ □	"On B and C Companies close to a frontage of two Companies."
		"A and D Companies, INTO FILE, INWARDS TURN. At the 'Short Trail,' Quick—March." (When in position) "HALT."
		"B and C Companies, INWARDS TURN; Battalion, STAND AT — EASE. STAND — EASY."
Words of Command. Positions 2 to 1.	┬ □	"Battalion—Attention. Re-form—Mass."
		"A and D Companies, About—Turn. Quick—March."
	┬ □	"A Company—Halt. Left —Turn" (when in position).
	┬ □	"D Company—Halt. Right —Turn" (when in position).
	┬ □	"B Company, Right — Turn."
	┬ □	"C Company, Left — Turn."

EXAMPLE 2.

Calling out Officers and N.C.Os. of Companies clear of Battalion to speak to them.

Position 1. *Mass.* Officers and N.C.Os. in correct positions.

Words of Command. "Officers and N.C.Os."
Positions 1 to 2. (On which the Officers and N.C.Os. will DOUBLE in front of the Battalion, and form up as in Position 2. The O.C. Company will, as soon as he DOUBLES out, face his Officers and N.C.Os., and when he sees that they are present will turn about, then Officers and N.C.Os. will salute together, the N.C.Os. will order arms, Officers and N.C.Os. stand at ease and stand easy.)

Position 2. Officers and N.C.Os. form up by Companies in front of Battalion as follows:—

Position II.

D. Coy. C. Coy. B Coy A Coy.

Words of Command. "**Dress up the Flanks.**"
Positions 2 to 3. (On which the Officers and N.C.Os. of "A" and "D" Companies will form to the Left and Right respectively at the DOUBLE, and carrying rifles at the "Short Trail.")

Position 3. Officers and N.C.Os. form inwards.

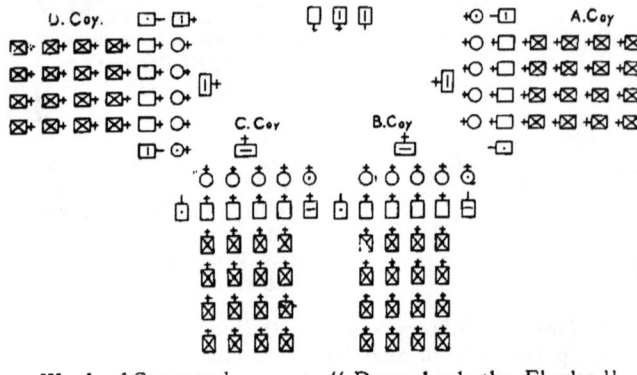

Words of Command. "Dress back the Flanks."
Positions 3 to 2. (On which "A" and "D" Companies will dress back in line with "B" and "C" Companies at the DOUBLE.)

Words of Command. "Fall in." (On which N.C.Os. will come to "Attention, Slope — Arms." Officers and N.C.Os. will then salute, turn about, and DOUBLE to their Companies.)
Positions 2 to 1.

EXAMPLE 3.
A Battalion in Close Column of Companies Closing in for the C.O. to Speak to the Battalion.

Words of Command. Positions 1 to 2.

"A and B Companies will retire. About—Turn. On B and C Companies close to three paces. A and D Companies at the 'Short Trail.' Quick — March (when at three paces distance). Halt. Battalion, Stand at—Ease. Stand—Easy."

Position 1. *Battalion in Close Column of Companies.*

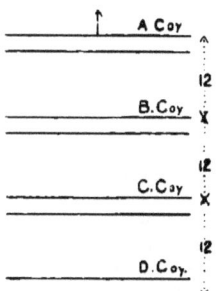

Position 2. Battalion in Close Column of Companies, three paces between "A" and "B," and "C" and "D," twelve paces between "B" and "C," "A" and "B" Companies turned about, facing "C" and "D."

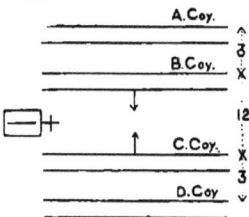

Words of Command. Positions 2 to 1.		
	┼⎵	"Battalion—Attention. A and B Companies will advance. D Company will retire. About—Turn. From B and C Companies form close column of Companies. A and D Companies, Quick—March."
	┼⎴⎵	"A Company (when at twelve paces)—Halt. Right—Dress."
	┼⎴⎵	"D Company (when at twelve paces)—Halt. Company will advance. About—Turn. Right—Dress."

EXAMPLE 4.

Officers falling out at the conclusion of a parade.

"*Battalion.*" (On which the Battalion will stand properly at ease, or the Battalion may be brought to the position of attention or to the slope.)

"*Fall out—the Officers.*" (On which Officers will come to attention, turn toward the Commanding Officer, and march out in quick time, and will form up in line at half-pace interval six paces from the Commanding Officer, mounted officers on the right. As soon as all Officers are in position, Officers will salute, taking the time from the mounted or dismounted Officer on the right; this Officer will be slightly in advance of the line so as to be able to give the time.) Officers will then march smartly to the rear of the Commanding Officer, turn about and face the Battalion, standing to attention until Battalion is dismissed.

CEREMONIAL.

Great value is attached to Ceremonial drill, especially at the conclusion of a morning's drill or field training. It is suggested that fifteen or even five minutes' Ceremonial at the conclusion of parades will do much to improve the spirit and Moral of all ranks.

Music, of course, is essential, even though, for a platoon, only a bugler, flautist, or piper is available.

The following are extracts from the "Ceremonial, 1912," provisional amendment, 1914.

Infantry.

55. GENERAL RULES.

1. *Formation of Companies.*—Companies will fall in in line, will be equalised and sized from flanks to centre, numbered from right to left, and told off into Platoons.

Company Commanders will not be mounted on ceremonial parades.

Section Commanders below the rank of Sergeant, Pioneers, and Signallers will be in the ranks. Signallers will not carry flags. The personnel of the Machine Gun Section will parade with their respective Companies unless the machine guns are specially ordered to be on parade. Company Sergeant-Majors and Company Quartermaster-Sergeants will be on the flanks of the front rank of their Companies, acting as right and left guide respectively, and will dress the Company as required. They will fix bayonets with the men. Sergeants, whether temporarily commanding Platoons or not, will be two paces in rear of the Company at equal intervals apart.

2. *Posts of Officers.*—In line, the Battalion Commander will be fifteen paces in front of the centre of the line. The senior Major will be ten paces in front of the right guide of the Battalion, the Adjutant ten paces in front of the left guide. Company Commanders will be ten paces, Officers Second-in-Command of Companies three paces, in front of the centre of their Companies. Platoon Commanders, when Officers, will be three paces in front of the centre of their Platoons. If there are less than four Officers Commanding Platoons in any Company on parade, the Officer Second in Command and the Platoon Commanders will divide the Company frontage equally between them.

In close column of Companies, which for ceremonial will be at twelve paces distance, measured from the heels of the front rank of one unit to the heels of the front rank of the next, the Battalion Commander will be fifteen paces in front of the centre of the leading Company. The senior Major will be on the right flank of the Battalion, three paces from a point midway between the first and second Companies, the Adjutant immediately in rear of him, between the third and fourth Companies, except that when the Battalion is on the move, it will be the Adjutant's duty to place himself in a position from which he can best superintend the direction of the advance and the covering of the guides on the directing flank. Company Commanders will be three paces from the left flank of their Companies. Officers Second-in-Command of Companies will be three paces in front of the centre of their Companies, Officers Commanding Platoons three paces in front of the centre of their Platoons.

If there are less than four Officers Commanding Platoons in any Company on parade, the Officer Second-in-Command and the Platoon Commanders will divide the Company frontage equally between them.

3. *Posts of Officers and other Ranks of the R.A.M.C. attached to Units.*—When the Battalion is formed in line or in marching past, the Medical Officer

will be two paces in front of the centre of the R.A.M.C. personnel, which will be five paces in rear of the Band when in line, or ten paces in rear of the centre of the rear Company when marching past. Not more than one Medical Officer will march past with each Battalion, the remainder, when more than one is present, taking post in rear of the saluting point. Medical Officers, when marching past, will salute with the right hand.

4. *Posts of Battalion Headquarters, etc.*—Posts of the personnel of Battalion Headquarters, band and drums (or bugles), machine guns, regimental transport, and cyclists, if present, and stretcher-bearers on parade as such, are shown in Plates 2 and 3.

5. *Marking Points and Markers.*—Flags or posts may be set up to mark the line on which troops are to form, or the line may be picked out, or marked by whitewash.

The Platoon Sergeants of the outer Platoons of a Company are available to act as markers. The words *on markers* should precede the command given when it is required to dress on markers. In such cases both markers of the Company of formation and the outer markers of the remaining Companies will double out in the case of deployments from close column on the command "Quick—March," and when forming line to a flank on the command "Left (or Right)—Form." Markers in giving points should turn towards the point of formation at arm's length in front of the alignment, with arms at the slope on the shoulder farthest from the alignment. When the men approach they will extend their inner arm at right angles to the body with the fist clenched, on which the line will dress. When the dressing is completed markers will resume their positions at the double on the command "Steady," changing their arms if necessary as they step off.

THE COMPANY.

67. *Sizing and Telling Off a Company.*

TALLEST ON THE RIGHT, SHORTEST ON THE LEFT, IN SINGLE RANK—SIZE.	The whole will break off and arrange themselves in single rank according to their size, the tallest on the right and the shortest on the left, carrying their rifles at the short trail, and will take up their dressing by the right.
NUMBER.	From right to left of the whole company.
SLOPE—ARMS. ODD NUMBERS ONE PACE FORWARD, EVEN NUMBERS ONE PACE STEP BACK —MARCH.	The odd numbers will take one pace forward and the even numbers will step back one pace.
NUMBER ONE STAND FAST. RANKS, RIGHT AND LEFT —TURN.	The odd numbers, with the exception of No. 1, will turn to the right, the even numbers to the left
FORM COMPANY QUICK—MARCH.	The whole will step off, the even numbers wheeling round to the right and following the left hand men of the odd numbers. No. 3 will form up two paces in rear of No. 1 ; No. 5 on the left of No. 1 ; No. 7 in rear of No. 5 ; No. 9 on the left of No. 5, and so on. The leading men of the even numbers will always form in the rear rank and the next man in the front rank. As the men arrive in their places they will turn to the left, order arms, and take up their dressing. NOTE.—If space is limited a company may be sized in two ranks, tallest on the flanks, shortest in the centre.

When the Company has been sized it will be numbered from right to left and told off into Platoons, Platoons being numbered from 1 to 4 within each

Company. When the number of files is not divisible by four, the outer Platoons should be the stronger. A Company will be told off into Platoons by calling out the numbers of the left-hand men: *e.g.*, *No. 21.* No. 21 of the front rank will then prove by extending his left forearm horizontally, elbow close to the side; *No. 21, left of No. 1 Platoon.* No. 21 will then drop his arm to the side. *No. 41, left of No. 2 Platoon,* etc.

68. *A Company in Line Saluting.**

Fix—Bayonets. Slope—Arms. General Salute. Present—Arms.	On the command Present—Arms, all officers will salute. The supernumerary rank and the guides present arms with the men.
Slope—Arms.	The officers will cut their hands away. Arms will then be ordered and bayonets unfixed.

69. *A Company Marching Past.*

For this practice the Company will be formed in line; arms will be at the *Order.* The posts of Officers are given in Sec. 55, 2.

Four points, numbered 1, 2, 3, and 4 (Plate 1), will be placed marking the angles of an oblong, of which the long sides will be 160 paces in length, and the short sides 80.

The Company will be in the centre of one of the long sides—the side opposite to the saluting base.

A point, termed the saluting point, will be placed ten paces outside the centre of the saluting base, turned towards the Company; and a point, lettered "A,"

---

* In this and the following sections dealing with ceremonial, the commands to *Slope Arms* and *Fix Bayonets* will not apply to men of Rifle Regiments, who will remain at the *Order* when halted, will *Present Arms* from the *Order* without *Fixing Bayonets,* and will march past at the *Trail.*

turned in like manner, on the saluting base, at ten paces to the left of the saluting point. As a rule all these points should be marked by camp colours.

Fix—Bayonets. Slope—Arms. Form—Fours. Right. Quick—March. Left—Wheel.	The company will step off, and will change direction to the left round the first point.
Company—Halt. Left—Turn. Right—Dress.	When the right of the company arrives on the saluting base, the commander will order it to Halt. Left—Turn. The company having turned to its front, the right-hand man of the front rank will immediately align himself on the right guide, and on the command Right—Dress, the right guide will dress the company and give the command Eyes—Front.
By the Right. Quick—March. Eyes—Right.	The commander, posted as in line—*i.e.*, ten paces in front of the centre of the company—will then give the command By the Right, Quick—March As he reaches the point "A" he will give Eyes—Right, upon which all, except the right guide, will turn their heads and eyes well to the right, looking the reviewing officer in the face, and the officers will salute.
Eyes—Front.	When the company is ten paces beyond the saluting point the commander will give Eyes—Front, upon which all will turn their heads and eyes to the front, and the officers will cut their hands away to side. *Note.*—The company, if required to resume its position on the original alignment, will be moved there from the second or third point in any convenient formation.

REVIEW OF A BATTALION.

71. *Formation.*

The Battalion will be drawn up in line as in Plate 2; bayonets will be fixed and arms sloped.

When the Colonel of the Regiment is present he will be ten paces in front of the Officer Commanding the Battalion. Should the Colonel-in-Chief also be present, he will be ten paces in front of the former.

72. *Receiving the Reviewing Officer.*

GENERAL SALUTE. PRESENT—ARMS.	When the reviewing officer reaches a point about sixty paces in advance of the centre of the battalion, he will be received with a salute, the men presenting arms, the band playing the first part of a slow march, and the drums beating. All officers will salute with the battalion commander.
SLOPE—ARMS. ORDER—ARMS.	

73. *Receiving the Sovereign or a Royal Personage.*

ROYAL SALUTE. PRESENT—ARMS.	As in preceding section, but the band will play the National Anthem or the first six bars of it.
SLOPE—ARMS. ORDER—ARMS.	

74. *Inspection in Line.*

The Reviewing Officer, accompanied by the Battalion Commander, who will ride on the farther side from the troops, will then pass down the line from right to left, returning along the rear, the men standing with ordered arms.

The band will play a march until he returns to the right of the line.

The Reviewing Officer will then give orders for the march past.

75. *Close Column.*

A Battalion may be formed up for inspection in close column of Companies, as in Plate 3.

76. A Battalion Marching Past.

1. Points will be placed on the principles described in Section 69; the points marking the saluting base will be covered in a line at a convenient distance from the saluting point.

2. *Posts of Officers.*—When marching past the Reviewing Officer by Companies, the Battalion Commander will be fifteen paces in front of No. 2 Platoon of the leading Company, the senior Major in front of No. 3 Platoon in line with the Battalion Commander. If the Colonel of the Regiment is present he will be twenty-five paces in front of the centre of the leading Company. Should the Colonel-in-Chief also be present, he will be ten paces in front of the Colonel. The Adjutant will follow ten paces behind the centre of the rear Company. Company Officers as in Section 69. When marching past in close column of Companies the Battalion Commander will be fifteen paces in front of the centre of the leading Company. The senior Major and the Adjutant will be ten paces in rear of the centre Platoons of the rear Company, the senior Major nearest the saluting base. Company Commanders will be three paces from the outer flank of their Companies. Officers second in command of Companies and officers commanding Platoons will be as in line, but dividing the frontage of their Companies equally between them.

3. *Officers' Salute.*—In marching past by Companies the mounted officers will salute when they arrive at point "A," Company Officers as in Section 69. Officers other than Company Officers conclude the salute when ten paces beyond the reviewing officer. The Battalion Commander, after he has saluted, will move out and place himself on the right of the reviewing Officer, and remain there until the Battalion has passed; the senior Major assuming command.

In marching past in close column the Battalion Commander only will salute.

If the Battalion marches past in column of route, all Officers will salute.

4. *Battalion Headquarters.*—Except when otherwise ordered, the personnel of Battalion Headquarters does not march past. The assistant Adjutant will march past with the Company to which he belongs. For the position of attached Medical Officer, see Section 55.

5. *Warrant Officers and Staff-Sergeants.* — The Sergeant-Major will be two paces in rear of the centre of the colour party. The Bandmaster and Sergeant-Drummer (carrying his staff at the *Trail* as he passes the saluting point), will salute with the outer hand on the first occasion of marching past.

6. *Drums and Band.*—For marching past the band and drums (or bugles) will move up to fifty paces in advance of the leading Company, both formed in two or more ranks. The band will commence playing as soon as the leading Company advances on the saluting base. When it arrives in front of the saluting point it will turn to the left, change direction to the right, and halt and turn to the right opposite to the saluting point, continuing to play until the rear of the Battalion has passed. The Bandmaster will face the saluting point.

7. Cyclist sections and stretcher-bearers, if ordered to march past, will be five paces in rear of the rear Company, or five paces in rear of R.A.M.C. personnel if the latter be on parade, cyclist section nearest the saluting base and on foot on the left of their cycles; stretcher-bearers on the outer flank. Should there be more than one cyclist section, cyclists will march past in column of sections ten paces behind the machine guns, etc.

8. Regimental transport, if ordered to march past, will be five paces behind the rear of the machine guns, cyclist section, and stretcher-bearers, carts nearest the saluting base, mules in centre, transport wagons on the outer flank.

77. Marching Past by Companies.

Fix—Bayonets. Slope—Arms. On the Right Form Close Column of Companies. Remainder Form—Fours. Right. Quick—March. Move to the Right in Fours. Form—Fours. Right. Number One will Direct. Quick—March.	
Change Direction Left. Left—Wheel Forward by the Left.	On the command Left—Wheel, which will be given when the battalion reaches the first point, a left wheel will be made, the battalion moving forward on the command Forward as soon as the change is completed.
Halt. Left—Turn. Battalion Right—Dress.	On the command Halt, which will be given when the battalion reaches the saluting base, the right guides will turn to the right and be covered by the adjutant, who will give the command Steady. On the word Steady the right guides will turn about, and the right-hand man of the front rank of each company will immediately correct his dressing by the right guide. On the command Right—Dress the right guides will dress their companies and give the command Eyes—Front.
March Past by Companies by the Right.	The commander of No. 1 will give the command No. 1, By the Right, Quick—March, the remaining companies following in succession at 40 paces distance, or as ordered, and acting as in Sec. 69.

78. Marching Past in Close Column of Companies after the March Past by Companies.

AT THE HALT CLOSE— COLUMN.	If the battalion be required to march past in close column, the leading company will be halted when it has moved to thirty-eight paces beyond the third point. Close column will be formed by order of the senior major, who will superintend the covering.
ABOUT—TURN.	
ORDER—ARMS.	
LEFT—DRESS	On the command LEFT—DRESS the left guides will dress their companies and give the command EYES—FRONT.
SLOPE—ARMS.	
ADVANCE IN CLOSE COLUMN BY THE LEFT. QUICK—MARCH.	
EYES—LEFT.	The battalion commander will give the command EYES—LEFT when he arrives at ten paces from the saluting point.
EYES—FRONT.	The battalion commander will give the command EYES—FRONT when the rear company has passed the reviewing officer. *Note.*—(i.) Left guides will not look to the left. (ii.) If required to resume its position on the original alignment, the battalion will be moved there from the second or third point in the most convenient and quickest formation. The Senior Major, Company Commanders, and Adjutant will resume their respective posts in close column.

79. *A Battalion Advancing in Review Order.*

ADVANCE IN REVIEW ORDER, QUICK—MARCH.	The battalion having been formed into line, with bayonets fixed and arms sloped, will advance by the centre, the band and drums playing, till within thirty paces of the reviewing officer, when it will be halted and ordered to salute in the same manner as when receiving him; after which it will be directed to order arms, and will wait for orders.

Common Faults. (General.)

1. Men taking up their dressing without words of command.

Common Faults. (At Review.)

1. Company Officer not falling out and reporting on approach of Reviewing Officer.

Common Faults. (March Past.)

1. Guide stepping too long.
2. Men not looking Reviewing Officer in the face.
3. The shoulder farthest away from saluting point not square, generally dropping back.

Key to Plates 1, 2, 3, and 4.

- BATTALION COMMANDER
- SENIOR MAJOR
- ADJUTANT
- COMPANY COMMANDER
- COMPANY SECOND IN COMMAND
- PLATOON COMMANDER
- QUARTERMASTER
- THE KING'S COLOUR
- REGIMENTAL COLOUR
- SERJEANT-MAJOR
- BATTALION QUARTER-MASTER-SERJEANT
- ARMOURER-SERJEANT
- COMPANY SERJEANT-MAJOR
- COMPANY QUARTER-MASTER-SERJEANT
- PLATOON SERJEANT
- BANDMASTER
- BAND SERJEANT
- BANDSMAN
- SERJEANT-DRUMMER
- DRUMMER
- PRIVATE, REAR RANK

PLATE I.

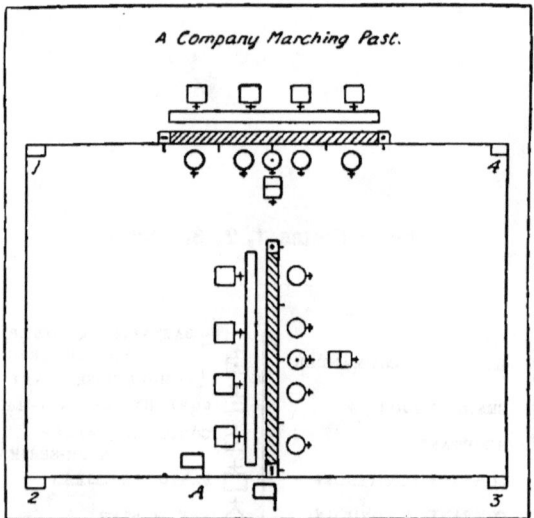

PLATE II.

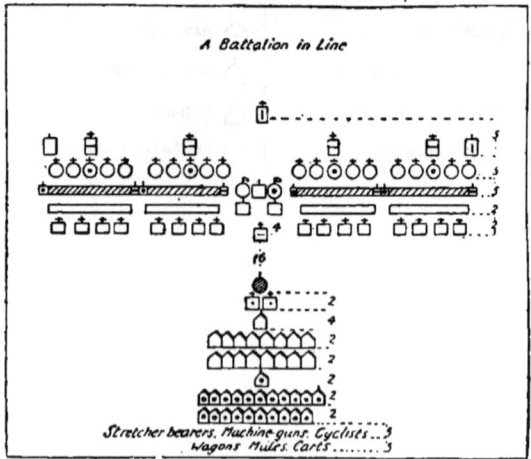

PLATE III

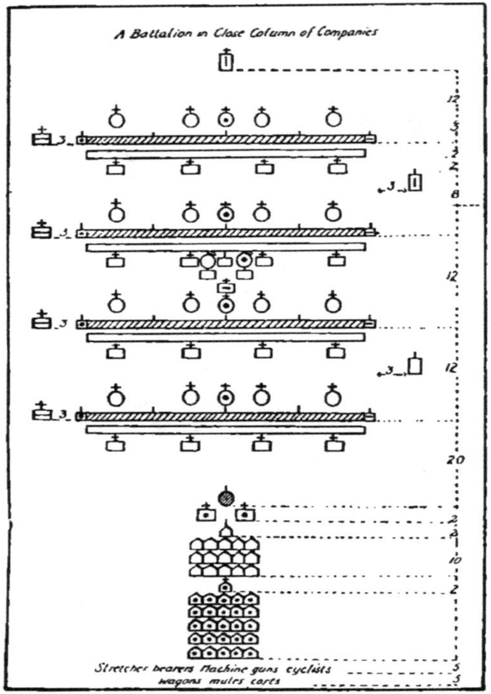
A Battalion in Close Column of Companies
12
3
3
2
8
12
12
20
2
3
10
2
5
5
3
3
3
3
Stretcher bearers Machine guns cyclists
wagons mules carts

PLATE IV

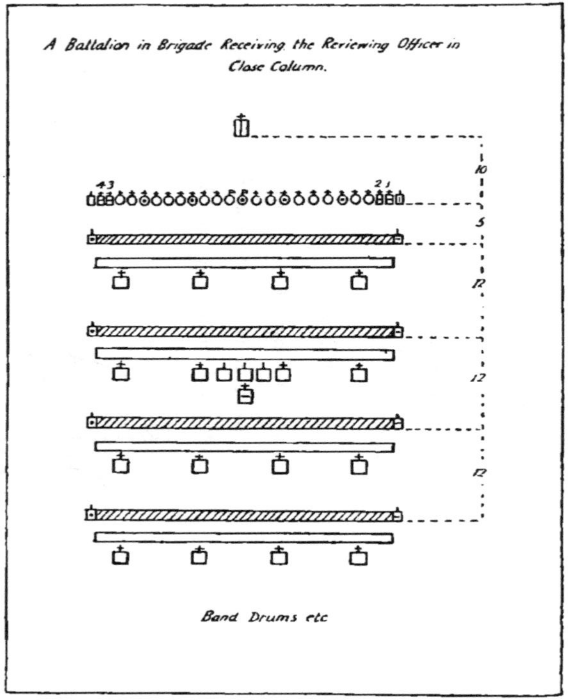
A Battalion in Brigade Receiving the Reviewing Officer in Close Column.
4 3
2 1
10
5
12
12
12
Band Drums etc

APPENDIX I.

Section Training (Drill).

Forty Minutes.

A
- 5 mins.   Inspection, telling off and proving.
- 5 mins.   Explanation of programme *and good news*.
- 10 mins.   The following movements in "Arm drill" :—
    - (i) Attention.
    - (ii) Slope Arms.
    - (iii) Present Arms.
    - (iv) Slope Arms.
    - (v) Order Arms.
    - (vi) Pile Arms. (Also practise with ranks turned about.)
    - (vii) Stand at Ease.
- 5 mins.   Games.
- 10 mins.   Section drill, practising the following movements :—
    - (i) Forming fours. (Also practised with ranks turned about.)
    - (ii) Marching in fours.

    In practising (i) change over odd and even numbers and blank file.

    In practising (ii) look to the correct covering of the fours, and see that they march by directing flank.
- 5 mins.   Conclude parade with "March past" in line and column of route. If possible obtain *music,* if only a bugler or a drummer or flautist are available, it will serve the purpose.

Platoon Training (Drill).

Forty Minutes.

B

10 mins. Inspection, telling off and proving.

5 mins. Explanation of programme, and *good news*.

10 mins. The following movements in "Arm drill" :—
- (i) Attention.
- (ii) Slope Arms.
- (iii) Present Arms.
- (iv) Slope Arms.
- (v) Order Arms.
- (vi) Pile Arms. (Also practise with ranks turned about.)
- (vii) Stand at Ease.

5 mins. Games.

5 mins. Platoon drill, practising the following movements :—
- (i) Forming fours. (Practise also with ranks turned about.)
- (ii) Marching in line.
- (iii) Marching in column of route.

In practising (i) look for correct covering.

5 mins. Conclude parade with " march past " in line and column of route, with music if possible.

In practising (ii) see that the guides select points to march on, and keep to those points. That the men put plenty of *dash and swagger* into their marching, **and in correcting intervals, they move to their places gradually.**

In practising (iii) see to the points connected with March Discipline.

Company Training (Drill).

Forty Minutes.

C
10 mins. The Company Commander takes over and looks around the Company, and if he chooses, inspects a section or platoon.

Tells off and proves the Company, closes them into a suitable formation and explains the Training programme, and lets them know the *good news*.

5 mins. Arm drill as follows :—
  (i) Attention.
  (ii) Slope.
  (iii) Order.
  (iv) Stand at Ease.

15 mins. Company drill, practising the following movements :—
  (i) Advancing.
  (ii) Retiring.
  (iii) Advancing in column.
  (iv) Forming close column, from (iii), and halting.
  (v) Advancing in column of route.

In the whole of the above the steadiness of the men can be tested, also the knowledge and ability displayed by the Section Commanders. In (iii), (iv), and (v) the Company Commander is testing the drill knowledge of his Platoon Commanders.

10 mins. " March past."
  (i) Column of platoons.
  (ii) Column of route.

If possible with *music*.

Battalion Training (Drill).

Forty Minutes.

D
10 mins. The Battalion Commander takes over and looks around his Battalion, and if he chooses, inspects a platoon here and there. Tells off and proves the Battalion. Closes the Battalion to a suitable formation, gives them *good news*, and tells them what they are going to do.

5 mins. Arm drill as follows :—
   (i) Attention.
   (ii) Slope.
   (iii) Present.
   (iv) Slope.
   (v) Order.
   (vi) Stand at ease.

15 mins. Battalion drill, practising the following :—
   (i) Advancing.
   (ii) Retiring.
   (iii) Halting.
   (iv) Dressing.
   (v) Column of route.
   (vi) Close column of Companies.

10 mins. "March Past" in close column of Companies.

Notes.—(a) The whole of the movements given in the (A), (B), (C), and (D) to be carried out with *absolute steadiness and precision*.

(b) Conclude parades with "*March Past*" with *music*, even though, in the case of a platoon, that be a solitary musician.

(c) Avoid getting into formations which will make control difficult. Remember that it is 40 minutes *drill*, not manœuvre.

PART II.

GAMES.

GENERAL REMARKS.

The essence of the following games is that they should be conducted with the utmost amount of energy and the rigid observance of all the details connected with them.

Executed in this way, they inculcate discipline and develop quickness of brain and movement, whereas, if carelessly carried out, they may do more harm than good.

A game may be introduced into the daily P.T. Table to prevent monotony, either before or after the Marching and Jumping Exercises or in place of them, according to the time available.

Games should not be continued for too long, and must not be carried out to the detriment of P.T. proper. Maximum time devoted to games during a Table should never exceed 10 minutes.

1. JUMPING THE BAG.

Formation.—The players stand in a circle at close intervals and facing inward.

Apparatus.—A light rope 5 to 8 yards long, to one end of which is attached a small bag of canvas or leather filled with sand and weighing about 1 lb.

Method of Playing.—The Instructor stands in the centre of the ring and swings the bag round, gradually paying out the rope until it becomes necessary for the players to jump to avoid it. The direction in which the bag is swung should be varied. The rate of swinging as well as height of the bag from the ground should be gradually increased. The object of the players is, of course, to avoid being caught by the rope or bag and brought to the ground.

Common Faults.

Some of the players stand outside the ring, the bag thus not passing under their feet.

2. SIMPLE RELAY RACE.

(a) **Formation.**—Two parallel lines are marked out about 20 to 50 yards apart.

Each team is divided into two parts containing an equal number of players.

These are drawn up on the parallel lines, facing one another and extended at intervals of about 1 yard.

Method of Playing.—On the word "Go," the left-hand man of each team drawn up on the one line races to and touches the outstretched hand of the man immediately opposite him. As soon as his hand has been touched, the latter races similarly to the next man opposite, and so on, the team whose last man first crosses the line being the winners.

(b) **Progression.**—Instead of touching a partner, a stick or other article may be carried and transferred, not thrown, from man to man.

Common Faults.

(1) Not waiting to be touched by a partner, or not waiting to receive the stick, etc., before starting.

(2) Standing in front of, instead of "toeing," the line.

3. THREE DEEP.

(a) **Formation.**—Players pair. One pair will be told off as "Chaser" and "Runner." Remaining pairs form a double ring, one man standing behind the other, with at least 2 yards between pairs who face the centre of the ring.

Method of Playing.—" Chaser " and " Runner " take up their positions just outside the ring at opposite points of it. On the word " Go," the " Chaser " pursues the " Runner " with the object of " touching " him. If he succeeds, " Chaser " becomes " Runner," and vice versa. " Runner " can take refuge by placing himself, facing inwards, in front of a pair, whereupon the rear man of this pair, now three deep, immediately takes up the rôle of " Runner."

(b) **Progression.**

Formation.—As above, except that the men of each pair face one another about 1 yard apart.

Method of Playing.—As above, except that the " Runner " takes refuge *between* a pair, when the one to whom he turns his back becomes " Runner," and the late " Runner " steps back into his place.

This form of the game requires continual alertness on the part of both men in each pair.

Common Faults.

(1) The " Runner " dodges about too long before taking refuge, thus making the game tedious for the others.

(2) In (a) the " Chaser " and " Runner " dodge between the two men forming a pair. This is often due to the outer man not standing close enough to the inner one.

(3) The ring is allowed to grow too small. This is bound to occur unless each pair is careful to step back a short pace to its proper relative position in the ring every time a " Runner " halts in front of it.

4. " UNDER PASSING " RELAY RACE.

Apparatus.—Two or more subjects about the size of a croquet ball, i.e., balls made out of rags or paper, boxing gloves, etc.

Formation.—Players are formed into two or more ranks (according to numbers of men and balls available), facing the flank.

Method of Playing.—All the players, excepting the last one of each row, stand with their feet at least three foot-lengths apart, bend forward from the hips and grasp the hips or belt of the man in front.

The leading player of each row holds the ball; the rear one bends down in a position of readiness to receive it.

At the word " Go," the leading man throws the ball, or other object, backwards to the rear man, between his own legs and those of the other players of his row. The ball should be thrown so as to skim the ground. Should it not reach the rear man in one throw, the nearest player must seize it and pass it on in the same way. As soon as the rear man receives it, he must run to the front of his row and go through the same procedure as No. 1, and so on until the last man gets it, i.e., the original leader. The latter races to the front and places the ball on the ground in front of his feet; the first rank to do this is declared the winner.

Should the ball go outside the players' legs, the player at that spot must fetch it, return to his place and pass it on as described.

Common Faults.

The ball is thrown to the side or too high, instead of straight and skimming the ground.

5. "PLACING THE INDIAN CLUB" RELAY RACE.

(a) **Apparatus.**—Two or more Indian Clubs or some similar objects.

Formation.—As in " Under Passing " Relay Race. Opposite, and at about 15 and 20 yards respectively from the front man of each row, two circles of about 8 inches diameter are marked on the ground, one straight behind the other. In the nearest of each of the circles an Indian Club or other object is placed standing on end.

Method of Playing.—At the word "Go," the first player of each row races to the first circle, seizes the club with the left (right) hand, and with the same hand stands it up in the second circle situated 5 yards off. He then races back and touches the outstretched hand of the next man of his row. The latter then races to the club and in the same way places it back in the near circle, and so on alternately until each man of the row has had his turn. The last man, having deposited the club in the circle, races back to the line which the front men were originally "toeing." The first row to finish are, of course, the winners. Each man, after having touched the outstretched hand of the "next to run," places himself at the rear of his row, which keeps moving forward so that the "next to run" is always "toeing" the original line.

Should the club fall over, the player responsible must replace it in position before the game may be continued.

(b) **Progression.**—Between the front man and the nearest circle of each row (which distances should be increased in this case to almost double) a circle of about 1 to 2 yards diameter is drawn.

Each player must, on his way to the club, run round this circle from left to right, and on his way back from right to left. Procedure otherwise as already described.

Common Faults.

(1) Using both hands or the wrong one to place the club.
(2) Players overstepping the line before being touched by the returning man.
(3) Running round the circles in the wrong direction.

6. "WHIP TO THE CAP."

Apparatus.—A knotted handkerchief, towel, or other suitable object.

Formation.—The players stand in a ring at close intervals, lean forward, look on the ground in front of them, and hold their hands behind their backs.

Method of Playing.—The Instructor walks or runs round the outside of the ring and as secretly as possible places the handkerchief in the hands of one of the players. The latter at once chases his right (left) hand neighbour, beating him with the handkerchief as he runs round the ring back to his place.

Both then take their places in the ring, and the Instructor proceeds again as before.

The latter should endeavour to deceive the players as much as possible as to whom the handkerchief has been given.

Common Faults.

Players looking round to see who receives the handkerchief.

7. CHANGING PLACES.

Formation.—All the players but one stand in a circle of about 7 yards or more diameter, facing inward. The odd player stands in the middle.

Method of Playing.—Each player is given a number, which he retains all through the game. The Instructor calls out two numbers (but not, of course, that of the player in the middle), and the players so numbered must change places in the circle. While they are doing so the odd player must try to get into one of the vacated places first, and if he is successful the ousted player then becomes the odd man in the centre.

8. CIRCLE TOUCH BALL.

Apparatus.—A football.

Formation.—Players stand in a circle 1 to 2 paces apart, facing inward, with one player inside the circle.

Method of Playing.—The football is passed, by hand, from one player to another, and the player inside the circle endeavours to intercept it. If successful, he changes places with the last thrower. If the ball falls to the ground, the player responsible either for the bad pass or missed catch—at the discretion of the Instructor—changes places with the player inside the circle.

Common Faults.
  (1) The ball is held too long before passing (about 3 seconds may be put as a time-limit for holding the ball).
  (2) The ball is kicked, which is wrong, and spoils the whole idea of the game.

9. MAZE.

Formation.—All the players, except two, stand in parallel ranks one behind the other. The distance between each player and each rank is that of "double arm's length," so that whichever direction the ranks may face with arms extended horizontally a line of players with finger tips touching will be formed. The ranks should be drawn up so as to form a square as nearly as possible.

Method of Playing.—The chaser has to pursue the runner up and down the lines until he catches him, neither being permitted to pass under the outstretched arms. The Instructor makes sudden changes in the lines by calling out "Right Turn" or "Left Turn," on which all turn in the required direction, still keeping the arms outstretched. These sudden changes alter the direction of the paths down which the two players may run. The interest depends greatly upon the judgment of the Instructor in giving the commands "Right (or Left) Turn." They should be given frequently and sharply, and often just at the moment when the chaser is about to catch the runner.

The game continues until the runner is caught or a time-limit reached, when a new chaser and runner are selected.

Common Faults.
  (1) Chaser or runner passing under outstretched arms.
  (2) Not changing the chaser and runner sufficiently often.

10. BOMB-BALL.

A game for bringing into play the muscles used in bombing, and for the development of quick and accurate throwing.

Ground. — Any football ground or open space, marked out as under; the size of the rectangle may be varied to suit the amount of ground available.

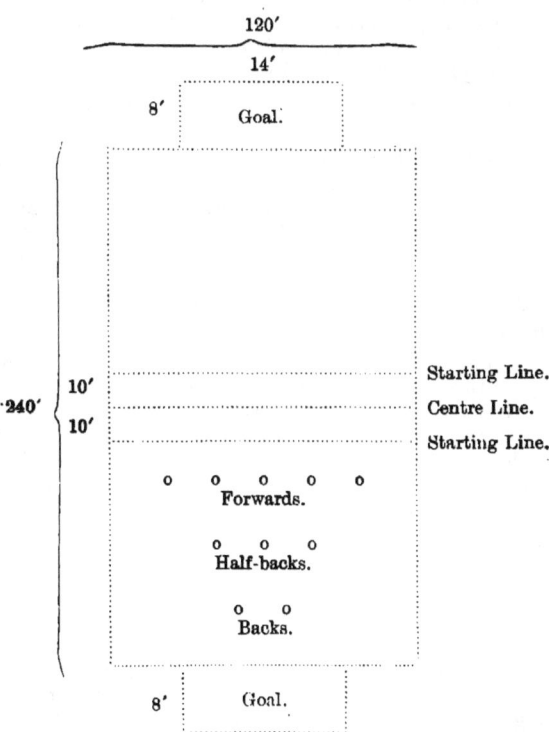

The goal should be marked out on the ground, no goal-posts being necessary.

Teams.—The players should be disposed as in Association Football, but a lesser number than eleven a side should take part if the ground be small.

Apparatus.—Some object approximating to the weight, size and shape of a grenade, care being taken that it is not such as to be likely to injure the players. The following is suggested: a small oval-shaped bag of canvas or thick calico, filled with sand or small shot to the required weight and securely sewn up.

Referee.—A referee should control the game, as in football.

Method of Playing.—The ball is passed from player to player by hand, the object being to land it in the goal. It may be passed backward or forward as in Association Football, and the " off-side " rule will apply in the same way. The passes are taken on the run, and the ball must not be held but passed on immediately. If dropped, the ball must be picked up and similarly passed on at once.

The ball may be caught with both hands, but must only be thrown by one. Only two methods of throwing are allowed: (1) For long distances, a full over-hand throw, as shown in the diagrams in " Training and Employment of Bombers," March, 1916; (2) for short distances, a " put," made in the same manner as " putting-the-shot."

In order to exercise equally both sides of the body and to develop skill and accuracy with both hands, the throwing-hand may be changed every 10 minutes or so, at the discretion of the Referee.

To start the game, Captains toss, and the winner has the first throw and the right to select the goal he wishes to defend. The teams are then drawn up, the forwards along their respective starting-lines. The Referee blows his whistle and the game commences by the centre-forward taking the first throw or " put."

In the course of the game, if the ball lands in the goal, or is caught in the goal and subsequently dropped within it by any player, a goal is scored.

If the ball is caught in the goal before touching the ground and thrown out at once no goal is scored.

If the ball goes " behind " or into " touch," it is thrown in similarly as in Association Football, but with one hand, and this also applies to a " corner."

After a goal has been scored, the game is started again as at the commencement.

Charging.—No charging or rough play is admissible. Passes may be intercepted, or throws frustrated, with the open hand.

Fouls.—Fouls may be given for (1) Running with the ball, instead of passing it at once as soon as caught or picked up; (2) Throwing the ball in any way but the two methods allowed; (3) Catching hold of a player; (4) Any form of rough play; (5) Being " off-side "; (6) Using the wrong hand for throwing.

Penalties.—A penalty for a foul will take the form of a free throw against the offending side from the place where the foul occurred. In the case of rough play, a goal may be allowed against the offending team for each similar offence after the first caution.

Duration of Game.—From 20 to 30 minutes each way, according to the condition of the men.

CHAPTER VII.

THE ATTACK IN THE OPEN.

Two forms of Drill Attack are advocated at the Senior Officers' School: The " Flagged Attack," for the purpose of teaching the uses of formations, dealt with in Part I, and The " Ground Attack," for the purpose of teaching the use of ground dealt with in Part II.

PART I.

THE " FLAGGED ATTACK."

The stages in the attack, at which hostile opposition necessitates a change of formation, are marked by flags. It is to be regarded purely as a drill which enables a Commanding Officer to satisfy himself that all his Officers, N.C.Os. and men are thoroughly grounded in the various formations necessary to an advance under fire.

It also has the advantage that the attack can be practised when the ground available for manœuvre is very limited, such as is often the case when training in billets in France.

1. The attached diagram shows how the course should be flagged and the formations to be adopted when carrying out a practice attack with flags.

2. Each of the flagged points should denote a stage. Care must be taken that the depth for each stage of the attack is sufficient to allow the practices being carried out without mixing up the stages, and so confusing the minds of those under instruction.

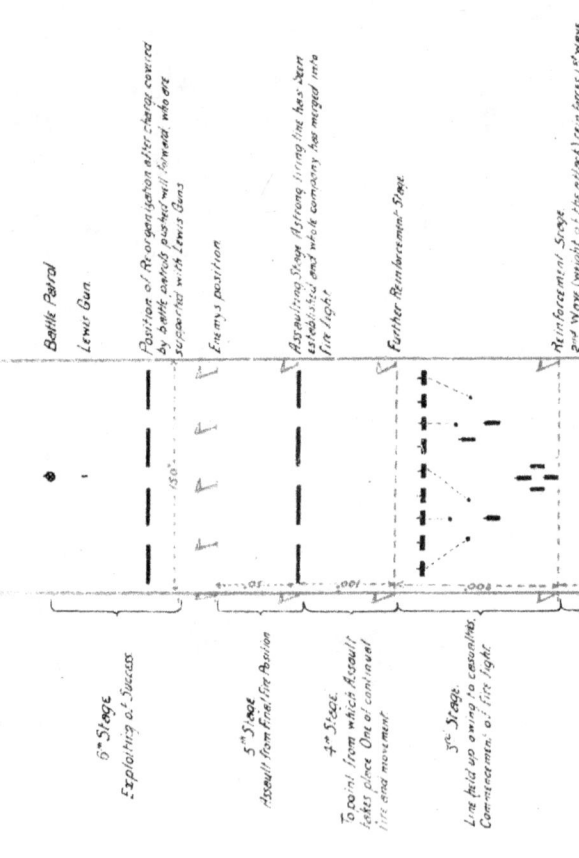

Diagram showing the formation of a Company during stages of practice in the flagged attack.
The distances shown in red are the minimum distances required to mark out a satisfactory course for this practice attack.

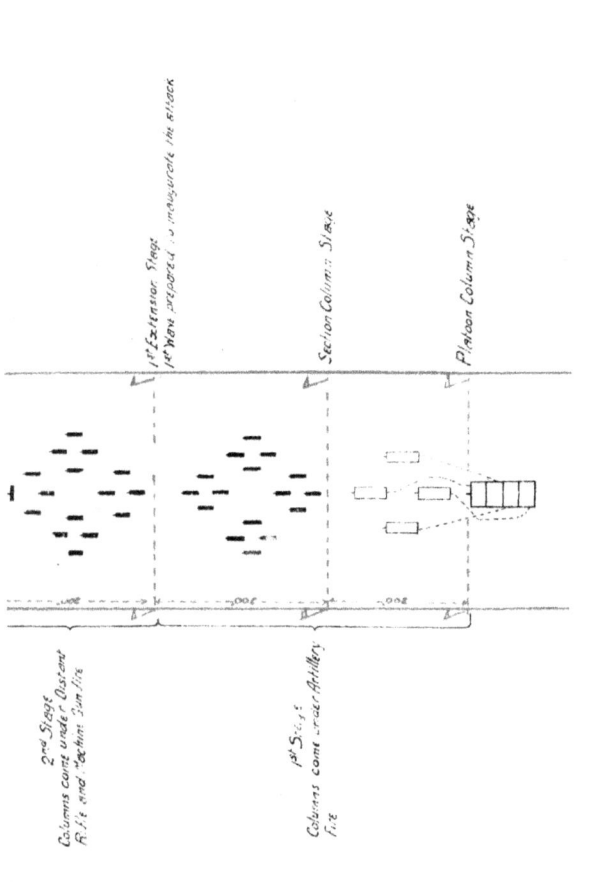

3. The frontage must, for the purposes of the exercise, be on the scale of about 150 yards per Company, and care should be taken to see that the distances between these flags at each stage are certainly not less than this distance.

4. The Instructor and the Officer Commanding the Company demonstrating should be mounted.

5. When one Company is demonstrating, and the other three looking on, the duty of ensuring that the other three are so placed and moved along that all may get a good view of the demonstration, etc., should be delegated to the Second-in-Command, who should also be mounted.

PART II.

THE "GROUND ATTACK."

This is not to be confused with the "Flagged Attack," which should be carried out on the flat, and where the flags have no reference to ground.

In the "Ground Attack" successive fire positions are marked by flags, and the points to be considered are as follows:—

(1) How ground affects the original advance—right or left leading, as the case may be.

(2) Fire positions—how they assist advance of unit, or co-operate with other units—actual firing position of each man in relation to the ground.

(3) How ground affects movement—rush over open ground—halt for a breather under cover, etc.

(4) How ground affects observation—false crest—gentle convex slopes, etc.

All these questions are carefully gone into by the Officer carrying out the instruction with his subordinate commanders. The subordinate commanders then take their men over the course, acting in the dual capacity of instructor and leader; that is to say, before leading them from one position to another they call their men round them and discuss the points enumerated above.

PART III.
THE ATTACK IN THE OPEN.
(References in the Margin refer to "Infantry Training.")

Various Stages.	Considerations on Each Stage.	
PREVIOUS TO MOVEMENT.		
Explanation of proposed attack.	Personal reconnaissance if possible, protected by Scouts.	**121 (4)**
(a) C.O. to Company Commanders.		
(b) Company Commanders to Platoon Commanders.	N.B.—Occasions will frequently arise when there will not be enough time for such detailed explanation.	**122 (4)**
(c) Platoon Commanders to Platoons.	Shows necessity of training subordinate leaders to grasp situation quickly and act quickly.	

(A) C.O. TO COMPANY COMMANDERS.

(1) Formation of Battalion.	(1) In this case presumably three Companies in firing line, of which one Company is in support.	**122 (1)**
	One Company in local reserve.	
(2) Compass Bearing.	(2) And intermediate direction marks.	**123 (11)** **122 (4)**
(3) Instructions as to time that the attack will take place.		
(4) Flanking Units and their objective.		**122 (4)**
(5) Position of enemy and objective.	(5) If possible, divide objective from the start.	
	Choose final fire positions.	**121 (3)**
	Note any covered lines of approach.	

Various Stages—*Continued.*	Considerations on Each Stage.—*Continued.*
(6) Method of Communication.	(6) Visual Signals, Dietz Discs, Telephone Runners, Flares and Aeroplanes. (Training of Runners and Observers.)
121 (11) (7) Ammunition Supply.	(7) Position of Pack Animals. Consider advisability of placing them under Regtl.-Sgt.-Major.
(8) Position of Lewis Guns.	(8) Whether in firing line. Importance of Lewis gun for rendering mutual support and in repelling counter-attacks.
(9) Arrangements for covering fire.	(9) Whether machine guns have been specially detailed for this purpose.
(10) Ranges.	(10) **Key Ranges** from ranges taken by Battalion Range-finders.
(11) Position of Dressing Station.	
(12) (a) Position of Commanding Officer.	12 (a) Normally in any position, whence he can best control use of his Battalion Reserve.
(b) Points to which messages and reports will be sent.	(b) Should Commanding Officer **decide to accompany** reserve, then decide on some fixed locality to which messages may be sent.
122 (4) **123 (9)** (13) Action when objective gained.	(13) Pursuit, or pursuit by fire alone.
(14) **A final word re the reputation of the Regiment.**	

Various Stages—*Continued.*	Considerations on Each Stage.—*Continued.*	
(B) COMPANY COMMANDERS TO PLATOON COMMANDERS.		
Includes all (A) **and also—**		
(1) How initial advance is to be carried out.	(1) Platoon, Section Columns, Intervals and Distances.	**123 (1)**
(2) Frontage of each Platoon.	(2) Whether Platoons to be in depth or width. Depth facilitates re-organisation, but complicates earlier command.	
	Good Formation:	**123 (2)**
(3) Selected non-commissioned officers for directing flanks.	(3) Loss of direction entails :— Masking fire of others. Bunching or flank movement across front.	
(4) Width of Extension, whether extension to right or left or outwards.		
(5) Arrangements for replenishing ammunition.	(5) Normally only means of getting ammunition to firing line is with reinforcements. Reinforcing lines must be issued with extra ammunition.	
(6) Position of the Company Commander.	(6) Moves up with final reinforcements of Company.	**123 (8)**

Various Stages—Continued.	Considerations on Each Stage.—Continued.

(C) PLATOON COMMANDERS TO THEIR PLATOONS.

Importance of the men in the ranks knowing detail, objective, direction of attack. Enables them to carry on without leaders.

FIRST STAGE.

When Company may or does come under Artillery Fire.

Moves from Column of Route to Columns of Small Units.

Points to be noticed:

(a) Scouts to protect formations.

(a) Danger of suddenly coming under Machine Gun or Rifle Fire in Column Formation. Scouts should preclude any possibility of attack thus.

(b) Celerity of movement, especially of leading Company.

(b) Rapid movement of leading Company into Artillery Formation does not delay remainder of Battalion under shell fire.

(c) Absence of noise or confusion.

(c) Ensured by good " Barrack Square " Training.

(d) Direction of Platoons.

(e) Irregularity of formation.

(e) Necessity of deceiving enemy artillery.

Various Stages—Continued.	Considerations on Each Stage.—Continued.	
	Give no regular frontage to range on. Line gives a regular front, easy ranging hard to control. Small Columns best for passing barrage or shell-searched area of ground.	**118 (3)**
(f) Necessity for keeping on move.	(f) Harder for artillery to range. Movement keeps offensive spirit going.	**116 (8)**

SECOND STAGE.

When Columns come under distant Rifle or Machine Gun Fire.

(a) Rapid orderly extension if forced to do so.	(a) Practised and perfected on Barrack Square.	
(b) Direction.	(b) Intermediate direction marks.	
(c) Position of Commanders, Runners and Observers.	(c) Best position for Commanders is slightly behind their command. Facilitates control. If troops require to be led at this stage attack bound to fail.	
(d) Fire.	(d) Only fire action developed at this period (excluding Artillery) would be that of specially detailed covering parties. Fire should not be opened if satisfactory progress can be made without it.	**116 (8)**

Various Stages—*Continued*.	Considerations on Each Stage.—*Continued*.
(e) Pace of advance.	(e) Must be steady and easy to control; opposing Infantry Fire will probably not be formidable at this range, except in reaching and passing across Ranging Marks. Doubling at this range will unnecessarily tire the troops.

THIRD STAGE.

When the first line is held up owing to casualties and needs support.
Second line reinforces first line commencement of Fire Fight.

(a) Inter-communication between firing line and supports.	(a) Observers of firing line and supports must be in communication. Reason for reinforcing:—Front line cannot advance without aid of fire, owing to casualties; has not enough rifles to make fire effective.
(b) Covering fire to aid advance of troops in rear.	(b) First line signals to second line to reinforce; covers advance of second line by a brisk, well-directed fire which unsteadies enemy's aim.

Various Stages— *Continued.*	Considerations on Each Stage.—*Continued.*
	At this range, if the rate of this covering fire exceeds five rounds a minute, it will not be sufficiently accurate to achieve its object.
(c) Re-distribution of Command and Re-organisation.	(c) Senior Officer in firing line takes command. If casualties amongst subordinate Commanders, tell off new ones.
	This re-organisation should be rapid rather than accurate.
	Flank men of fire units " Proving " after re-organisation.
(d) Dividing fire frontage.	(d) Necessity of keeping whole of the enemy front under fire.
	To accomplish this, enemy front to be divided amongst units.
	Whether fire should be delivered obliquely or direct to front.
(e) Opportunities for closing up.	(e) Take every opportunity of getting supporting lines close to front line when cover admits.
	Facilitates control and communication of orders.
(f) Nature and method of further advance.	(f) Choosing of intermediate fire positions.

Various Stages—*Continued.*	Considerations on Each Stage.—*Continued.*
FOURTH STAGE. **STILL FURTHER REINFORCEMENT REQUIRED.** **Points to be noted:**	
(a) Position of Commanders.	(a) Company Commanders, with Third or Fourth Line. Section Commanders, when halted slightly in rear of line. Facilitates control, enables Officers to see whereabouts of Section Commanders. Unit Commanders behind centre of their unit.
	Commanders and observers not bunched together.
(b) Length and strength of rushes.	(b) A rush must be to the next fire position, or, if that is too far, to a position of safety short of it, where men can get their breath under cover before making another rush towards the next fire position.
	The section is the unit for both fire and movement; therefore section rushes.
	Methods of rising and falling quickly.
	Give enemy no notice of your advance.

VARIOUS STAGES—*Continued.*	CONSIDERATIONS ON EACH STAGE.—*Continued.*
(c) Co-operation of fire and movement.	(c) Never open fire if troops can advance without covering fire before advance commences. Consider desirability of Lewis guns being used for this purpose. If another part of your line held up, try to advance yourself, attracting fire from them. Shouting out that your unit is about to advance.
(d) Irregularity of formation.	(d) Regular line easy to range on, section rushes not necessarily to reach same alignment. Avoid systematic advance from same flank.
(e) Continual movement.	(e) Flusters enemy more, necessitates continual change of sights. Keeps your troops' blood up. Impresses enemy. Quicker advance less time under fire. Object of advance is to **close with enemy.**
(f) Covering fire from covering troops.	(f) Best aid to movement, their fire more effective. They are not blown, range fixed. Firing line must husband ammunition. Every round wanted for final fire fight.

116 (8)

Various Stages—*Continued.*	Considerations on Each Stage.—*Continued.*
(g) Continual re-organisation.	(g) Any individuals not told off to sections must attach themselves to one.
(h) Strength of reinforcement.	(h) Not less than a Platoon at a time, moving forward by section rushes. Don't dribble away your reinforcements.

123(7)

FIFTH STAGE.
When line decides to assault.

(a) This point under cover, if possible.	(a) If possible assaulting point not more than 50x from position. If more, troops will be too blown to use bayonet. Also enables final dispositions to be made. Enables line to thicken up. Enables men to get a breather.
(b) Futility of assaulting with inadequate numbers.	(b) Inadequate numbers for assault, due to faulty leading and fire discipline. Aim at weight one point, rather than mild blow over whole line.
(c) Fixing Bayonets.	(c) If attack started at 600x or less, fix before starting, otherwise fix by alternate sections, so as not to seriously diminish fire. Rifles at "High Port" in first stage of assault.

124 (3)

Various Stages—*Continued*.	Considerations on Each Stage.—*Continued*.
(d) Final fire preparation.	(d) Of most intense and accurate disciplined description. Fire control in hands of individual.
(e) Cohesion in assault rather than pace.	(e) **Straggled assault enables enemy to deal with individuals.**
	Straggled assault does not impress enemy.
	Straggled assault more difficult to control.
	Difficulty of subsequent re-organisation.
	Whole Companies rise simultaneously.
(f) Cheering, bugles, etc.	(f) Heartens your men and demoralises enemy.
(g) Co-operation with flank units.	(g) Assault simultaneous as far down line as possible. Warn flanking units of intended assault, so that they can co-operate by fire or movement.
(h) Signal for assault.	(h) Not necessarily from Company Commanders. Probably from some individual who possesses most dash, and who feels instinctively that the time is ripe.

Various Stages—*Continued.*	Considerations on Each Stage.—*Continued.*
SIXTH STAGE. **Capture and consolidation of position.**	
(a) Rapid telling off of pursuing party.	(a) Preferably freshest troops **pursue by fire.** All must be prepared to pursue, however fatigued. Danger of infantry pursuit who run into enemy shell fire and their own. Pursuing party performs rôle of covering party during re-organisation and consolidation.
(b) Rapid re-organisation.	(b) Difficulty of this after successful assault. Men hard to restrain. If under fire, has to be done roughly and lying down. More complete re-organisation at nightfall or when opportunity arises. Men must be drilled in this. Non-commissioned officers call out Regiment first, Company after, then Platoon. Otherwise confusion.
(c) Rapid decision of method of re-organisation.	(c) Whether convert enemy's position. Whether to dig another line and where. Consolidation to be regarded as temporary; must be ready to advance at any moment.

VARIOUS STAGES—*Continued.*	CONSIDERATIONS ON EACH STAGE.—*Continued.*
	Pursuit carried out with fresh troops if possible.
(d) Battle patrols.	(d) Infantry patrols, accompanied by a Lewis gun, if possible, sent out to cover the consolidation; also question of an Officer's patrol to exploit success. Can these be detailed beforehand, or must they be detailed by the Senior Officer on the spot?
(e) Senior Officers assume Command.	(e) Officers must endeavour to find out what Officers are remaining.
(f) Communication with Officer Commanding Battalion or Artillery and flanking units.	(f) Situation must be communicated immediately to enable fresh troops to come up. Artillery must be acquainted with situation. Value of Artillery screens. Units on flanks communicated with. They may want assistance.

CHAPTER VIII.

MARCHES.

PART I.

NOTES ON MARCHES AND MARCH DISCIPLINE, By LIEUT.-COLONEL J. F. C. FULLER, D.S.O., p.s.c., The Oxfordshire and Buckinghamshire Light Infantry.

The March the Foundation of all Operations.

"Movement is the soul of War." The March is the foundation of all operations, as it enables the initiative to be seized. "To conquer is to advance" (Frederick the Great). "The secret of manœuvres and combats lies in a man's legs and not in his arms" (Napoleon). If men cannot march well they cannot carry out the fundamental principles of war: "To be stronger at a given time and place than the enemy."

Factors Marching depends on:

(i.) Time. (ii.) Distance. (iii.) Endurance.
Endurance depends on Mental and Bodily Vigour.
Mental Vigour depends on Discipline and Moral.
Bodily Vigour depends on Exercise and Training.

Four requisites:—(1) Rest; (2) Food; (3) Discipline; (4) Esprit de Corps.

(1) Rest.

The soldier on the march cannot get too much sleep. He should not be kept waiting about. Fatigues should be most carefully regulated. The soldier should sleep when he can; old soldiers should instil this idea into the younger, and not leave them to learn it after a sad experience.

Rest often requires cover; without cover much sleep may be lost; without sleep there is no good marching.

Bivouacs.—Every Unit should be prepared to bivouac itself at a moment's notice. Requisites to each 4 men : 4 ground sheets, 2 short poles, tackle, and 10 wire skewers; 3 sheets laced together form a roof. Bivouacking should be reduced to a drill. A Battalion should be able to bivouac itself in five or six minutes.

(2) Food.

Directly a march is completed a meal should be served. If a delay occurs soldiers will turn in and go to sleep without waiting for dinners. Sleep refreshes, but it cannot invigorate the body as food does. A weary man who has slept on an empty stomach derives little benefit from his sleep.

Drink.—On the march drinking must be most carefully regulated; at times, however, it is absolutely necessary. Sipping must be strictly forbidden, but whenever a long halt takes place men should be allowed to have a good drink. A long drink before starting a march helps to keep down thirst. Thirst is increased by smoking, spitting, and incessant talking. There should be no cigarette smoking on the line of march.

(3) March Discipline.

Bad march discipline is more destructive than the enemy's fire. " To be footsore is to be wounded."

Preparations for a March.

(i.) Previous to a long march a careful medical inspection should be made, at which men should not make light of small ailments, for it is better to fall out before a march begins than during it.

(ii.) Half an hour before a march the Company Officers should visit their Companies and see that non-commissioned officers and Officers are doing their duty.

(iii.) A quarter of an hour before a march all transport must be drawn up at the appointed place.

Formation and Station of Officers.

(i.) When marching in fours not more than four men, including supernumeraries, should march abreast.

(ii.) Columns of fours will march on the right-hand side of the road in France. If the men on the extreme right are caused inconvenience, they should change places after each halt.

(iii.) Exact distances and covering must be maintained.

(iv.) Captains in front of their Companies, one Subaltern in rear.

Marching At Ease and Halting.

(i.) Men must march at Attention until ordered to march At Ease.

(ii.) When marching At Ease fours are not to open out.

(iii.) When the Halt is signalled the head of the Battalion should stand fast, and although the Battalion should not be closed up on the preceding one, the rest of the Battalion should be closed up on its head.

(iv.) Halts should take place 10 minutes before the hour, and the march should be resumed at the hour.

(v.) When halted men should take off their pack equipment, and, if weather permits, open their jackets and shirts, so that the air may freshen up the body. They should lie or sit down.

Defiling to be Prevented.

(i.) No unit should diminish its front, or attempt to avoid a bad spot in the road unless the preceding unit has done so.

(ii.) When defiling is necessary it must be executed with order and precision.

(iii.) Whenever a stream, ditch or bank is to be crossed, the front should be increased and not diminished, by an extension before arriving.
(iv.) When a very bad place has to be crossed, an Officer should superintend the crossing.

Stragglers.

(i.) No man is to quit the ranks for any purpose without permission of his Captain.
(ii.) Every man unable to keep up must receive a ticket: " The Bearer marched off with the ....Battalion, but was unable to keep up with it. Signed .... Commanding .... Company."

Stepping out to be prevented.

(i.) Men are never to step out beyond the regulation pace, unless ordered to.
(ii.) If distance has to be made up, the head of the Battalion or Company must step short.
(iii.) After passing an obstacle the leading Company must step short until the rear is closed up.
(iv.) When a central or rear Company cannot keep up, its Captain must pass word up for Companies in front to step short.

(4) Esprit de Corps.

Moral, Esprit de Corps, and the example of the Officers, are the mainstays of good marching. On the line of march the Officers must perpetually be watching their men. The Captain must frequently ride up and down his company, and the Platoon Commanders must keep their Platoons closed up. It is an historical fact, proved over and over again, that " Soldiers who will not be beaten cannot be conquered; they may be annihilated, but not subdued." When this unconquerable spirit possesses a Battalion men do not fall out on the line of march. They may fall dead, but they do not fall out, because they belong to an invincible Army, a splendid Regiment, and a fine Company, and would rather die than disgrace either one or the other.

Boots.

" Shoes help on marches, and marches win battles " (Napoleon). " The first requirement of a soldier is a pair of boots, the second a pair of boots for a change, the third a pair of soles for repairs " (Wellington). Boots should be worn before being used on a march. The boots should be loose rather than tight. Toes and heels should be protected by plates. Boots should be well greased, not blacked.

Socks.

Socks and feet must be frequently washed. When washing is impossible, socks should be beaten out, and rubbed until all hardness due to moisture is removed. On a long march it is a good thing when a long halt takes place to change socks from foot to foot. If the skin of the feet is tender, rub socks with soft soap. If skin blisters, run needle and thread through blister and let water out. Boracic powder is good for hardening feet. If socks are wet, place them over shoulders under jacket, heat of body will dry them.

Uniform.

Company Commander should see all boots and uniform fitted. Uniform should be loose. On march collars should be unhooked and cuffs should be turned up.

Equipment.

All equipment should be inspected before march to see that it fits properly. Packs should hang comfortably. Authorised articles only should be carried.

Praise.

On the completion of a long or difficult march the Commanding Officer should never forget to give the men a word of PRAISE or encouragement.

PART II.

A MARCH DISCIPLINE DEMONSTRATION.

This demonstration was carried out by a Brigadier for the benefit of the whole of the Officers and non-commissioned officers of his Brigade during the period the Brigade was out for training immediately prior to proceeding to the SOMME in June, 1916. The points brought out subsequently proved of the greatest assistance to the four Commanding Officers of the Brigade when marching both to and away from the SOMME area, especially the latter when the Brigade had undergone a complete change. This demonstration especially enables the untrained Officer to realise the importance of certain points in their relationship to efficiency on the march from the time the orders relating to the hour of parade are issued to the hour of arrival in billets or camp at the end of the march.

Preliminary Stage.

(a) All the Officers and non-commissioned officers of the four Battalions are assembled, if possible, the day before in some convenient hall, and the Brigadier addresses them on the points he proposes to demonstrate.

(b) The Officers and non-commissioned officers are then formed into one Battalion, and the Battalion is taken through every one of the stages.

(c) If the Commanding Officer desires to carry out the exercise, he first of all assembles all his Officers and non-commissioned officers, and similarly explains the points, and then carries out the demonstration with the four companies of his Battalion.

First Stage.

The hour the Battalion, Company and Platoon Commanders order their parade, to fit in with the time of the higher parade, e.g., if the Battalion has to carry out a Brigade route march and to pass the starting point at a certain hour, then the orders of the lesser Commanders *re* the hour of parade of their commands must be well thought out, to avoid parading the men either too early or too late.

A golden rule to aim at is to give the soldier one clear hour between his breakfast and the hour he has to parade with his platoon.

Second Stage.

When the platoons fall in, are inspected and told off, the following points to be noted:—

(i.) Correct formation of sections.
(ii.) Correct words of command—superfluity of words of command unnecessary.
(iii.) Rear rank stands easy whilst front rank is being inspected, and vice versa.
(iv.) Forming fours with ranks changed. This is a very necessary movement.
(v.) Celerity of inspection. A well-trained Officer in a well-trained unit ought to be able to carry out his inspection very quickly.

Third Stage.

When the company marches to join the Battalion on the Battalion parade ground:—

(i.) The right Section Commanders of the companies going on ahead and taking up their correct position in whatever formation is ordered.
(ii.) The companies dressing according to the methods laid down in " Infantry Training."
(iii.) The Company or Platoon Commander bringing his men to the " Stand Easy " position with the least delay possible.
(iv.) The Commanding Officer rides on to parade, the whole Battalion being called to " Attention," and then to the " Slope," by the Second-in-Command, who reports " All present " or otherwise. The Commanding

Officer rides along the front and flanks of the Battalion, and takes in at a glance the general appearance of the men, and whilst doing so insists on the most perfect steadiness in the ranks, and the correct position of "Attention" of everyone. (If there is time, and he wishes to do so, he can dismount and inspect either one company, one platoon, or one section in each company.) Before moving off, the Commanding Officer takes this opportunity of speaking to his Officers and men, telling them anything that he thinks may interest them, and giving them any information he can regarding the exercises, etc., he proposes to carrry out.

(v.) The Commanding Officer tells off the Battalion, viz., "Tell off by companies."

(vi.) The Battalion moves off. The *whole* Battalion is *not,* except for some very special reason, brought to the " Slope," and kept there whilst the Battalion marches off. Each company is in succession brought to " Attention," arms are sloped, and each platoon moves off by word of command of the Platoon Commander. By so doing the men are saved from the unnecessary fatigue of standing strictly to " Attention " for the five minutes or so it takes for a Battalion 800 to 1,000 strong to pass a given point.

N.B.—The Drums and Fifes, Pipes, Bugles or Band of the unit play lively airs before and during the forming up of the Battalion. *Music is a great incentive to Moral,* and good, popular and lively airs at the forming up of the Battalion put everyone in good spirits and give the day a good start.

It should also be a golden rule for the Band to play its Regiment through a town or village. The inhabitants like it, and the men like it, it is the duty of the Drum and Pipe Major to see to this.

Fourth Stage.

When the Battalion is on the march.

(i.) The Battalion remains at "Attention" with arms correctly sloped for perhaps five minutes, and the Commanding Officer with his Staff takes up his position in some convenient position, in order to see the Battalion pass him. On this occasion it is not a bad custom for the whole Battalion to give "Eyes—right" to their Commanding Officer.

(ii.) The Battalion marches at ease by order of the Commanding Officer, the order being repeated by the Company Commanders, and the men not acting until they get the command from their Platoon Commanders.

(iii.) The Regimental Sergeant-Major is told off to keep and to check the pace throughout the march.

(iv.) The Second-in-Command looks out for oddments, stragglers, etc.

Fifth Stage.

When the Battalion Commander wishes to halt and fall out for the customary halt of ten minutes, or so.

(i.) One whistle denotes "Come to attention." The hand put up signals the halt, and the direction of the hand the side of the road to which the men are to fall out.

(ii.) Celerity of movement to the side of the road denotes a well-trained Battalion.

Sixth Stage.

When the Battalion falls in previous to marching on, and when it marches on.

(i.) One minute before the hour for moving on arrives the word to get dressed is given by the Platoon Commanders.

(ii.) One whistle denotes "Fall in," and the men fall in at the "At Ease" position.

(iii.) A second whistle denotes "Advance at ease," and the Battalion moves on.

(iv.) Celerity of movement and absence of noise and paper after the Battalion has marched on denotes a well-trained Battalion.

Seventh Stage.

When the Battalion forms up for a mid-day halt, and to get their dinners.

(i.) A mounted Officer rides on to select or to be shown the field, etc., and rides back to meet and conduct the Battalion.

(ii.) The Regimental March Past is played, and on that, without any further word of command, the Battalion comes to attention, putting their caps on properly, buttoning up their coats, tightening up their slings, etc., and stepping out with arms swinging and heads up, giving the impression of men who are proud of themselves and of their Battalion.

N.B.—The Band must be told when to strike up.

(iii.) The Battalion forms up *vide* THIRD STAGE (i.), (ii.), (iii.), the Company Commanders getting their men to the "Stand Easy" position at once. There is nothing so irksome as for men to be kept after a long and strenuous march standing to attention, whilst the whole Battalion is forming up and getting dressed, etc., and especially irksome is it to the leading Companies. They must be brought to a position of relaxation immediately.

(iv.) The Commanding Officer sends for his Second-in-Command, his Company Commanders, and his Medical Officer, and issues instructions on information he receives from his Staff (i.e., Quartermaster and Adjutant), viz.,

   (a) Hour dinners will be ready.

   (b) Hour Battalion will move off. *N.B.*—Always give the men time to have their dinners in comfort. There is nothing worse than hurrying Officers or men over their meals, when there is no necessity for it.

   (c) Position of Water, Latrines.

   (d) Estaminets or Inns. If the opportunity presents itself, halt near a town or village, and give the men the chance of getting a glass of beer, and of mixing with the inhabitants. It is a mistake not to do so. We have suffered in the past from our failure to bring the soldier into closer touch with the civilian, and especially has this been the case during the manœuvre period.

   (e) Company Commanders report on the numbers of men who have fallen out, and the Battalion Commander calls for special report from the Medical Officer at once.

(v) The Company Commanders return to their companies, issue the necessary orders to their men, and withdraw to the place selected for the Officers' Mess. Officers should take the earliest opportunity of lying down well clear of the Right Flank of the Battalion, pending the final instructions being received from the Company Commanders.

(vi.) The Company Commander will arrange that either he or the Company Orderly Officer or both see that their men's dinners are all right before commencing their own.

Eighth Stage.

When the Battalion moves off (*vide* THIRD STAGE) (v.).

N.B.—The Second-in-Command satisfies himself that the Battalion has left its bivouac ground scrupulously clean, and reports the same to the Commanding Officer. If any company has not done so, a party is marched back to clean up.

Final Stage.

After the Battalion halts in Billets or Camp for the night (*vide* SEVENTH STAGE). All holds good if the Battalion is going into camp, and practically all if going into billets, the only alteration being that the Officer in charge billeting party will meet and guide the companies to their billets, and the Company Commanders will meet the Battalion Commander at some central spot to receive their orders.

The foregoing take the Officer through all stages of a march, from the orders to move until the order to turn in, and if added to this it is remembered that *every single Officer and man* right down to the cooks must be uniformly dressed from the head of the Battalion to the end of the Transport, and that all must keep their badges and buttons clean, and themselves cleaned and shaved every day during a march, the March Discipline in that Battalion will be of the highest order.

Before the Battalion marches off for a march of some days' duration, a word from the Commanding Officer to his Officers and men to remember the reputation their Battalion enjoys for its excellent marching powers, and the necessity that exists for every member of it to live up to that reputation, and also a word of praise at the end of each day's march before the Battalion dismisses, does no harm.

CHAPTER IX.

PART I.

OUTPOSTS.

(*Battle Outposts, F.S.R., Part I, Chap. V, para. 89.*)

If the enemy is close at hand, and battle imminent, or if the battle ceases only at nightfall to be renewed next day, the whole of the troops must be in complete readiness for action. There may not even be room for outposts, and the troops will have to bivouac in their battle positions, protected only by patrols and sentries. In such cases the firing line takes the place of the piquets. It will often occur in these circumstances that no orders can be issued by superior authority as to measures of protection, and in any case nothing can relieve the commanders of advanced battalions and companies of the responsibility of securing themselves from surprise, and, unless circumstances forbid, of keeping touch with the enemy.

A Company on Outposts.

The following is the sequence of events that has to be carried out by Officers when employed on outpost duty (references in the margin refer to "Infantry Training") :—

1. **Officer Commanding Company.**

    (a) On receipt of orders from the Officer Commanding Outposts he will explain the situation to his Company. The Company will then be moved, precautions being taken to guard against surprise, to the ground allotted to it, where the men will be halted under cover.

    150 (2)

    (b) The Commander will then carry out a rapid reconnaissance of his ground under cover of his scouts, when he will decide ROUGHLY AND QUICKLY on the number and positions of the supports, and will issue orders accordingly. These orders should include :—

    (i.) Situation.
    (ii.) General line.
    (iii.) Dispositions by day and night.
    (iv.) Action in case of attack.
    (v.) Any details regarding cooking, etc.
    (vi.) Relief.
    (vii.) Position of Commander.

(c) The line of piquets must correspond roughly with **150** (3) the line of resistance indicated in the Outpost Commander's Orders.

(d) He will decide what patrols are to be sent out, **150** (5) and whether they will be found by the piquets or supports.

(e) He will communicate with Companies on either **148** (2) flank, and also with the Outpost Commander.   **150** (3)

(f) As soon as piquets and sentries are posted, he will arrange for the withdrawal of the covering troops.

2. Piquet Commander.

(a) The Piquet Commander, having received his orders, will move his command, under cover if possible, to a spot in rear of the position of the piquet line to which he has been detailed. He will then examine the **151** (1) ground and decide on the number of sentry groups required, keeping the number down to a minimum. Having made up his mind, he will then issue his orders, explaining to his men :—

    (i.) Direction of the enemy.
    (ii.) Position of neighbouring piquets.   **151** (3)
    (iii.) Position of supports.
    (iv.) Action in case of attack.
    (v.) The necessity that no movement, except what is actually necessary, should take place either in front of, or behind, the outpost line.

151 (3)   (vi.) Detail various sentry groups and patrols, with their reliefs; a sentry over arms.

(b) The Piquet Commander, having issued his orders, will then post his sentry groups, and see that they understand their orders, viz.:—

    (i.) Regarding direction of enemy.
    (ii.) Position of sentries on right and left.

152 (4)   (iii.) Position of piquets, and any detached posts in vicinity.
    (iv.) Extent of ground to be watched.
    (v.) Regarding people approaching outpost line.
    (vi.) Regarding any patrols out in front.
    (vii.) Names of villages, rivers and places to which roads and railways lead.

(c) The Piquet Commander is responsible for strengthening his position, and allowing room in his defences for the support as well as his own men.

(d) Men on piquet will not remove their equipment.

3. **Officer Commanding Support.**

Officer Commanding Support will see that all his men understand what to do in case of attack, and that the route from his position to the piquet is marked out in such a way that it can be followed at night without confusion.

4. **Sentries.**

(a) Sentries are posted in groups, either single or double sentry groups. If no non-commissioned officer is with the group, the oldest soldier takes command. Groups remain out for at least twelve hours, so no relief **152** is required if force is only halting for one night. Groups should remain quite close to the sentry, within a few yards; not, as is sometimes done, 50 yards or so away.

(b) Sentries are not allowed to lie down without the special sanction of the officer posting the group, owing to danger of falling asleep. At night they must *never* lie down.

(c) Except at night, or in a fog, bayonets of sentries should not be fixed.

5. Method of Challenging.

(a) On the approach of anybody the sentry warns his group.

(b) When nearest person is within speaking distance, the sentry will call out " HALT " in a *low* tone of voice. take cover himself, and get ready to fire.

(c) If sentry's order is disobeyed, shoot without hesitation.

(d) If order obeyed, Group Commander will order person to advance and give an account of himself.

6. Numbering of Piquets, Sentry Groups, etc.

Outpost companies are numbered from right to left throughout the sector.

Piquets are similarly numbered from right to left of their respective companies, and sentry groups of their respective piquets.

They are not numbered consecutively through the front.

7. A Platoon Commander, when detailing his troops for outpost duty, as in any other military operation, should always bear in mind the importance of maintaining his sectional organisation.

All sentry groups are doubled by night, and it is preferable to detail a complete section to a double sentry group.

8. Another point requiring consideration is the number of troops that should be detailed to form a piquet.

Should the particular piquet front require anything over two double sentry groups, it would be advisable to detail more than one platoon for that particular piquet.

The question of who shall find patrols has also to be decided by the Company Commander.

As the piquet duties are heavy and arduous, it is suggested that these patrols may well be found from the supports in preference to taking them from the piquets.

9. Should a Battalion be detailed for outpost duty, it is recommended that each Company should find its own piquets and supports, the outpost line being thus organised in depth.

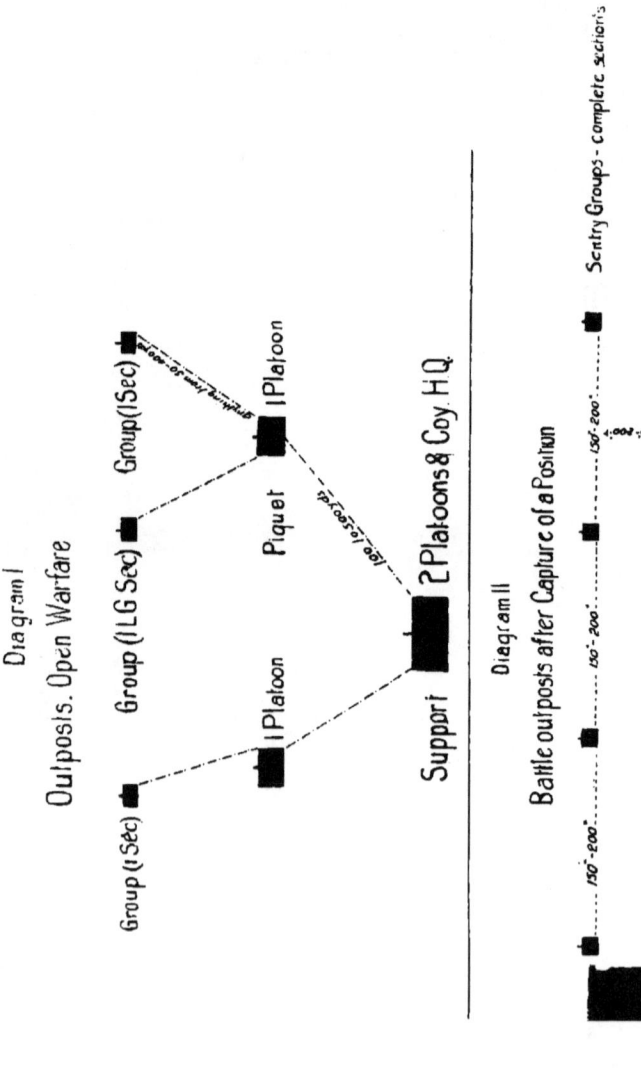

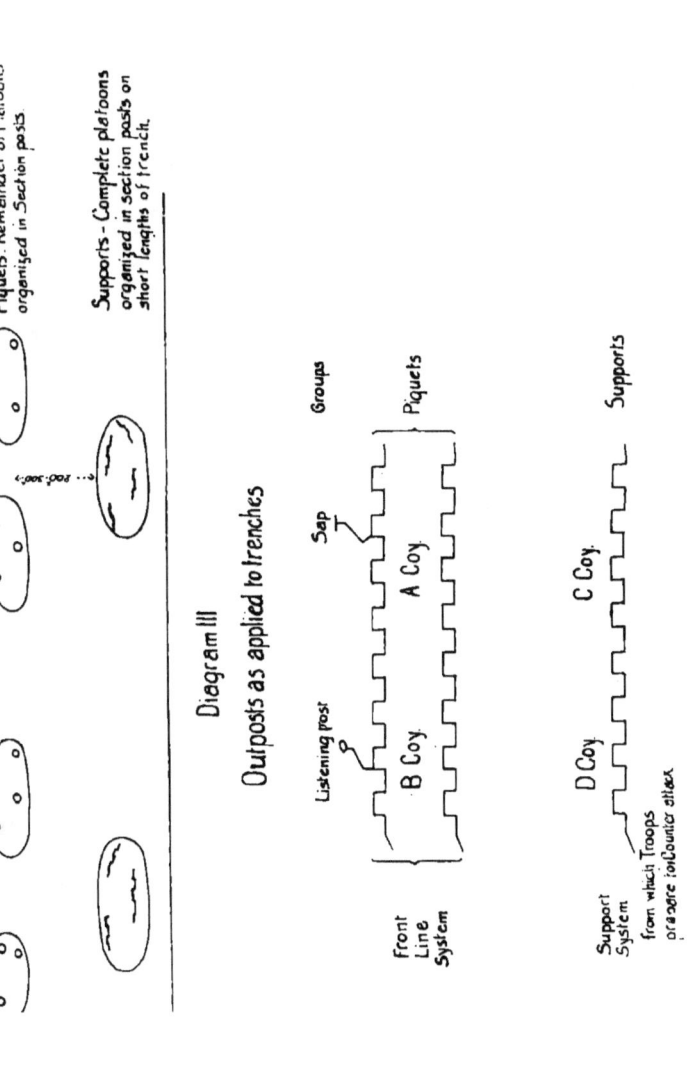

Diagram III
Outposts as applied to trenches

Piquets. Remainder of Platoons organised in Section posts.

Supports - Complete platoons organised in section posts on short lengths of trench.

PART II.

ADVANCED GUARDS.

(*F.S.R., Part I, Chap. V.*)

1. The duties of a Tactical Advanced Guard are threefold:—

- (i) Protection of the force it is covering from surprise or interference.
- (ii) Obtaining information of the enemy and country.
- (iii) In the event of the enemy being met with in force, to gain time for the Commander of the force to develop his plan. To this end tactical features which may assist the future action of the main body should be seized.

2. These duties can only be carried out by *fighting*, therefore the Advanced Guard must be constituted as a fighting force.

- (i) An Advanced Guard secures the protection of the force it is covering by driving off small bodies of the enemy in the vicinity of the route of the Main Body, and by holding tactical features until the passage of the column is secured. In this connection it must be remembered that if the Advanced Guard has no mounted troops, the area within which it is possible to hold tactical features without danger of delaying the advance of the column is very limited. That is to say, with an Advanced Guard composed solely of Infantry, certain risks must be taken.
- (ii) To obtain information of the enemy it is nearly always necessary to fight. The

Advanced Guard, let us say, meets with opposition. How can the strength of the enemy be determined unless he is attacked? It is the duty of the Advanced Guard to do so in order to give the Commander of the Force timely information as to the disposition of the enemy.

(iii) If in the course of the advance information is obtained either by fighting or otherwise which shows that the enemy is in the immediate vicinity of the line of advance in such strength that the Advanced Guard cannot brush him aside without the assistance of the Main Body, it becomes the duty of the Advanced Guard Commander to hold the enemy at arm's length, so to speak, until the Commander of the force has been able to develop his plan. This action may entail a defensive attitude, but whether offensive or defensive, the Advanced Guard Commander should seize and hold any tactical features in the vicinity, the possession of which may assist him in carrying out his own duties or facilitate the execution of the general plan.

(iv) In short, an Advanced Guard must at all times act with vigour and without hesitation, remembering that its actions must be controlled by the interests of the force it is covering.

3. (i) The Commander of the Advanced Guard, who should be named in the orders of the formation detailing him, must know sufficient of the plan of the Commander of the force to enable him to carry out his duties intelligently, and must receive clear instructions as to engaging the enemy should he be met in any force.

(ii) The Commander of the Advanced Guard is responsible for :—

   (a) The issue of orders to his Advanced Guard, explaining the general situation, the route to be followed, the composition of the vanguard and the main guard, the order of march and the hour of starting.

   (b) The maintenance of the proper distance and of communication between himself and the Main Body. That is to say, if the " starting time " is mentioned in the orders of the formation to which he belongs, the Advanced Guard Commander must see that by that hour his command is disposed to cover the advance of, and is in communication with, the Main Body.

(iii) The position of the Commander of the Advanced Guard is normally at the head of the Main Guard, but he must be prepared to move to any point to control the situation, or to give a rapid decision.

4. (i) Advanced Guards are divided into :—

   Van Guard—Whose duties are mainly reconnaissance.

   Main Guard—Whose duties are mainly fighting.

   The Van Guard, therefore, will be composed mainly of mounted troops, if they are available, and should also include a party of R.E. to clear the road. The Van Guard is responsible for the protecton of the Main Guard from surprise.

> The Main Guard will comprise the remainder of the Infantry and such Artillery and other troops as may be allotted to the Advanced Guard.
>
> (ii) The strength of the Advanced Guard may vary from $\frac{1}{8}$ to $\frac{1}{4}$ of the strength of the force it is covering. The smaller the force the greater the proportion required for the Advanced Guard.

5. Formation of an Advanced Guard is shown in Plates A, B, and C.

PLATE A

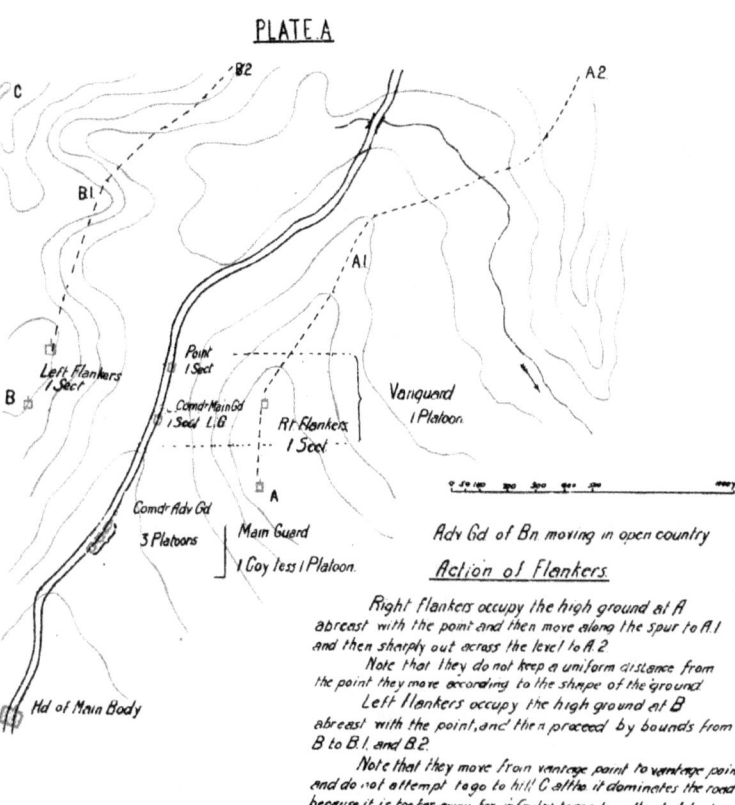

Adv Gd of Bn moving in open country

Action of Flankers

Right flankers occupy the high ground at A abreast with the point and then move along the spur to A.1 and then sharply out across the level to A.2.

Note that they do not keep a uniform distance from the point they move according to the shape of the ground.

Left flankers occupy the high ground at B abreast with the point, and then proceed by bounds from B to B.1. and B.2.

Note that they move from vantage point to vantage point and do not attempt to go to hill C altho it dominates the road because it is too far away for infantry to reach without delaying the march of the main body.

PLATE B

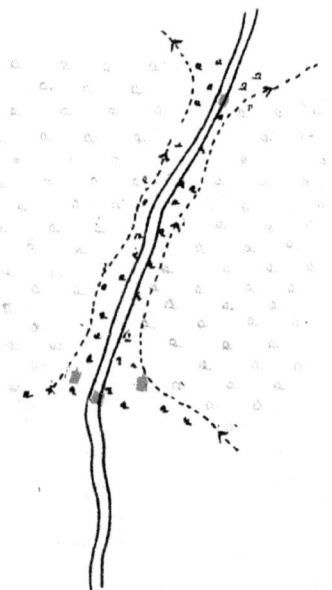

Action of an Infantry vanguard on reaching a wood or other obstacle so large that it is impossible to search it thoroughly. Object is to secure the exit and make certain that no parties of the enemy are lurking in immediate vicinity of road. Point pushes through to far edge, flankers close in parallel to road and within sight of it, remainder of vanguard supports the point. Note that it is impossible to thoroughly search a wood of this size within the time or with troops available, therefore compromise-

PLATE. C.

Suggested form of an advanced guard to a Battalion advancing in semi-open warfare on Western Front. The Advance will be carried out by bounds from one tactical feature to the next.

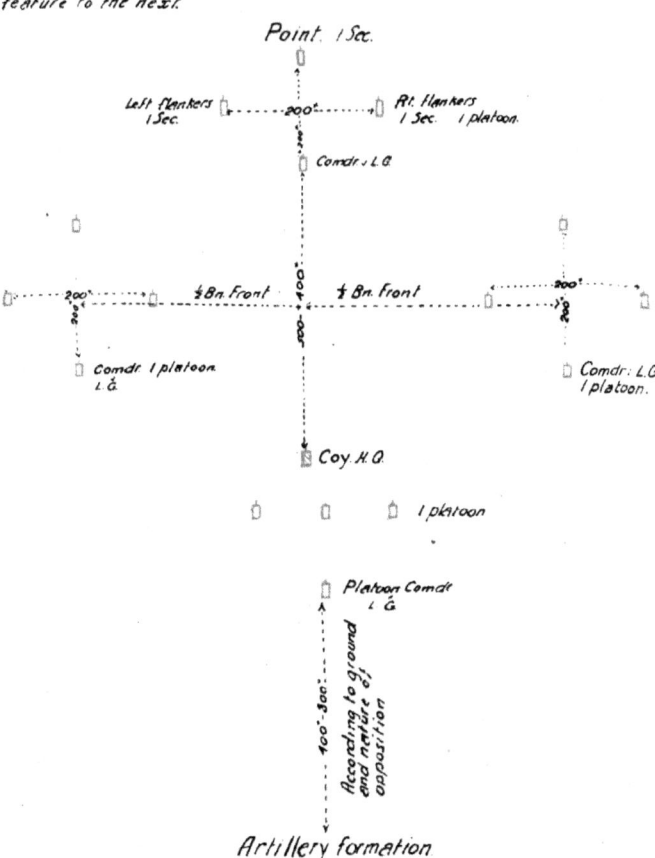

PART III.

NOTES ON RECONNAISSANCE.

1. (a) A Reconnoitring Patrol or Detachment bases its movement entirely on the enemy or on the information it is required to obtain. It is a pure and simple information seeking patrol. No Commander can in any way count for protection on the fact that a reconnoitring patrol has been sent out.

(b) A Protective Patrol or Detachment bases its movement entirely on the force it is covering, and must never uncover that force under any circumstances.

2. By day both classes of patrols move by bounds from Tactical point to Tactical point.

3. A Reconnoitring Patrol halts on completing the bound until the Leader has—

(a) Received reports from advanced scouts.
(b) Got into communication with detached scouts.
(c) Examined the country foreground, background, right, left, centre.
(d) Decided where the next bound will take him and how he will advance.
(e) Decided whether he has any information to send back.

4. A Protective Patrol halts on completing the bound until the leader has dealt with the points enumerated in para. 3, and <u>until he has corrected his distance with the force he is covering</u>.

5. By night, when feeling forward in close contact with the enemy, protective patrols must advance a given number of paces, say 200 to 400, and halt until the body in rear closes up. They are then again pushed forward. Unless this methodical method of advance is carried out, patrols will get lost, and the troops in rear will be surprised. A rate of advance of a

quarter to one mile per hour is the most that can be expected. A reconnoitring patrol, on the other hand, can be pushed well ahead, according to the skill and training of the Leader, but very careful arrangements must be made to receive its reports.

6. Patrols must invariably cover themselves with protective scouts, but care must be taken not to get the patrol so scattered that the Leader cannot rally it if necessary to do so.

7. The following information must be given to every leader of a reconnoitring patrol :—

>**T**ime to be away.
>**O**ther troops and what is known of them.
>**R**eports and where to send.
>**I**nformation on what points required.
>**D**irection and distance to go.
>**E**nemy and what is known of him.
>Aid to memory—TO RIDE.

8. A Reconnoitring Patrol must be given a simple question to answer :—

>(a) Is MERCATEL occupied by the enemy or not?
>(b) Is the enemy occupying the HINDENBURG TRENCH between.........................:..............and
>............................
>(c) Are our troops in occupation of BEAURAINS?

Patrols must never be told to reconnoitre in a certain direction without being given definite questions to answer.

Information may be asked for under the heading " IN GENERAL " and " IN PARTICULAR."

" IN GENERAL " to report the location or movement of any (large) hostile bodies in such and such an area.

" IN PARTICULAR " (a) Is the enemy retiring from

>(b) Is.............occupied by the enemy?

9. It is essential to recognise the difference between a reconnoitring patrol and a reconnoitring detachment.

- (a) A Reconnoitring Patrol consists of one leader and the men of the patrol.
  Having only one leader, it cannot reconnoitre more than one objective at a time.
- (b) A Reconnoitring Detachment consists of two or more patrols, and so can reconnoitre two or more objectives simultaneously.

10. The best results will generally be obtained by sending a detachment forward under a capable leader to some central point from which he will detach the patrols, keeping at the same time some troops in hand, for:—

- (a) Supporting the patrols.
- (b) Forwarding messages.
- (c) Covering the retirement of the patrols.

11. ALL Officers and N.C.Os. must be trained to write messages in proper form.

PART IV.

NOTES ON RAIDS.

1. Impossible to standarize raids—originality and surprise.

2. Different sorts of raids, but all forms of reconnaissances—
    (i) To secure identifications.
    (ii) To ascertain damage done by bombardments.
    (iii) To inflict loss and damage on enemy and lower his moral.
        All above three can be combined.
    (iv) To increase our own moral. This latter should invariably be of simplest character, and as fool-proof as possible.
    (v) Night or daylight. All big schemes by day must have adequate artillery support.

3. All raids, to be successful, must be founded on sound principles, same as major operations of war :—
    (i) Simplicity of scheme.
    (ii) Punctuality.
    (iii) Must be carried out by complete tactical units.
    (iv) Everybody taking part must be imbued with determination to get there and carry out his job.
    (v) Artillery co-operation must be suitable to the general scope of the plan.

Reference the above—
    (i) No bombing inwards, or changes of direction at night. Everybody must be able to go straight to his appointed objective.
    (ii) Applies to infantry and artillery—careful estimate of time required not only to cross No Man's Land, but to get into position, and also to return. Patrolling.

(iii) Danger of "storm troops." German moral destroyed.
(iv) Closely allied with (iv) a question of moral.
(v) If too great, give show away; if not enough, machine guns may hang up the show. Normally not open till zero. If it opens before zero Boche must have been taught to regard it as a normal "strafe."

4. **Orders for Raids.**

Who issues? Action of Brigade and Battalion—
Must state—

Area to be raided and object of raid.
Unit and strength of raiding party.
Artillery, machine guns and trench mortar co-operation.
Any special directions as to carrying out raid, including signal for return.
Equipment to be carried.
Special signal arrangements.
Disposal of prisoners — immediate report — papers.
Removal of papers and identification before going over.
Zero hour.

5. **Preparation for Raids.**

Careful reconnaissances of ground and wire; wire-cutting.

Best method is to concentrate on cutting Boche wire all the time with Stokes and trench mortars, so that there are always some gaps ready made.

Practice trenches and wire. Best if you can get a piece of the old Boche trench and wire to practise over.

Get them to go quicker than artillery barrage table in practice, so as to ensure plenty of dash and go. Men to carry bombs, etc., must carry them in practice. A night raid must be practised in dark as well as by daylight. Men must be in hard condition. Importance of taking prisoners much better than stories of dead Boche.

6. **Equipment.**

No fancy articles. A man is trained to use rifle and bayonet in all conditions, and should be encouraged in every way to gain confidence in the use of his weapons.

Box Respirators in accordance with Standing Orders.

Demolition Parties.—Mills', smoke, and Stokes' bombs.

Rifleman.—Rifle, bayonet, bandolier.

Blocks.—A minimum of 2 riflemen, 2 Lewis gunners, 2 rifle-bombers No. 23. That is, in effect, a Lewis gun section. Don't employ blocks unless Boche is likely to *counter-attack* the raiding party—only wastes men. If counter-attack is likely, then "block" must be organized to fight.

CHAPTER X.

ORDERS AND MESSAGES.

By LIEUTENANT-COLONEL A. C. BAYLEY, D.S.O., p.s.c., The Oxfordshire and Buckinghamshire Light Infantry.

1. The first and most important point to be observed in the writing of Orders, Messages, and Reports, etc., which should be short and concise, is to write them in a clear and legible hand.

The second, which, if observed, will ensure this being done, is always to keep at hand a supply of good, well-sharpened BLACKLEAD Pencils. Do not depend on an indelible pencil, for it is practically impossible to use it in wet weather.

The third point is always to keep at hand an A.B. 152.

2. Style of a Report or Order.

When writing orders and messages in the field, under conditions when a typewriter is not available, it is a great advantage if a uniform system is adopted in the Battalion as to the style these orders should take.

For instance, it is recommended **that a Commanding Officer should normally make use of A.B. 152,** in preference to using a smaller type of notebook.

A.B. 152 is a most convenient size, and it allows sufficient room for a *small* margin to be left for remarks.

Should the order take the form of a signal message, then make use of the Signal Message Form C 2121.

In writing orders or instructions always number your paragraphs, and give the heading in the margin in Block Type, so that the subject matter of your instructions can be seen at a glance.

3. Preparation of Orders.

For details as to the rules regarding the preparation of orders and reports, read F.S.R., Part 1, Sect. 9. Sect. 12 in the same book gives you the necessary instructions regarding the form that these orders should take.

4. Orders.

The important thing in Operation Orders is to keep the main object of those orders clear.

Verbal orders are dangerous, and if given should always, when possible, be confirmed later on in writing.

Orders should, as far as possible, be framed in accordance with the stereotyped form, so that Officers are readily familiar with it. In war this is most important, as orders have to be read and digested very often under the most disturbing circumstances. No single precaution should therefore be avoided which will aid a subordinate in grasping his instructions without trouble and delay. They should be as short as possible, **especially in open warfare, when time does not permit of the detailed orders used in trench warfare.**

5. Warning Order.

Particular attention is drawn to F.S.R., Part 1, para. 13 (3), regarding the issue of a " Warning Order." This should be done whenever possible, so as to give subordinates not only the necessary rest, but an opportunity of making any arrangements required to carry out the subsequent operation order.

6. Messages.

1. Address message to unit. Do not address it to an Officer by name. Then follow with your registered letter and number, and if necessary quote the number of the message you are referring to. (See Message Form C 2121.)

2. If to be delivered to more than one addressee, say so in space provided for address, and add information at end of message as directed in F.S.R., Part 1, para. 16 (6), viz., addressed to people who have to take action on it, and repeated to people who require it for information only.

3. Important numbers written in words.

4. Word **" NOT "** in block.

5. Authorised abbreviations only, F.S.R., para. 16.

6. Always put time of message at end—most important.

7. In reporting on a situation remember that in an engagement, whatever you do, inaction is sure to be wrong. Say in your report, "I am going to do so and so."

7. Obedience of Orders.

Every Officer must know F.S.R., Part I., ch. II., para. 12 (13), beginning, " A formal order is never to be departed from when . . . , etc."

8. Sketches.

(a)) When submitting reports on any tactical situation, nothing assists the recipient of that report so much as a clear and simple sketch. By means of such a sketch it is possible to save a great deal of writing, as, for example, to describe the actual position and distribution of your troops in detail requires a lot of writing in a report, but can readily be shown with very little trouble on a sketch, and in a manner that is far more readily seen and understood. [See F.S.R., Part I, 15 (7).]

(b) On the attached diagram a series of three sketches is shown, each of which was intended to accompany the same report.

Sketches Nos. 1 and 3 were drawn by Lieutenant-Colonel L. H. Jardine, New Zealand Expeditionary Force, and Sketch No. 2 is one that actually was received with a report, and has not been **exaggerated** in any way.

The following criticisms are made as regards these sketches :—

(i.) *Sketch No. 1.*

In this sketch a great deal of trouble has been taken to show as accurately as possible all the topographical features of that particular bit of country. It entailed a lot of time being devoted to this work, which often is not available when one is employed on reconnaissance work against time. Not only that, a sketch of this nature, if carried out by anyone who is not an expert draughtsman, soon becomes a mass of detail, so that it is exceedingly difficult either to locate what are the chief **military tactical features** or to see at a glance what is the **actual** distribution of the troops.

(ii.) *Sketch No. 3.*

In this sketch no attempt has been made to do anything more than show approximately the main tactical features.

In deciding upon what features should be shown, two points should be kept in mind. First, show some of the important features which are shown on your small scale map, so that your sketch may be afterwards read in conjunction with that map. It then becomes possible to locate with fair accuracy all information shown on your rough sketch. Secondly, show any features which you consider of real tactical importance, but which are not shown on the map. By confining oneself within these limits the map is not obscured with detail, and sufficient room is left for marking down the dispositions of the troops.

It is important that the formation to which any particular body of troops belongs should be indicated, and this is best done by marking down, in the first instance, the headquarters of a unit. Then, it is suggested, the position of any detachment found by that unit should be connected up with a dotted line, or by means of arrows, so that the Officer who has to examine the report can see at a glance exactly what your distribution is and how it has been arrived at.

A scale of yards has not been shown, for it would very likely be misleading. Actual distances would be obtained by reference to the map. An occasional range to some important point may be useful.

Other points requiring attention are that the top of a rough tactical sketch should be the direction of the enemy, and all printing and writing kept horizontal, except that indicating roads, rivers and railways.

NOTE.—If a sketch has to be made by several Officers with the intention of joining them up into a combined sketch, then the top of your paper will always be **True North.** This hardly, however, comes under the heading of a Rough Sketch.

A sketch of this nature, showing only approximately the chief tactical features and disposition of troops, is one that **any** Officer should be able to complete in the shortest possible space of time, and however roughly done, if carried out on these lines, adds very considerably to the value of any report.

(ii.) *Sketch No. 2.*

The chief points in connection with the sketch are :—
- (a) Troops most indistinct, no strength shown.
- (b) No tactical features regarding the ground shown.
- (c) Detail incorrectly expressed, such as roads, woods, hedges, etc.
- (d) Writing facing in all directions.

9. The following are examples of—
- (a) An operation order dealing with a Simple March.
- (b) An operation order dealing with an Attack.
- (c) An operation order dealing with Outposts.
- (d) A Battalion Routine Order.
- (e) An official message.
- (f) A memorandum.

EXAMPLE A: An Operation Order for a March.

Secret. Copy No 8.

10th Bn. THE BUFFS, Operation Order 75.

Ref.: 1" Aldershot Manœuvre Map, North. 12/1/17.

INFORMATION. 1. Small hostile patrols were reported by our Cavalry in the LONG VALLEY at 8.0 a.m. on 11th inst. Otherwise touch has not been obtained with the enemy.

INTENTION. 2. The Battalion will march to CRONDALL to-morrow

DETAIL. 3. (a) Advanced Guard:—Commander, Major JACKSON, A Company.

(b) Main Body:—H.Q., C, D, & B Company less 2 Platoons.
1st Line Transport.
Baggage Section of Train.

Starting Point:—Railway Level crossing at ASH JUNCTION STATION.

Time:—10.0 a.m.

Route:—BADSHOT LEA — FARNHAM — DIPPENHALL.

(c) Rear Guard:—Commander, Lieut. P. JONES. 2 Platoons, B Company.

REPORTS. 4. Reports to head of Main Body.

J. H. THOMAS, Capt. & Adjt
10th Bn. The Buffs.

Issued personally at 4.15 p.m.

Copy No. 1. A Company.
No. 2. B ,,
No. 3. C ,,
No. 4. D ,,
No. 5. Transport Officer.
No. 6. Quartermaster.
No. 7. Office.
No. 8. War Diary.

NOTE:—Regimental Routine Orders. The heading for such Orders is 'Battalion Orders by Lieut.-Col. (name) Commanding (name of Battalion)."

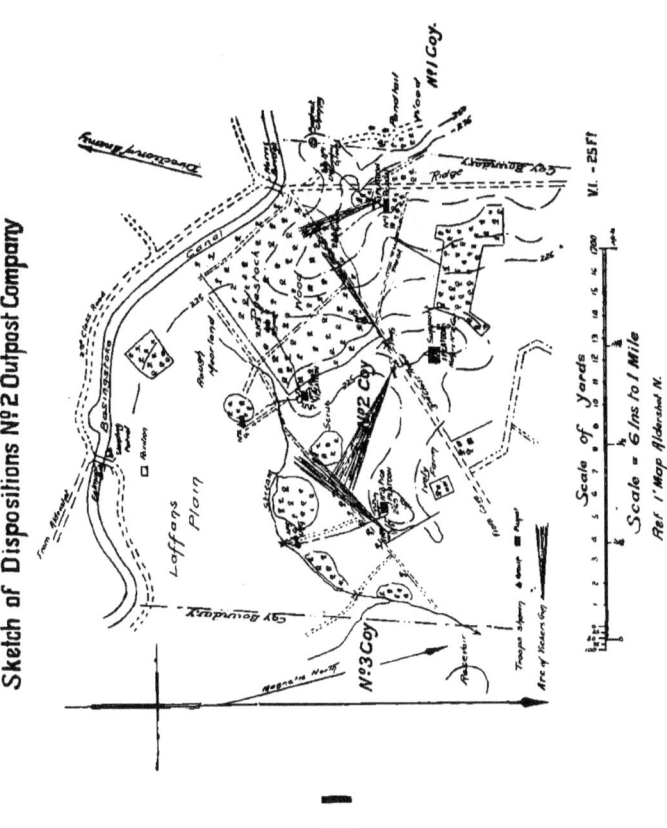

SKETCH I

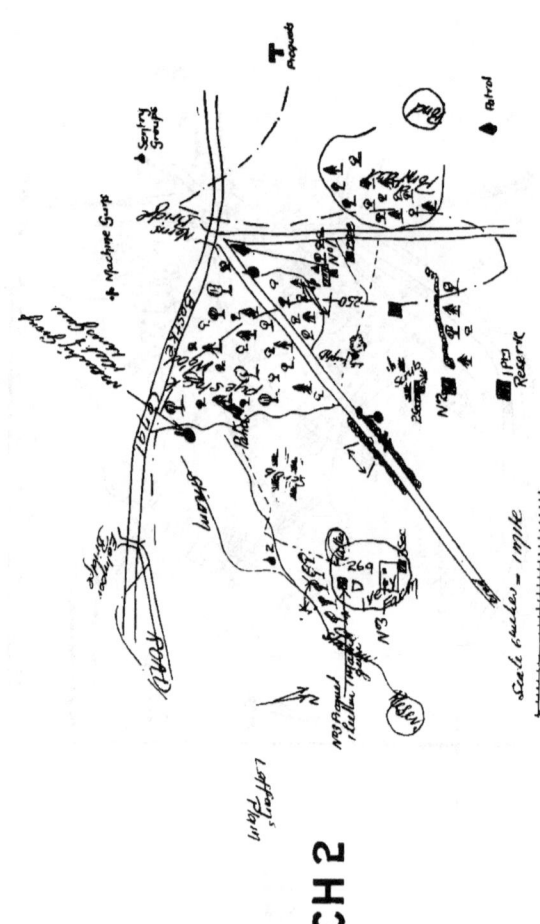

SKETCH 2

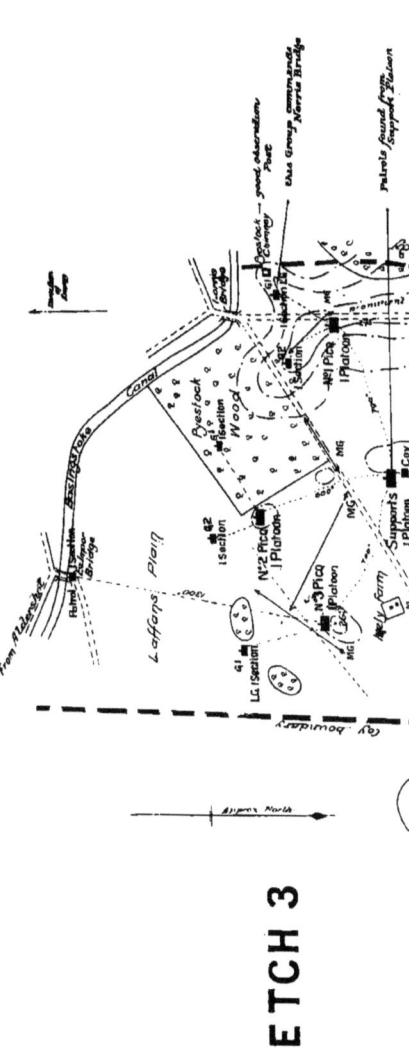

SKETCH 3

EXAMPLE B: An Operation Order for an Attack.

Secret. Copy No. 10.

35th Bn. MIDDLESEX REGIMENT, Operation Order No. 11.

Ref.: Aldershot Map, N. 17/8/17
1 inch to 1 Mile.

INFORMATION. 1. (a) Enemy are reported on MILES HILL, LONG HILL and JUBILEE HILL, and are strongly entrenched along the line of the FLEET—TWESELDOWN—HEATH HOUSE road.

(b) Our advanced troops have reached the line of the main LONDON—FARNHAM road.

INTENTION. 2. The Battalion will take part in a Brigade attack. Battalion Objective : JUBILEE HILL.

DETAIL. 3. (a) Battalion will assemble for attack immediately EAST of point 340 at D.7.b 6.5, and will form up in three lines.

(i) Firing line { A Company on right.
                 { B Company on left.
(ii) Support   C Company.
(iii) Reserve D Company.

(b) (i) Companies in firing line will each advance on a front of 300 yards. B Company will direct with the left along the WELLINGTON MONUMENT—BOURLEY HILL road.
BEARING of ADVANCE—255°.

(ii) C Company will follow firing line after an interval of 10 minutes.

(iii) D Company will follow the supports after an interval of 10 minutes.

(c) 35th Bn. Royal Fusiliers will co-operate on our right, 35th Bn. The Buffs on the left.

(d) *Time of Attack.*—Attacking troops will debouch from the line of WOODS from D.7.b.3.4 to D 7.b.3.8 at 11.30 a.m.

LIAISON. 4. D Company will detail two officers with suitable escorts to keep up liaison with battalions on both flanks.

S.A.A. 5. Ammunition pack animals will concentrate at point 340 and come under the orders of the Regimental Sergeant-Major.

AID POST. 6. At WELLINGTON MONUMENT.

TRANSPORT.	7. Will remain at its present position ready to move at half an hour's notice.
REPORTS.	8. Report centre at point 430. When objective has been captured and consolidated report centre will move to point where stream crosses BOURLEY HILL road at D.7.a.9.3.

(Sgd,) F. BICKNELL, Lieut. & Adjt.,
35th Bn. Middlesex Regt.

Issued at 9 a.m. by runner.

Copy No. 1. A Company.
    No. 2. B Company.
    No. 3. C Company
    No. 4. D Company.
    No. 5. 200th Infantry Brigade.
    No. 6. 35th Bn. Royal Fusiliers.
    No. 7. 35th Bn. Buffs.
    No. 8. Quartermaster.
    No. 9. Medical Officer.
    No. 10. Office.
    No. 11. War Diary.

NOTE :—The most satisfactory way to maintain liaison in open warfare is to arrange for officers with a suitable escort to meet at stated times and places.

EXAMPLE C. An Operation Order for Outposts.

Secret. Copy No. 5.

2nd SUFFOLK REGIMENT Operation Order No. 1.

Ref. Aldershot Map, N. 6/8/17.
1 inch to 1 mile.

INFORMATION.
1. (a) Enemy is reported in FLEET, covered by Outposts on the line TWESELDOWN HILL—PONDTAIL BRIDGE—EAST edge of FLEET POND.

    (b) Our troops are billeted in the area NORTH CAMP STATION—ASH VALE STATION, with Outposts from E in COVE (B.31.d 7.3) — Reservoir (D.1.b.6.4) — Second A in CANAL (D.1.d.7.4) to WELLINGTON MONUMENT.

    (c) The 1/Bn. Border Regt. are on our right, the 2/Bn. Welsh Regt. on our left.

INTENTION.
2. The Battalion will hold No. 2 Section of the above Outpost line, from a point 100 yards N. of the road at D.1.d.7 8 to the CANAL at D.1.d.5.4.

DETAIL.
3. (a) A Company : No. 1 Outpost Company from the road inclusive at D.1.d 7.8 to a small bridge (not on map) at D.1.d 7.6.
    B Company : No. 2 Outpost Company from D 1.d.7 6 small bridge to CANAL inclusive at D.1.d 5.4.

    (b) C and D Companies will be in reserve at BLANDFORD HOUSE (D.2 c.2.5).

    (c) Bn. Headquarters at BLANDFORD HOUSE.

    (d) Piquet Line will be line of RESISTANCE.

    (e) No fires in the Piquet line and no smoking after dark.

    (f) Outpost Companies will not be relieved before 2 p.m. 7th inst.

TRANSPORT.	4.	In small wood EAST of FARNBOROUGH—ALDERSHOT ROAD at D.2.c.2 3.
AID POST.	5.	BLANDFORD HOUSE.
REPORTS.	6.	BLANDFORD HOUSE.

(Sgd.) G. C. HAMILTON, Capt and Adjt.,
2/Bn. Suffolk Regt.

Issued at 4 p.m. by runner.

Copy No. 1. A Company.
No. 2. B Company.
No. 3. C Company.
No. 4. D Company.
No. 5. Filed
No 6. Medical Officer.
No. 7. Quartermaster.
No. 8. Transport Officer.
No. 9 Border Regt.
No. 10. Welsh Regt.
No 11. Brigade
No 12. War Diary.

EXAMPLE D.

Battalion Order No. 100,
By LIEUT.-COL. A. G. BROWN, D.S.O., M.C.,
Comdg. 10th (S.) Battn. The Royal Fusiliers.

9/12/16.

PART I.

DETAIL FOR TO-MORROW. 1. Orderly Officer—Lieut. P. A. Smith, M.C.
Supernumerary—2nd Lieut. J. J. Jones.
Next for Duty—Lieut. J. Bull.
Battalion Orderly-Sergeant — No. 102 Sergt. O. Green.
Rouse, 7 a.m. Breakfasts, 7.45 a.m. Orderly-room, 9 a.m.

TRAINING. 2. Companies will be at the disposal of O.C. Companies.

BATHS. 3. Companies are allotted the Baths to-morrow as under:—
½ Bn., Headquarters, and A Company, 9 a.m.
B Company, 11 a.m.
C Company, 2 p.m.
½ Bn., Headquarters, and D Company, 4 p.m.

ADVANCED PARTIES. 4. All parties detailed to proceed to the trenches will assemble at Battalion Headquarters at 8.30 a.m. Those detailed to remain in the trenches will parade with kits packed. All will take a haversack ration.

CASH REQUISITIONS. 5. Will be submitted to Orderly-room by 9 a.m. to-morrow.

PAY. 6. The Battalion will be paid on the 11th inst.

J. A. BAYNES, Captain & Adjutant,
10th Royal Fusiliers.

PART II.

PROMOTIONS. 1. No. 106 Corpl. P. L. Brown, A Coy., to be sergeant, vice Sergt. J. Pike appointed provost sergeant. 8/12/16.
No. 1068 L.-Cpl C. D. Silcock, A Coy., to be corporal, vice Corpl. Brown. 8/12/16.

APPOINTMENTS.

2. No 256 Sergt. J. Pike, A Coy., is appointed regimental provost sergeant 7/12/16.

No. 502 Pte M. Bullock, B Coy., No 6002 Pte N. Tod, C Coy., No. 2005 Pte. J. Gunn, A Coy., are appointed lance-corporals. 9/12/16.

DIPRIVATIONS OF PAY.

3. No 100161 Pte. G. G. Brownlow deprived 10 days' pay for absence from parade.

J. A. BAYNES, Captain & Adjutant
10th Royal Fusiliers.

NOTICE —There will be a performance by the Divisional Follies in the Y.M.C.A. Hut at 6.15 p.m. to-morrow evening.

NOTES.

(a) No mention of the date you are taking over trenches is put in Routine Orders. This will appear in your Operation Order, which is a secret document.

(b) No mention has been made in these Orders of Gas Helmet Drill. With such large reinforcements arriving, it has been assumed that the Commanding Officer has already issued instructions to his Company Commanders on the vital importance of this particular duty.

(c Companies have been placed (Order 2) at the disposal of Company Commanders, so that they may inspect and see that their men are thoroughly equipped before proceeding to the trenches. The Commanding Officer has explained his views to his Officers at a Conference.

EXAMPLE E: An Official Message on A.F. C 2121.

The message has been addressed to three Battalions, viz.: The 10th Buffs. 5th Gloucestershire, and 6th Worcestershire Regiments. The message has reference to a Brigade Operation Order No. 75 which affects the Buffs. It is also desired to let the other two Battalions mentioned know of the change in programme. This is done as indicated in para. 6 (2), on page 98.

"A" Form — Army Form C. 2121.

MESSAGES AND SIGNALS. No. of Message............

Prefix... Code...m. Office of Origin and Service Instructions	Words	Charge	This message is on a/c of	Recd. at .... m.
		Sent	Service	Date...........
	At .... m.			From ....
	To			
	By		(Signature of "Franking Officer")	By ....

TO	10/BUFFS
	5/GLOUC
	6/WORC

Sender's Number	Day of Month	In reply to Number	
BM 76	5		A A A

Ref	para	3	Operation	Order
75.	aaa	Column	will	proceed
via	HUNGRY	HILL	and	NOT
via	FARNHAM	as	stated	aaa
Addressed	10/BUFFS	repeated	5/GLOUC	6/WORC

From 50th INF BDE
Place
Time 8.20 P.M.

The above may be forwarded as now corrected.

(Z) A.E. Sanderson Major

Censor — Signature of Addressor or person authorised to telegraph in his name

* This line should be erased if not required.

EXAMPLE F: An Official Memorandum.

Narrative.

You are Colonel X, commanding the 10th Battalion The Buffs, and you are out of the line training for a month. As a result of a ride through the billets, round the companies training, and back through the billets, where you arrive in time to see the Battalion at dinners, the following points come to your notice :—The guards all through were very bad at turning out, and when they did turn out the non-commissioned officers in charge had a very vague idea either of their duties or of the recognised procedure. The work being carried out by the companies was most satisfactory, and showed that the Officers had taken much trouble in preparing their plan beforehand, and in doing so were making it interesting for the men, who were working with a keenness that was quite a pleasure to see. The only thing wrong was the presence in the ranks of one Company ("A") of several rather dirty-looking men, with bad clothing, no cap badges, and unshaven faces. In the rest of the companies the men presented a smart, clean, and soldierly appearance. The dinners were excellent, but the billets were, with the exception of " B " Company, not as clean as they might have been, paper and refuse lying about, and the whole pointing to the fact that either the men had not been given time to clean up, or the Officers and non-commissioned officers were not fully alive to the importance of cleanliness in billets. The billets of " B " Company were excellent.

Memorandum (on above narrative).

    To O.C. " A " Company.
     „ O C. " B " Company.
     „ O.C. " C " Company.
     „ O.C. " D " Company.

The following points came to the notice of the Commanding Officer during his inspection of the companies at work and during dinner :—

GUARDS.   1. The guards were universally bad. Neither the non-commissioned officers in command nor the men themselves gave any proof that they knew their duties.

TRAINING.   2. The training all through was most satisfactory and the Commanding Officer wishes Company Commanders to tell their companies how satisfied and pleased he was to see the sound system that was evident throughout, and the keen and willing manner in which the men were working.

APPEARANCE.   3. The general appearance of the men on parade was, with one exception, most excellent. That exception was "A" Company, and the Commanding Officer was rather sorry to see in that company a good many rather dirty-looking men, with bad clothing, no cap badges, and unshaven faces in the ranks.

DINNERS.   4. The dinners all through were most satisfactory, the men expressing themselves thoroughly satisfied with their food and the manner in which it was served.

BILLETS.   5. The billets of "B" Company were excellent, but the same cannot be said of the remainder. Their state with paper and refuse lying everywhere, and the men's kits in disorder, pointed to the fact that, either the men were not being given sufficient time to clean and tidy up their billets before going on parade, or the Company Officers were not fully alive to their responsibilities in this direction.

The Commanding Officer, wherever he has referred in complimentary terms to the work, etc., of the companies, wishes you to bring the same to the notice of all concerned, and similarly, where he has found occasion to offer adverse criticism on certain points that came under his notice, he desires you to take whatever action you think necessary to effect improvement.

(Sd.).........................Capt. and Adjt.
The 10th Battalion The Buffs.

Date...........................

CHAPTER XI.

TACTICAL EXERCISES.

By LIEUTENANT-COLONEL A. C. BAYLEY, D.S.O., p.s.c., The Oxfordshire and Buckinghamshire Light Infantry.

1. For official information on this subject see "Training and Manœuvre Regulations."

2. From the definition of a Regimental Exercise, viz., an exercise in which the force actually dealt with on the ground does not exceed that likely to be commanded by a Lieutenant-Colonel, it is seen that what is required are schemes dealing with small forces such as a battalion or company.

3. **Regimental Exercises** are an excellent means of training Officers and non-commissioned officers in :—

    (a) Study of ground.
    (b) Making up their minds quickly.
    (c) Issuing orders quickly and concisely.
    (d) Topography and map reading.

(a) Study of Ground.

> An operation with troops is usually carried through to its conclusion with only a few checks. Time on these occasions is not always possible for a study of the tactical possibilities of any particular bit of ground. Moreover, a Commander's time is partly taken up in maintaining control of his troops. This is different on a Regimental Exercise, as ample time can be allowed for the study of ground and a full discussion take place. This is a great asset from an instructional point of view.

(b) Making up their Minds Quickly.

> Instruction in this respect can be progressive, as the time limit allowed for any particular problem can gradually be decreased as Officers and non-commissioned officers taking part in the exercise get more experienced.

(c) **Issue of Orders.**
> When operating with troops situations take time to develop. During an exercise TIME can be advanced as required, and ample opportunities created for the writing of orders and messages.

(d) **Topography.**
> A Regimental Exercise is primarily intended for the study of ground, and a map should only be used as a means of finding out the names of different tactical features and identifying them. This in itself forms the very best practice in map reading.

4. **Regimental Exercises** may be considered under three headings, namely, those intended for :—
   i. Senior Officers.
   ii. All Officers and senior non-commissioned officers.
   iii. Junior Officers and non-commissioned officers.

A suitable type of exercise for senior Officers is one dealing with reconnaissance, for this type of exercise is often beyond the scope of Junior Officers. On the results of these reconnaissances may be based Regimental Exercises of the second type.

In the second type of exercise problems should be set requiring orders to be dictated, messages written, formation of troops discussed, the actual method in which troops move across any particular bit of country considered, practice in fire direction and fire control, handling of Lewis guns, action and position of scouts, and a hundred and one other things connected with the movement of troops against an enemy.

The third type of exercise, namely, one intended for Junior Officers and non-commissioned officers, requires very little preparation. It should be confined chiefly to the action and movements of platoons and sections under varying conditions, and is such that any Officer of experience can improvise the problems to be set while the class is actually out on the ground.

The following notes on the preparation of schemes apply therefore to the first two types of Regimental Exercise which require previous preparation if full instructional value is to be obtained.

5. When drawing up a scheme, first consider the type of operation you wish to demonstrate, e.g., Advanced Guards, Defence of a Locality, Village or Wood Fighting, Consolidation of a Captured Position, or Crater Fighting.

Then select the best available bit of country for the purpose. Ground with numerous tactical features, such as hills, woods, houses, etc., is generally best, as situations can more frequently be changed, but as fighting may have to be carried out over any type of ground, it is therefore always possible to carry out a Regimental Exercise wherever you may be.

6. Formerly it was the practice to start schemes with a GENERAL *and* SPECIAL IDEA.

This is a needless complication as regards a Regimental Exercise, and it is far simpler to issue a short **narrative** containing everything that you consider necessary for the Officers taking part in the exercise to know.

Should the scheme be intended for Senior Officers, it is advisable to consider the force you are dealing with as forming part of a larger force, e.g., in an exercise dealing with the reconnaissance of a position consider your force as the Battalion forming the Advanced Guard to the Brigade. This helps to make the situations more real, for it is difficult at times to explain why a solitary Battalion should be attacking a strong position with no other troops in the neighbourhood to support it.

7. As regards the third type of exercise, namely, one intended for Junior Officers and non-commissioned officers, the following notes by Major-General D. M. Campbell, C.B., Commanding a Division in France, on the method of conducting such exercises, should be carefully studied :—

(a) "A Tactical Exercise may be carried out in anything from 10 minutes to 2 hours. It should seldom last longer than 2 hours.
(b) "The following is an example of a Company Tactical Exercise, class consisting of "A," "B," "C," "D," etc.

EXAMPLE :—

A Company Tactical Exercise.

PROBLEM SET.

"A" asked for solution. "A" gives "B" (who represents Platoon Commander) his *actual orders*. "B" decides to cover his advance with, say, a section. "B" must give "C" (representing Section Commander) his *actual orders*. "C" decides to cover his advance with two scouts. "C" gives "D" and "E" (representing Scouts) their *actual orders*.

Class now proceeds to scout's first objective and discuss manner in which scouts would approach—position and action of remainder of section—action of scouts on reaching objective, etc.

By working on the above lines the most systematic grounding can be given without employing a single platoon.

Whether an order is clear or not must frequently be tested by asking the recipient to explain what he thinks he is expected to do.

In giving orders at Tactical Exercises great care must be taken that the Commander always gives—

(i.) Information about the enemy,
(ii.) Information about own troops.
(iii.) His intention,

before detailing his orders. The above information is often omitted at Tactical Exercises, and a very bad and dangerous habit is acquired.

To get full benefit from a Tactical Exercise members must be encouraged to ask questions. Everyone must realise that the Instructor is out to help and not to find fault.

The above method of conducting Tactical Exercises has never failed to give the best results.

8. The following points should be carefully attended to when carrying out any Tactical Exercise :—

(a) **Preliminary Instruction.**

Before any Tactical or Regimental Exercise is undertaken the Directing Officer must ensure that those taking part in it have a very perfect idea of the strength, composition, method of movement and manœuvre of the unit they are to deal with. For instance :—

If the exercise is of an elementary nature, such as the rôle of a company in the Advanced Guard, the Officers and non-commissioned officers should be taken out and shown on the ground first a company at full strength in column of route, then moving off as an Advanced Guard, then disposed and halted on the ground as an Advanced Guard, and in such a way that every Officer and non-commissioned officer can, after seeing the demonstration, never forget the rôle and disposition of every Officer, non-commissioned officer and man in that Advanced Guard.

(b) **Size of Party.**

The numbers under one instructor should, if possible, not exceed fifteen. Even this number is too large if written solutions have to be handed in. In such cases it helps the instructor if the party is sub-divided up into groups, each group only submitting one solution.

The advantages of the group system are that it enables the instructor to return Officers taking part in the exercise their corrected solutions within a short space of time, while the situation is still fresh in their minds.

It also helps to promote discussion, for each problem must be fully discussed by the group before their solution is submitted to the instructor.

On the other hand, if problems requiring rapid appreciations and decisions are being set, then the group system should not be adopted, whatever the numbers of the party.

When the group system is adopted, each particular member of the group should be nominated to act in some particular capacity, e.g., one member as Battalion Commander, the remainder Company Commanders.

Each member should, in turn, be appointed to act as leader and spokesman for the group.

(c) **Formation of Party.**

The party must be assembled so that everyone can hear what is said. If working in groups, then the groups should be kept together.

Any remarks made by the instructor should be addressed to the whole party, and not to any particular individual or group.

Likewise any question raised must be addressed to the whole party, and not to the instructor only. It is the duty of the instructor to see that only one member of the party is allowed to speak at a time.

If these rules are not strictly enforced the exercise soon becomes a conversation between the instructor and an odd member or two of the party, and the instructional value of the exercise soon vanishes.

(d) **Dictating Orders.**

When an Officer is called upon to dictate orders to meet a certain situation, certain members of the party should be nominated to act as the subordinate commanders of that Officer.

The Officer should then be made to dictate his orders direct to these Officers.

It is only by acting thus that Officers can obtain practice in giving their orders quickly, clearly, and with a decided tone of voice.

The practice of addressing remarks to the instructor and saying, "I should do this or that," affords no training to Officers in the giving out of orders, and should, consequently, never be allowed.

(e) **Writing of Appreciation (with Special Reference to Tactical Problems).**

1. The object of an appreciation is to assist the writer of that appreciation in arriving at a decision as to the best course to adopt in certain given circumstances.

Any Officer, when he is faced with a tactical situation during operations, has to make up his mind as to a certain line of action he intends to adopt. In arriving at this decision, he considers certain factors, no matter how simple that problem may be. He, in fact, carries out a mental "appreciation of the situation."

2. The same process of reasoning is required when Officers are asked to write an appreciation dealing with a Tactical Problem.

What is required is a short statement of the facts dealing with the situation, and as a result of those facts a simple plan of action giving **sufficient details for an operation order to be drawn up** on the information given.

The important point to remember is that **rapidity is all important,** therefore facts which are obvious and do not deal directly with the case need not be stated.

3. In drawing up these appreciations the following points should be considered :—

- (a) The object you have to carry out.
- (b) Any **special** consideration either as regards the enemy or your own troops which may affect the attainment of your objective.
- (c) The various tactical features from the map, and how they may affect the particular operation.
- (d) After consideration of these points, note down anything you consider should be brought to the notice of the Officer who detailed you to carry out the particular task, such as points dealing with your instructions which you consider impossible to carry out, giving your reasons.
- (e) What you consider the enemy would like to do; and, finally,
- (f) A simple plan of action based on the above considerations.

4. **Before writing orders** for any tactical problem, an Officer should always "appreciate the situation," if not in writing, at least mentally.

To do this with any success he should accustom himself to follow some logical sequence, just as an Officer does when he writes out an Operation Order.

It is therefore suggested that the sequence stated in para. 4 will help Officers in this respect, viz. :—

    (a) Object.

    (b) Troops.

    (c) Tactical features.

    (d) Points for notice of Officer who issued instructions.

    (e) Enemy action.

    (f) Plan.

Seven Tactical Exercises, by Lieutenant-Colonel H. W. M. Watson, D.S.O., K.R.R.C. These are samples of the type of simple exercises that may be given to Officers and N.C.Os. in a Battalion. They indicate the lines on which a series of small military problems may be based :—

Outdoor Exercise "A."

The 180th Brigade, which consists of the 7th and 8th Battalions Royal Scots, the 7th and 8th Battalions A. and S. Highlanders, and the 180th Machine Gun Company, is marching from WOKING to FLEET *via* FARNBOROUGH, EELMOOR HILL.

The enemy is reported to be near BASINGSTOKE.

A. What proportion of the Brigade would you order for the Advanced Guard?

B. The head of the advanced guard has reached WHARF BRIDGE.

What is :—

    (1) The strength and formation of van guard, its position as regards main guard, and how would it move?

(2) Formation of main guard and position as regards main body?

(3) Your own position?

(4) Method of communication between van guard and main guard, and main guard and main body?

Outdoor Exercise "B."

You are commanding "A" Company, finding the van guard of the advanced guard, formation as follows:—

> Two platoons, one on each side of the road, moving parallel to it and 300^x to 400^x from it.
>
> Yourself and remaining 2 platoons on the road 400^x behind.

Officer Commanding No. 2 Platoon on left of road signals:—

> "My scouts fired on from COPSE East of BOTTOM in CLAYCART BOTTOM. No movement visible."

What action do you take?

What action does Officer Commanding No. 2 Platoon take?

As Section Commander in No. 2 Platoon, you are advancing with your platoon, and see five or six of the enemy running from the Southern Copse towards the road.

What orders would you give?

Outdoor Exercise "C."

Your Brigade has bivouacked in the OFFICERS' CLUB one hour before dark. Your battalion is ordered to hold the outpost line from Bridge at C in WATTS COMMON to the track at first O in CLAYCART BOTTOM inclusive.

How would you divide this frontage, and where would the reserve be, supposing you have decided to have one?

You are commanding "A" Company, and are allotted a line from the Bridge to the FLEET—ALDERSHOT ROAD inclusive.

What number of piquets do you think necessary?

What precautions would you take while examining the ground?

Where will you have your supports?

How will your company get their dinners?

Outdoor Exercise "D."

You are Commanding No. 1 Platoon, finding piquet on the Bridge.

What Sentry groups will you find by night and day?

What should every man in the piquet know?

You are a Section Commander, and are sent out two hours before daylight to reconnoitre in front of the line. You take two men with you. You reach the corner of PYESTOCK WOOD and spot a sentry, and six or seven men near him sitting down.

What would you do?

Outdoor Exercise "E."

Your Brigade is ordered to attack PYESTOCK WOOD from direction of GOVERNMENT HOUSE.

The objective given to your Battalion is from east corner of the wood to the track south of first o in Wood.

Write briefly your orders for the attack.

You are commanding "A" Company on the right of the Battalion.

What verbal orders would you give to your Platoon Commanders?

You are a Section Commander in the 1st line of "A" Company, which has just been reinforced by the 2nd line.

What is your duty?

You are ordered by your Platoon Commander to open fire on the front edge of PYESTOCK WOOD.

What exact fire orders would you give?

You are a Platoon Commander in "A" Company, and you have captured the enemy's trenches on the fringe of the Wood. No other Officer is up, and you can get hold of about 50 men, your own company, "B" Company, and some few of the Battalion on your right.

What do you do?

Outdoor Exercise "F."

Your Brigade is marching from WOKING to FLEET.

You are in command of the leading Battalion of the main body.

When you reach the point 266, you receive orders to be responsible for the right flank of the Brigade till it reaches PONDTAIL BRIDGE.

What would your flank guard consist of, and how would it move?

Outdoor Exercise "G."

Enemy are reported in neighbourhood of FLEET.

You as Battalion Commander have been ordered to make preparations to deny the enemy the high ground of FARNBOROUGH COMMON from an attack from the west (shown on ground).

Draw rough sketch showing disposition of your companies.

You are commanding "A" Company, and have been shown by the Commanding Officer what frontage you are responsible for.

What defensive works would you make? All necessary picks and shovels available.

You are commanding No. 1 Platoon, strength 32.

How exactly would you start your men working? And what is a reasonable task in this soil in four hours?

You are a Section Commander, and are given a working party of systematic wiring.

Where will you put your wire?

How do you organise your party for systematic wiring, and what system of working will you have?

CHAPTER XII.

MISCELLANEOUS EXERCISES.

By BRIGADIER-GENERAL R. J. KENTISH, D.S.O.

The following pages contain a series of exercises that were set from time to time, and are dealt with under three headings:—

Part I.—An exercise in the issue and writing of Orders for a Peace March, where the comfort of the troops is the predominating factor.

Part II.—Exercise to illustrate situations such as might confront a Commanding Officer from the time he marches his Battalion from the Battle Area and takes over a line of trenches in a new sector.

Part III.—An exercise dealing with the various problems a Commanding Officer must consider in anticipation of his Battalion being relieved in the trenches.

PART I.

An Exercise in the Giving and Writing of Orders for the March of a Battalion, Company, Platoon, Etc., under Peace Conditions, when Tactical Conditions do not require Detachments, such as Advanced Guards, Flank Guards, Etc.

Reference: ½-in. Country round Aldershot Map.

A Battalion of Infantry is marching from LONDON to BASINGSTOKE, and reaches ALDERSHOT at 10 p.m. on the 16th inst. Here it billets, and is distributed as follows :—

Headquarter and Headquarter Company in QUEEN'S HOTEL, FARNBOROUGH.

" A " Company in OUDENARDE BARRACKS.

" B " Company in HEADQUARTERS GYMNASIUM.

Two Platoons, " C " Company, in PRINCE CONSORT'S LIBRARY.

Two Platoons, " C " and " D " Company, in OFFICERS' CLUB.

The Transport in SOUTH CAVALRY BARRACKS.

Its average daily march has been 12 miles.

An hour before reaching Aldershot the Commanding Officer receives orders that his Battalion will march to FARNHAM on the 17th, and billet there for the night of the 17—18th. He is also told that he can march at his own time.

PROBLEM " A."

You are Colonel X., commanding the Battalion Write down the orders, and how you would issue and transmit them to your Battalion for the march of the 17th.

PROBLEM "B."

You are Captain Y., commanding " C " Company, and you and all your Officers are billeted in the Officers' Club. Similarly as in Problem A, write down the orders you would issue to your Company on receipt of the orders you receive from the Battalion.

PROBLEM "C."

You are Captain Z., commanding " A " Company. Similarly as in Problem B, write down your orders.

Note.—(1) The orders you issue on Problems B and C are to be based on those contained in your own solution of Problem A.

(2) In all these Problems state how the orders would reach those for whom they are intended, viz., Problem A, the Captains of the Companies and others concerned, and Problem B, the Platoon Commanders, non-commissioned officers and men of the Platoons.

SOLUTION TO PROBLEM "A."

1. On receipt of my orders, I send for Company Officers and the Transport Officers to ride to the head of the Column, and give them the following verbal instructions:—

   (a) We only have a short march to-morrow (viz., $4\frac{1}{2}$ miles) to FARNHAM. The Battalion will not move before 10.30 a.m.

   (b) Detailed orders will reach you at 9 a.m. to-morrow. You can all sleep until then. Tell the men they have marched splendidly. Sick parade will be at the Prince Consort's Library at 9.30 a.m.

2. At 11 p.m. after a meal I order my Adjutant to write the orders for the march to-morrow. These orders would be:—

Copy No. 5.

2nd Somersetshire Light Infantry Operation Order No. 1.

17th November, 1916.

Ref.: ½-in. Country round Aldershot Map.

INTENTION.   1. The Battalion will march to FARNHAM to-day and billet there for the night.

DETAIL.   2. (a) Order of March :—Hdqrs., A, B, C, D Companies, and Transport.

           Starting Point :—Cross roads by Church, just south of the "T" in ALDERSHOT.

           Time :—11 0 a m.

       (b) Baggage will be stacked ready for loading by 10.30 a.m.

       (c) Sick Parade will be at the Prince Consort's Library at 9.30 a.m.

       (d) Billeting parties will rendezvous at the Prince Consort's Library at 9.0 a.m.

REPORTS.   3. To head of column.

           K. JACKSON, Captain and Adjutant,
                           2nd Somersetshire Light Infantry.

Issued at 8 a.m. by Orderly.

Copy No. 1, Filed.
    ,,   ,,   2, A Company.
    ,,   ,,   3, B Company.
    ,,   ,,   4, C Company.
    ,,   ,,   5, D Company.
    ,,   ,,   6, Transport.
    ,,   ,,   7, Quartermaster.
    ,,   ,,   8, Medical Officer.
    ,,   ,,   9, War Diary.

SOLUTION TO PROBLEM "B."

1. On receipt of the Commanding Officer's verbal instructions I should, after halting the Company opposite the Officers' Club, issue the following orders to my Platoon Commanders, and in the hearing of my Company Sergeant-Major and Company Quartermaster-Sergeant :—

"We only have four miles to march to-morrow, and the Battalion will not move before 10.30 a.m. Give the men a good long night's rest. Tell them that the Commanding Officer is very pleased indeed with their marching, and that so am I. The Medical Officer will see any sick at the Prince Consort's Library at 9.30 a.m. to-morrow."

Note.—The Company Officer will visit the billets of his Company before he turns in for the night, and will satisfy himself that all is correct.

2. On receipt of the march orders the following morning at about 9.30 a.m. I should send for my Company Sergeant-Major, and issue the following verbal orders :—

"The Battalion is passing the cross roads by the Church just South of the Prince Consort's Library at 11 a.m. to-day in the following order :—H.Q., "A," "B," "C," "D." The Company will parade in front of Prince Consort's Library at 10.50 a.m. Baggage must be stacked ready for loading by 10.30 a.m.

3. In the first case the orders will reach the non-commissioned officers and men from the lips of the Platoon Commander before dismissing, and in the latter case from the Company Sergeant-Major to the Platoon Sergeants, who would inform both their Platoon Commanders and their men of the orders,

SOLUTION TO PROBLEM "C."

1. *Vide* para. 1 of Solution to Problem B above.

2. On receipt of the march orders, I should send for my Company Sergeant-Major and give him the following verbal orders :—

" The Battalion is marching to FARNHAM to-day.

" Starting Point : Cross roads by Church, just south of Prince Consort's Library.

" Order of March, H.Q., ' A,' ' B,' ' C,' ' D.'

" The Battalion will pass the Starting Point at 11 a.m.

" The Company will parade ready to march off at 10.30 a.m.

" Baggage must be stacked ready for loading by 10 a.m."

3. *Vide* para. 3 of Solution of Problem " B " above.

PART II.

Exercises to illustrate situations such as might confront a Commanding Officer from the time he marches his Battalion from the Battle Area and takes over a Line of Trenches in a New Sector.

NARRATIVE "A."

Reference: ½-in. Country round Aldershot Map.

You are Temporary Lieut.-Colonel BROWN, Commanding the 10th Service Battalion Royal Fusiliers, and your Battalion, after severe losses in a recent engagement, has, with the remainder of the Third Division, been withdrawn. On the 3rd December, 1916, your Battalion commenced its march North, to take over a sector of the Line. You have no Regular Officer with you, but your Second-in-Command, your Adjutant, and two of your Company Commanders have been with the Battalion since the date it was raised in August, 1914. Previous to commencing the march you have had two days' rest, during which period 10 Officers and a Draft of 300, made up of :—

(I) 120 Royal Fusiliers,
(II) 110 Royal West Kents (Bantams), and
(III) 70 King Edward's Horse (London Yeomanry),

joined as reinforcements. Your men, though badly in need of a bath and clean underclothing, have been unable to obtain either before commencing the march. You have been told that the men will receive both before going into the line. Your Battalion is marching independently.

PROBLEM "A."

I. Write your orders for the march of your Battalion on the 3rd December from ALTON TO ODIHAM. (These places, though in reality close up to your eventual destination, are supposed to represent the first day's march from the battle area. Your Battalion is somewhat scattered in its billets.) You can march in your own time.

II. Previous to commencing your march North, which you knew was going to take several days, what general action would you take with a view to enabling your Battalion to complete the march with the minimum of falling out, straggling and discomforts to the men?

Solution (I).

Secret. Copy No. 1.

10th (Service) Battalion The Royal Fusiliers, Operation Order No. 27.

2nd December, 1916.

Ref : ½" Aldershot Map.

INTENTION. 1. The Battalion will march to-morrow to ODIHAM.

DETAIL. 2. (a) Order of march :—Hdqrs., A. B, C, and D Companies and 1st Line Transport.

Starting Point :—Road junction half-mile south of the " A " in ANSTEY.

Time :—10 a.m.

Route :—JORDAN'S FARM—BLOUNCE FARM—FOUR LANES END.

(b) Baggage will be stacked ready for loading by 9 a m.

(c) Sick Parade TOWN HALL, ALTON, at 9 a.m. to-morrow.

(d) Billeting parties, as already detailed, will report at Battalion Headquarters at 8 a.m. to-morrow.

REPORTS. 3. To head of column.

(Signed) Captain & Adjutant,
10th (Service) Battn. The Royal Fusiliers.

Issued by Cyclist Orderly at 4 p.m.

Copy No. 1 Filed.
,,   ,,   2 to A Company.
,,   ,,   3 ,, B Company.
,,   ,,   4 ,, C Company.
,,   ,,   5 ,, D Company.
,,   ,,   6 ,, Transport Officer.
,,   ,,   7 ,, Quartermaster.
,,   ,,   8 ,, War Diary.

Solution (II).

1. I should get all my Officers and non-commissioned officers together, and go very closely into each point on March Discipline with them before starting off, and I should see that they were fully conversant with the system which obtains in my Battalion.

2. I should arrange that men who are not fit to march with their Companies are collected and are marched as a separate party, either well in advance of the main body or just in rear. But see that their march is so arranged that if they start in front they are not overtaken by the main body.

3. I should speak to the whole Battalion in the following manner :—

"We are going to commence a nine days' march the day after to-morrow. The average distance which we have to march daily is about 10 miles. We shall only go through the march with credit provided all ranks are determined to do their level best to turn out well, and to march well throughout. One man falling out may at once start many others doing the same, and very quickly the Battalion will consist of four weak Companies and many stragglers. Such a spectacle is not creditable to anyone. I have made arrangements that your comfort will be attended to throughout the march, and I hope you will do your level best to get to the end of it with as few men falling out as possible."

4. I should speak to my Second-in-Command, or some reliable Officer (who should be able to speak French), and arrange with him to do the billeting of the Battalion during the march. I would talk to him as follows :—

"I wish you to make every endeavour to see that the men have good places for their mid-day halts (when I decide to have mid-day halts). If possible, select places which are near towns or villages where those men who have money can obtain beer on payment, or buy other necessities.

" As regards the actual billets, I want you on every occasion, if possible, to select a building big enough for all the Officers to mess together; also a similar room for the Sergeants of the Battalion. If you hear of any band or concert troupe being in the vicinity, or in the town itself where we may be billeted, try and arrange for their services. Don't take ' NO ' for an answer from the Mayor of any town or village, or the owner of any building who might say ' NO ' to your request that a certain building should be placed at your disposal. Get the men billeted as comfortably as possible wherever they are."

5. I arrange for an ambulance to accompany the Battalion on the march.

6. I see that the Quartermaster does everything possible in refitting men, and insist upon uniformity of dress. Uniformity of dress is most important.

The Quartermaster should also obtain ample supplies of hot water so that men can get their feet washed and put in proper order for a march. He should obtain a supply of dubbin.

7. I make arrangements to see that my men get beer when they get in. If the estaminets are closed, I arrange for one to be kept open; and if there is any difficulty, I issue instructions for men to be marched under supervision to get their beer. I am prepared to accept responsibility for my action, but I insist upon seeing that my men's wants are attended to.

NARRATIVE (Continued) "B."

On the afternoon of 9th instant, at about 3 p.m., you reach FLEET, where you are to billet for the night of 9/10th. FLEET is a good-sized town, where the Headquarters of the outgoing Division, with its baths, cinema and canteen are established. Orders from the Brigade reach you here to the effect that your Battalion will remain in FLEET until the evening of 11/12th.

The Brigade Order also states that a motor-bus to hold up to 30 will be at your Headquarters at 8.30 a.m. on 10th instant, to convey you and those you tell off to accompany you to FRIMLEY GREEN, where you will find the Headquarters of the 100th Infantry Brigade and guides to take you to the Headquarters of the Battalion you are going to relieve. Your Specialists are to go into the line on the evening of the 10th.

PROBLEM " B."

(I) Write down the Officers, non-commissioned officers and men (if any) you would select to accompany you.

(II) Write down your Battalion Orders for the 10th. N.B.: When writing your Orders bear in mind the fact that your Battalion will not be required to move before 4 p.m. on the 11th instant.

Solution (I).

The following are selected to proceed by motor-bus to reconnoitre the line :—

1.	Commanding Officer	1
2.	Adjutant	1
3.	Transport Officer	1
4.	Orderlies	3
5.	Four Company Commanders	4
6.	A N.C.O. from each Company (to be a Sergeant)	4
7.	Signal Officer and 1 N.C.O.	2
8.	Sniping ⎫ Scouting ⎬ Officer and 1 N.C.O. ... Intelligence ⎭	2
9.	Lewis Gun Officer ...	1
	Total ...	19

Solution (II), see page 227.

NARRATIVE (Continued) " C."

You, with your party, arrive in due course at Brigade Headquarters, at FRIMLEY GREEN, at 9.30 a.m., where you are met by the Brigade Major, who tells you that the guides are ready, and that you can start at once.

PROBLEM " C."

What action do you then take?

Solution.

1. I ask to see the Brigadier and get him to show me on the map the trenches I am about to take over. I get him to point out the various communication trenches, and ask him which are the communication trenches most generally in use. I also ask the Brigadier tactfully what sort of a fellow the Commanding Officer is whom I am about to relieve.

2. Whilst I am engaged with the Brigadier my Adjutant interviews the Brigade Major and gleans all the information he can from him regarding the line.

3. My Transport Officer gets into touch with the Staff Captain and makes enquiries regarding the Q side of the Brigade Area, e.g., baths, canteen, beer, transport accommodation, etc. He also finds out what ground is available for training purposes, what areas are usually shelled, and the time this shelling normally takes place.

4. Before leaving Brigade Headquarters I make absolutely certain that the guides placed at my disposal really know the way to Battalion Headquarters, and that the Battalion we are relieving has been notified and is expecting us.

5. Ask the Brigadier what time you are likely to get back, and tell your Transport Officer to inform the Battalion accordingly when he returns.

6. Having obtained all the information we require at Brigade Headquarters, we proceed on our way in

small parties (formation usually recommended by Brigade). It is generally advisable for the Commanding Officer to lead the way with the first party. Arrange for these parties to meet at the Battalion Headquarters.

NARRATIVE (Continued) " D."

After hearing what the Brigadier has to tell you, you start off for the line in the manner approved, and at 11 a.m. you arrive at Battalion Headquarters, which you find established in a big, deep and perfectly safe dug-out, capable of holding from 10 to 12 persons. The Specialists have already gone off with their opposite numbers, according to your instructions given to them before leaving Brigade Headquarters, and you have with you at Battalion Headquarters your Adjutant, your Signalling Officer, your Company Officers, and 4 Company non-commissioned officers—a party of about 18 altogether. Colonel WHITE, Commanding the Battalion you are to relieve, has the guides all ready for you and wishes you to start off at once. He himself has only been in the line two days, and knows very little about it, and so he does not propose to accompany you. He has, however, detailed his Intelligence Officer to accompany you.

PROBLEM " D."

(a) What would you think of the situation?
(b) What action would you take?
(c) What orders or directions would you give to your Officers?

Solution.

1. I do not start off round the trenches at once, but I insist on going into the dug-out with my four Company Commanders, and when all are seated with their maps out, I ask Colonel WHITE, from whom I am

taking over, to give us briefly a general idea of the line, its weak and strong points, etc.

2. I ask which is the most difficult sub-sector, the **number of rifles** holding the front line, and I enquire particularly as to what the strength of the Companies in the line actually is. I then tell off my Companies on this information.

3. I then send my Officers off with instructions to rendezvous at Battalion Headquarters by a certain time (the time will depend on what Colonel WHITE tells me).

4. I then arrange a definite plan of action with Colonel WHITE. I get him to show me his WORK Scheme before moving off, so that I may notice what is being done in that way while I am going round. I ask if it is possible to visit an O.P., from which I could get a general view of his sector. We then start off together, leaving my Adjutant behind to talk matters over with his opposite number.

5. The Adjutant makes it his duty to find out all details regarding the office, defence scheme, method of carrying up rations, water, etc., position of dumps, tram lines, etc.

NARRATIVE (Continued) "E."

You have now cleared up the situation and given your orders, etc., to your Officers, and you start off at 11.30 a.m., with Lieut.-Colonel WHITE, to obtain the information referred to in Solution "D" above.

PROBLEM "E."

On your way down the communication trench, which, from Battalion Headquarters to the front line, is about 800 yards, what would you expect a Commanding Officer who knew his line to point out to you?

Solution.

I expect Colonel WHITE to stop at two or three points on the way up the communication trench, and point out to me the tactical points of importance from the front to the rear of the line, and also on that particular flank.

NARRATIVE (Continued) " F."

Lieutenant-Colonel WHITE has stopped at three or four points on the way up the communication trench, and from these points he has pointed out to you the tactical features and other points of importance referred to in Solution " E " above.

PROBLEM " F."

Are you satisfied with all the information contained in this Solution, or would you desire information on other points? If so, state what these points are?

Solution.

I pay particular attention to the state of defence of the left flank communication trench along which we are proceeding, viz. : whether it is fire-stepped; whether it is wired on one or both sides; and whether it is well traversed, etc. I ask who are the neighbouring troops on the flank. I also pay particular attention to the state of cleanliness of the trench, and if it is dirty I bring it to the notice of Colonel WHITE.

NARRATIVE (Continued) " G."

You arrive in the front line, and on the extreme left of it Lieut.-Colonel WHITE turns sharp right-handed and moves along the line. His pace is too fast for your purpose, and you are not obtaining the information you require. He, however, is considerably your senior in age and service, and is, so to speak, your host.

PROBLEM "G."

What action do you take?

Solution.

I stop Colonel WHITE and tell him that I have come up the line because I want to make sure of certain points, and that if we keep up the pace he is going I shall not effect my purpose. Perhaps you can regulate the pace by getting in front of Colonel WHITE and leading the way.

NARRATIVE (Continued) "H."

You are now proceeding along the line in a more satisfactory manner, and you have got both Colonel WHITE and his Intelligence Officer in a chatty and communicative mood.

PROBLEM "H."

What are the cardinal points that you give your attention to in making this inspection?

What information do you especially try to obtain, and from whom do you try to obtain it? (Apart from the Commanding Officer and his Intelligence Officer who have been accompanying you.)

Solution.

1. I pay particular attention to the state of the wire at all parts of the front, and if it is bad I get Colonel WHITE to agree that it is bad.
2. I note the average distance between the German trenches and our own.

I ask him for any information regarding any nasty points of the line, e.g., salients, craters, etc.

3. I pay particular attention to the sanitary state of the trenches; and if they are dirty, and there is paper, tins, etc., lying about, I make a point of asking Colonel WHITE to have those cleaned up before he hands over.

4. I make a point of talking to the Captains or Subalterns of the Companies of Colonel WHITE'S Battalion, and I glean any information I can from them.

5. Remember that during this preliminary reconnaissance you require to get a general idea of the line you are to take over. You cannot, therefore, pay attention to every detail.

Such things as the siting of Lewis Guns, position of Observation Posts, etc., all require detailed reconnaissances on future occasions.

NARRATIVE (Continued) " J."

On approaching a part of the line you find that the enemy are trench-mortaring and shelling it—not very badly, but sufficient to make the trench unhealthy. You are anxious to see that part of the line, but you don't want to get knocked out. Colonel WHITE says, "Oh! we will go on; it is ten to one against their getting us."

PROBLEM " J."

What will you do, bearing in mind again the circumstances mentioned in Narrative " G " above?

Solution.

I tell Colonel WHITE that if he likes to go on and get his head blown off by a shell he can do so; I am not going to follow his example. I therefore wait until the shelling stops and then go on. If he does not stop I try to circumvent the danger point; and go on to another part of the line.

NARRATIVE (Continued) " K."

You persuade Colonel WHITE to wait, and in time the shelling ceases. You then complete your tour to the extreme right flank, and then return by the extreme right flank communication trench, taking stock of the same points on your way back as on your way up in the morning. You arrive back at Battalion Headquarters at 2 p.m., where you find half your party is assembled.

PROBLEM " K."

What action do you take?

Solution.

1. I first of all send the non-commissioned officers back to Brigade Headquarters, and I enter Colonel WHITE'S dug-out again with my Company Commanders.

2. I find out from my Company Commanders if they have any points they wish to bring forward with reference to their walk round the trenches.

3. I then formulate my plan for taking over the line. I make sure that the two Adjutants, in consultation with the Company Commanders, have made proper arrangements regarding guides. This is most important.

4. I arrange with Colonel WHITE that he should leave one Officer (preferably the Intelligence Officer) to remain with my Headquarters for 24 hours after the relief is completed.

If this is a new sector I am taking over, I ask that one Officer per Company may be left behind.

5. I ask Colonel WHITE if he can produce by the time I come in to-morrow night a WORK PLAN of the Sector, showing the work done and work in hand as it actually is.

6. I arrange with Colonel WHITE that we shall move our Mess in to-morrow evening, and that we shall be very pleased if he and his Staff will dine with us.

7. And, lastly, if I have found the trenches dirty, I tell Colonel WHITE so, and express a hope that he will have them cleaned up before we move in.

NARRATIVE (Continued) "L."

You arrange everything to your satisfaction; you thank Colonel WHITE for his kindness, and you return to Brigade Headquarters, where you find the bus waiting for you.

PROBLEM "L."

What action do you take?

Solution.

1. On arrival at Brigade Headquarters I personally see the Brigadier, and if the arrangements have been good and worked well, I thank him.

2. If they have been bad I tell him so, but I am very careful to have my points clear in my head first.

3. In either case I inform him that the arrangements for the relief appear to be in order, and that Colonel WHITE understands the situation perfectly.

4. Whilst I am seeing the Brigadier I tell my Adjutant to see the Brigade Major or Staff Captain and to make any final arrangements.

NARRATIVE (Continued) "M."

You arrive back with your party at Battalion Headquarters about 5 p.m. Your Officers are messing by Companies, owing to the scattered position of the billets.

PROBLEM "M."

What do you do first of all? Write out your orders for the march to, and the taking over of, the trenches on the night of the 11/12th.

State what further instructions, if any, either verbally or otherwise, you would give to either the Officers, non-commissioned officers and men previous to the Battalion marching off on the 11th.

Solution.

1. I invite all my Officers in to have tea at my Headquarters.

2. I then go through, roughly, the details of the relief for to-morrow, and after asking them whether they have any points to put to me, I leave them to write my orders for the actual relief, which are as follows :—

COPY No. 1.

10TH (SERVICE) BATTALION ROYAL FUSILIERS.

OPERATION ORDER No. 28.

10/12/16.

1. The Battalion will relieve the 50th (Service) Battalion Warwickshire Regiment of the 761st Infantry Brigade in the FRITH HILL sector to-morrow night.

2. The Battalion will parade at 2.45 p.m. to-morrow on the Battalion Parade Ground, and will proceed as a Battalion as far as the cross roads at FRIMLEY GREEN.

N.B.—This place has not been selected tactically, but is taken at random, to illustrate the principle that it is necessary to split up into small parties when you get within the shelled area.

From this point Companies will move off to the rendezvous at F 25a 1.9 (cross roads) at 10 minute intervals, in the order stated below :—

- " B " Company to relieve " C " Company, Warwickshire Regiment, in trenches T16—T24.
- " C " Company to relieve " A " Company, Warwickshire Regiment, in trenches T25—T32.
- " A " Company to relieve " B " Company, Warwickshire Regiment, in trenches T33—T40.
- " D " Company to relieve " D " Company, Warwickshire Regiment, in the reserve trenches.

3. 50th Battalion Warwickshire Regiment has arranged for guides to be at the rendezvous, F 25a 1.9, as under :—

Advanced Party at 11 a.m. on 11th inst.

Battalion Headquarters and Companies at 6.30 p.m on 11th inst.

4. *Advanced Party.*—Signallers and Bombers detailed as such have proceeded to the line to-night. Non-commissioned officers for taking over trench stores will parade at Battalion Headquarters at 9 a.m. on the 11th inst., and will proceed under the Battalion Signal Officer to meet guides at F 25a 1.9, as detailed above.

5. Arrangements have been made to issue rations and trench boots to Companies at FRIMLEY GREEN.

(There is no need for a forward dump of this nature, unless the march to the trenches is likely to be a long and arduous one.)

6. Code word for reporting relief complete is " Your AK 57 received."

Issued at 8.30 p.m.

(Signed)   Capt. & Adjt.,
10th Battalion Royal Fusiliers.

NARRATIVE (Continued) " N."

You have written your orders for the taking over of the trenches, and you have seen all your Officers and non-commissioned officers together, and you have gone through all the important points in connection with the line you are taking over, and also other points of importance connected with Trench Warfare. Your men, thanks to your system, which provides a copy of your Battalion Trench Orders for every man on joining the Battalion, have been taken through each order by their Platoon Commanders during the time you and your Officers were inspecting the trenches, and with the additional words of advice you gave to them this morning you feel confident that the Battalion will acquit itself well. At any rate, you feel that you have done all that is humanly possible for any Commanding Officer to do, and so your Battalion proceeds to the trenches, you easy in mind, and your men in good heart.

You arrive at Colonel WHITE'S Headquarters at 8 p.m., and you are told by him that relief is going on well. The Specialists have already left the line, and the Right Company Commander has just reported his Company relieved all correct.

PROBLEM " N."

What action do you take on arrival?

Solution.

(i.) I report my arrival by telephone to Brigade Headquarters, irrespective of whether my Brigade has taken over from the outgoing Brigade or not, and I take this action so that in the event of any emergency both Brigadiers may know exactly where I am.

(ii.) I ask Colonel WHITE if anything of importance has occurred during the preceding 24 hours.

(iii.) I go through the Log Book with him, and also study the work map showing work in progress and work contemplated, etc., etc.

(iv.) I take over all maps of importance and all secret documents which refer to the Sector.

(v.) I ask for the Defence Scheme, and go through it with Colonel WHITE.

(vi.) By this time dinner is ready, and Colonel WHITE sits down with me and my staff to an excellent dinner.

NARRATIVE (Continued) "O."

At 10 p.m. the relief is reported completed. Colonel WHITE wishes you the best of luck, says "Goodnight," and departs. You have the following with you at your Headquarters:—Your Second-in-Command, Adjutant, Grenadier, Signalling and Intelligence Officers, and the Intelligence Officer of the outgoing unit, and the Artillery Officer in liaison.

PROBLEM "O."

What orders or instructions do you issue both for the night of the 11/12th and for the following day?

Solution.

(i.) I ascertain from the Royal Artillery Officer whether everything is in order, so far as concerns the liaison with the Batteries and Battalion Headquarters.

(ii.) I send (or do not send) my Second-in-Command up to the front line to see both Company Commanders, and to find out whether they are all right.

N.B.—I do not go round myself, because no good purpose is to be served by doing so, and it is more important for me to be present at Battalion Headquarters on the **first night,** so that should an attack take place I am in a position to control matters.

(iii.) I arrange to visit the front line at "Stand to" the following morning, and I give orders that the Company and Platoon Commanders shall meet me on the right flanks of their units at 7.0 a.m. and wait for me until I arrive. The men are not to "Stand down" until I have given the order myself.

(iv.) I give orders for my Second-in-Command to visit the support Company at the same hour, and he visits the Headquarters Units (Pioneers, Signallers, Orderlies, Grenadiers, etc.).

(v.) I arrange with Brigade Headquarters for the Officer Commanding Field Company to meet me in my Headquarters at 11.0 a.m., and for my Second-in-Command, whom I have appointed as my Field Works Officer, to be present at the same hour and place to discuss the work on the line and the system whereby it is to be carried on expeditiously and well.

(vi.) I tell my Adjutant to arrange for the Company Commanders' Conference at Battalion Headquarters at 2.0 p.m., and for the Intelligence and Grenadier and Scouting Officer to be present at the same time.

(vii.) I ascertain from my Adjutant that he has a list of returns required, and how they are to be dispatched.

I then have a whisky and soda or a cup of coffee with some rum in it, say good-night, and turn in.

NARRATIVE (Continued) "P."

According to your orders, the whole Battalion is standing to at 6 a.m., and you arrive on the extreme right of the line at 7 a.m., just as it is light. According to your orders Captain P., Commanding the Right Company, and Lieutenant G., Commanding the Right Platoon of that Company, meet you, and you commence your tour of inspection.

PROBLEM "P."

(I) State whom you take with you on this inspection.

(II) State what points you will give especial attention to on this, your first inspection of the front line.

Solution.

(a) I take both the Intelligence Officers and one of my personal Orderlies.

(b) (i.) I make this inspection primarily with the object of seeing how the line is held, so that I may alter the dispositions if I consider it necessary. For this reason I ordered the whole front line to "Stand to" until the order comes from me to "Stand down."

(ii.) I make a careful inspection of the wire on my front with a view to giving my Company Commanders a good sound system of getting to work on the wire. This work should be continued until it reaches a minimum depth of 10 yards from end to end. After that a second line of similar thickness and depth is commenced.

(iii.) I am shown by the outgoing Intelligence Officer all the tactical points in the line, e.g., forward saps, mine shafts, craters, salients, etc.

(iv.) I ask one or two men if they know where their reserve ammunition and bombs are, and other such points as position of Company Headquarters, Latrines, etc.

(v.) I take with me the Captain of the Right Company along the front of the Left Company, and then together we go to the dug-out of the Officer Commanding Left Company, and there decide on any alterations in the dispositions of the men in the whole line.

N.B.—During my visit to the line I make a special point of saying " Good morning " to the non-commissioned officers

and men, and I stop every now and then
and have a chat with them. This is
where my fund of good stories comes in.
Contrast my action with that of Colonel
BLUEFACE, who goes round the line
with a very blue face, without a word to
the men from end to end, except possibly
to speak in rough terms to some unfortunate man, in the trenches for the first
time, who does not get out of his way
quick enough.

NARRATIVE (Continued) " Q."

You finish your inspection of the front line at about 8 a.m., and you give certain verbal instructions to the two Captains in Captain A.'s dug-out. (*N.B.*—You had previously told Captain P. to accompany you to see Captain A.'s line.)

You gladly accept Captain A.'s invitation to have breakfast with him, taking care to see that your Orderly gets his breakfast too. At 10 a.m. you return to Battalion Headquarters, taking full stock of the tactical features of that part of the sector you pass through on your way back. At your Battalion Headquarters you find your Adjutant, all the remaining Officers having, according to your orders, gone to the line or elsewhere to make themselves acquainted with the situation.

PROBLEM " Q."

What do you do?

Solution.

(i.) I tell my Adjutant to have all correspondence ready for me at 12 noon, and I then wash and shave.

(ii.) At 11 a.m. I meet the Sapper Officer with my Second-in-Command, and we discuss very fully the work in hand and work contemplated, Colonel WHITE'S Intelligence Officer being present. The Sapper states his requirements, and the Adjutant has the list of parties ready for the Company Commanders' Conference at 2 p.m.

NARRATIVE (Continued) "R."

After washing and shaving, your Adjutant shows you a mass of correspondence which has just come in from the Brigade Office. One document states that " It has been decided to issue mincing machines to Battalions, for the benefit of those men whose molars cannot cope with the ration biscuit," and the Staff Captain wants the number of mincing machines required by each Battalion by 10 a.m. the following morning. Another document forwards some comments by the General Officer Commanding-in-Chief, Central District, on the unsoldierly appearance in the streets of Birmingham and other places in that district of both Officers and Privates of the British Expeditionary Force when on leave from France, and the General Officer Commanding-in-Chief particularly draws attention to the colour of the socks worn by some of the Officers when wearing trousers. The minute of the Staff Captain forwarding this to you states that the Brigadier wants you to bring these points to the notice of all concerned in your Battalion.

PROBLEM "R."

1. What action do you take with reference to both these two communications?

2. What action do you take with regard to your correspondence generally when in the trenches?

Solution.

(i.) I do not bother my Company Commanders with either. The former I answer at once by giving a round number, say 6, and the latter I mark B.C., which means Billet Conference, which I hold the day after coming out of trenches.

(ii.) My general policy with regard to correspondence is not to harass my Officers and Warrant Officers, when they are fighting the enemy, with a single piece of paper more than is absolutely necessary. I know and appreciate to the full what it means, both for myself and my Adjutant to receive a mass of paper from the Brigade, and how I should appreciate it if the Brigade retained certain matters not of immediate importance until my relief from the trenches; I therefore mark all such papers B.C., and tell my Adjutant to bring them to my notice in billets.

(iii.) With regard to other correspondence, which requires immediate action, I mark T.C. (Trench Conference), and bring it up then.

NARRATIVE (Continued) " S."

The hour is now 2 p.m.; all the Officers have returned, and you have had lunch. You particularly looked after the Sapper Officer and Colonel WHITE'S Intelligence Officer, who are your guests. Your four Company Commanders have arrived, and your Conference commences.

PROBLEM "S."

How do you conduct this Conference, and what purposes can it, if properly conducted, serve?

Solution.

(i.) I have my four Company Commanders, Second-in-Command, Adjutant, Scouting and Intelligence Officer present.

(ii.) I expect my Adjutant to have prepared a list of those points I wish to bring up; also to have the daily report ready for me to fill in.

(iii.) I first of all discuss the preceding 24 hours and fill in the report required by the Brigade from information received verbally from the Company Commanders.

(iv.) I then discuss the action proposed for the following 24 hours, e.g., "Strafing," Trench-Mortaring, Patrolling, etc.

(v.) I ask the Royal Engineer Officer who has remained for the Conference to explain, in general terms, the work in progress on the line and the number of men he requires daily (day and night) to carry it on.

(vi.) I invite my Officers to raise any questions they wish to bring forward.

(vii.) I make reference to any point I wish to, e.g.,

    (i.) The disposition of the units holding the line.

    (ii.) Matters I have noticed during my visit to the trenches.

    (iii.) General topics, such as telling the Company Commanders to tell their men how pleased I was with the expeditious manner in which the relief was carried out.

        N.B.—The advantages of such a system are obvious :—

(a) The amount of paper and correspondence saved is beyond belief.

(b) The power of the tongue over the pen is brought out in full relief.

(c) The pleasure of getting all the Company Commanders together, of having a chat with them, and of asking one or two to lunch every day.

NARRATIVE (Continued) " T."

At 3 p.m. your Conference is over, and you are satisfied that you have made a real good start with the defence of your sector generally, and that all your Officers have a very good idea what is expected of them and their Companies in certain emergencies.

PROBLEM " T."

State how you think your orders and directions given at the Conference will reach the men?

Solution.

The system of having a Commanding Officers' Conference at Battalion Headquarters is further applied to the Companies. The Company Commanders in their turn return to their Companies, and have their Platoon Commanders' and Platoon Sergeants' Conference, at which all my orders and directions are interpreted to them, with orders to pass them on to the men. If there is any point of great importance, I issue it at the Conference in the form of an order or direction in writing and emphasise it verbally; for the rest, I leave it to the Company Commanders, who have heard my wishes from my very lips.

NARRATIVE (Continued) " U."

As your Officers leave you, you say to the Adjutant—who has been trained and brought up by your predecessor as a clerk and not as a fighting Adjutant, and who consequently is hardly ever to be seen in the line—" I want you to go up now and have a look at the men, and see if there is anything you think might be done for them." And your Adjutant says, " I am afraid I cannot go up now." And you say, " Why not?" He replies, " Well, there is a lot of correspondence to be dealt with, and I may be rung up by the Brigade Major or the Staff Captain, etc., etc."

PROBLEM " U."

What do you say to this?

Solution.

You say to him, "Give me any very important papers, and tell Lieutenant K. (who is the young Officer understudying your Adjutant) to answer for you, and go round as I wish."

NARRATIVE (Continued) " V."

It is now 7.30 p.m., and the time for the rations to be arriving, etc.

PROBLEM " V."

(i.) Who are you expecting to come with the Transport?
(ii.) What do you propose to do to-night?

Solution.

(i.) The Transport Officer or the Quartermaster, and the four Company Quartermaster-Sergeants.

(ii.) (a) I see and personally thank the Officers left behind by Colonel WHITE, who have by your order reported at Battalion Headquarters on their way out of the trenches.

(b) I spend the rest of the evening in going through and mastering the details of the Defence Scheme.

> N.B.—My Second-in-Command is with the Royal Engineer Working Parties, seeing that all is in order and cheering up the men.

NARRATIVE (Continued) " W."

You have seen your Quartermaster or your Transport Officer, and your Second-in-Command has just returned from seeing the working parties at certain points on the sector. Many minor and one or two major irregularities come under his notice. These irregularities affect different Companies. The time is 11 p.m.

PROBLEM " W."

What action do you take to put a stop to these irregularities and when do you take it?

Solution.

Unless there is any matter of very great importance which requires immediate action, I tell my Second-in-Command to have the points in sequence for the Conference the next day, which will be at 12 noon in future daily.

NARRATIVE (Continued) " X."

The hour is 6 a.m. on the 13th instant, and you, in accordance with your plan, are inspecting the Support and Reserve Companies. Here again you notice more irregularities, some whilst you are with the Captain of the Companies concerned, and others after you have left him.

PROBLEM "X."

What action do you take to get these irregularities remedied and when do you take it?

Solution.

Those which come to my notice whilst I am with the Company Commanders I remedy on the spot, and the others I mark down for the Conference.

NARRATIVE (Continued) "Y."

You return to your Battalion Headquarters, wash and shave, deal with the correspondence, and prepare for the Conference which to-day and on all other days is at 12 noon. Your Adjutant, mildly protesting, is going round the line, and Lieutenant K., a young promising Officer belonging to "A" Company, is answering for him and learning the duties. At 12 noon the Conference begins, and at 1 p.m. it ends.

PROBLEM "Y."

Whom do you invite to lunch with you, and what do you suggest would be a profitable method of spending the afternoon?

Solution.

(i.) One of my Company Commanders and a Subaltern Officer from the Reserve Company.

(ii.) To visit the line at 3 p.m., approaching by a communication trench leading up to the centre of the sector, and having a good look at the tactical features again on the way. I should have tea with the Officer Commanding Support Company, and then arrive in the line just before the "Stand to." I should then turn left or right, as the case might be, and see one of the Companies at "Stand to," passing down the line slowly, and having a word with the men on my way. I should probably return to Battalion Headquarters in time for dinner at 7.30 p.m.

NARRATIVE (Continued) "Z."

You know you are to remain in the line for one week.

PROBLEM "Z."

You have already told us how you would spend the first two days, i.e., 12th and 13th. Now write down your programme for the remaining four days, i.e., 14th, 15th, 16th, and 17th, bearing in mind that you come out on the 17th.

Solution.

My general policy is, on going into a new line, to master the situation as quickly as possible; from experience I know that this can only be done by working on a system, and my system is as follows :—

(i.) First of all to get a rough idea of (a) the Enemy's trenches; (b) NO MAN'S LAND; (c) my front line; (d) the area near my front line.

(ii.) Then to take each part of the Sector separately and to study it in detail. For instance,

I devote two days to getting a rough general idea of the sector. Then I devote, say, one morning in daylight to doing one half of the front line only and noting the wire on that particular part of front, taking on my way, up and down, a different Communication Trench and noting its general state, defects, etc. Then I devote another morning to the other half. Then I take the support and Reserve lines in turn, and, having mastered these lines and the intervening ground and its tactical features, I go into further detailed inspection of such things as :—

- (a) Machine and Lewis Guns.
- (b) Bomb and Bomb Stores.
- (c) Communications.
- (d) Trench Mortars.
- (e) Ammunition question.
- (f) Artillery.
- (g) Cooking arrangements.
- (h) Water supply.
- (i) Dumps.
- (j) Intelligence work generally, including Snipers, Scouts, and Patrols.
- (k) Gas Measures.
- (l) Accommodation of garrison, etc.

And I emphasise this fact, viz., that I select as my guide the Officer concerned with each of these matters, but only when I am sure that he has grasped the situation himself.

(iii.) At each Conference I bring out all points I have noticed in my inspection of each portion of the

Sector, and I am able by these means gradually to master the line and to impress on my Officers my system of doing things, and of the necessity of Company and Platoon Commanders working exactly on the same methodical lines.

(iv.) Whilst I am doing this I am getting a very clear idea of the Defence Scheme, adding to or suggesting any necessary alteration.

When I have mastered the line, and all details connected with it, I ask the Brigadier to accompany me round, and, with a clear plan in my head, I point out to him what I consider to be the weak points in it, and I ask his advice on the same.

My programme for the following four days would therefore be:—

THIRD DAY.—In the morning the wire in front of and No. 1 Sub-sector, front line fire-trench only. In the afternoon No. 1 Sub-sector Support line.

FOURTH DAY.—In the morning the same as the THIRD DAY. In the afternoon same as for THIRD DAY.—In No. 2 Sub-sector.

FIFTH DAY.—In the morning whole of Close-support line. In the afternoon Artillery O.Ps. and Reserve line.

SIXTH DAY.—In the morning work done in the front line system. In the afternoon work done in the rear system.

N.B.—During my inspection of the various parts of the sector I ascertain the position of machine guns and trench mortar emplacements, etc., and I take careful stock of the same, and of the teams and guns occupying them.

It will be seen that at the end of the Sʊᴏᴛʟ Dᴀʏ, when **Colonel White** and his advanced party arrive, they are given a very clear idea of the situation and of the progress made in the work. **The result is that an " Entente " springs up between the two Battalions, and the duty of handing over the line is very much simplified.**

PART III.

An Exercise on the Duties of a Commanding Officer about to Come Out of the Trenches.

NARRATIVE.

You are Lieut.-Colonel X., commanding the 11th Battalion the Buffs, occupying a sector of the line. Your Battalion has recently been heavily engaged. Your Battalion marched straight from the HAPPY VALLEY and took over the line of trenches you are holding to-day on the 18th November. On the 22nd instant you receive orders that you are to be relieved on the night of the 26/27th, and that you will go back for a week to the Reserve Battalion Billets at CRECY, where you are to rest, refit, and train your Battalion. CRECY is four miles behind the line.

PROBLEM.

What action do you take on receipt of the orders referred to above, so far as concerns the Training, Resting, and Refitting of your men, and when do you take it?

NOTES TO AID YOU IN YOUR SOLUTION.

1. Your Battalion is to return to the trenches on the night of the 3/4th December.

2. With regard to the training part of the solution, you are only required to state what orders you would give for the 27th instant, i.e., the day after you come out of the trenches.

3. Your solution should take the following form :—

" I should give the following orders to the following Officers :—

(i.) My Second-in-Command.
(ii.) My Adjutant.
(iii.) My Quartermaster.
(iv.) My Transport Officer.
(v.) My Medical Officer.
(vi.) My Padre.
(vii.) My Regimental Sergeant-Major."

This Exercise was drawn up with the intention of assisting Commanding Officers to make proper and suitable arrangements for the training and comfort of their Officers, non-commissioned officers and men when they come out of the trenches, either for a short rest period of a week or less, or when they come right out of the line to train.

The point which it has been desired to emphasise is the necessity for the Commanding Officer to *prepare his plan immediately he receives definite orders* that the Battalion is coming out of the line, instead of waiting until the Battalion arrives in the rest area before taking action.

SOLUTION.

I send for my Second-in-Command, Transport Officer, Quartermaster, Padre and Adjutant on the evening of Wednesday, 22nd, when I issue certain instructions (*vide* paper " A "). These I issue personally the first time, because, in the Battalion I am commanding, there has been no proper system, and my Officers do not know my views on what can and should be done when a Battalion receives orders to go into Rest Billets. On all subsequent occasions I expect my instructions to be carried out. Therefore I have Paper " B " typed, and copies issued to all Officers for reference on future occasions.

PAPER " A " (Verbal Instructions).

The Second-in-Command.

(a) You will proceed to CRECY at 6 p.m., Friday, the 24th, to arrange for the arrival and stay of the Battalion in that town on the night of the 26/27th for a period of one week.

(b) You will see the Staff Captain of the Brigade, and arrange that two companies bathe in the morning and two Companies in the afternoon of the 27th.

(c) You will at the same time arrange that the whole Battalion is paid during the day.

(d) You will also arrange for the whole Battalion to attend a concert, given by the Divisional Concert Troupe, on one evening during the week.

(e) You will also find out whether there is any other Divisional Troupe near at hand, the Officer in charge of which would, as a change, be prepared to come over and give a concert to the Battalion, and if there is, arrange a day.

(f) You will also arrange with the Officer-in-charge of the Divisional Band to play once or twice during the week at suitable hours. (N.B.—Ask the Regimental Sergeant-Major beforehand what is the most suitable hour of the day for this performance.) At the same time arrange for the Band to stay on and play for the Officers at dinner, and see that the Band receive supper or refreshments at the end of their performance.

(g) You will find out whether there is any town or place of interest near the billets, and if beyond walking distance arrange with the Division for lorries to take parties of non-commissioned officers and men in on certain days during the week.

(h) You will also ask the Brigade what can be done with regard to giving leave to deserving Officers to such places as Paris, and to a percentage of all ranks to visit Amiens, St. Omer, etc.

(i) You will also arrange for a Battalion concert, and, if the Companies are scattered, for the Battalion Concert Troupe to visit each Company in turn.

(j) You will go into the beer question. If there is none in the estaminets, arrange to send to the nearest town for it, and have it ready for the men on arrival. Ask the Brigade, if necessary, to place lorries at your disposal for this purpose.

(k) You will find out about the Musketry conveniences, e.g., Ranges, where they are and how they can be obtained. Targets, etc. I want Ranges every afternoon.

(l) You will find out what conveniences there are for the men to buy food, cigarettes, writing material, etc. If there is a Divisional or Brigade Canteen, go to it and see that they have, or will have, plenty of everything in by the time the Battalion arrives in billets. If there is not, select a room, and in conjunction with the Padre turn it into a Regimental Canteen and stock it with everything the men require.

(m) You will be ready to give me a detailed account of the facilities in the way of ground, etc., which exist for training purposes.

(n) You will tell the Mess Sergeant from the Mess President to have a meal in a room ready for all Officers on our arrival in billets on Sunday night.

The Adjutant.

Prepare the usual programme for the Battalion resting for one week behind the line.

The Quartermaster.

(a) You will arrange with Major X., my Second-in-Command, that Officers and men are comfortably billeted. I insist on my Officers being billeted in comfort and in a manner becoming their rank and position.

(b) If it can be possibly arranged, I want one Mess Room, where all my Officers can mess together. If not all the Companies, then as many as possible.

(c) You will see that you have a sufficient store of clothing, etc., in your stores to meet requirements. The men are very badly off. If there is any difficulty, go to the Division and interview the D.A.D.O.S.

(d) You will arrange that there is plenty of fresh straw ready by Sunday morning; keep it dry, and ask the outgoing unit to clear out their old straw and put down our fresh, and tell them we will do the same for them 14 days hence.

(e) You will arrange for the men to have hot tea, OXO, and, if a wet night, RUM on arrival. If any trouble, go to the Brigade.

(f) The Companies complained of a shortage of candles in their billets last time. See that there is plenty of light, especially the first night coming into new billets.

(g) I have given detailed instruction to Major X. You will be able to assist him in many points. Work together, especially with regard to the beer question. Should it be necessary to do so, I do not mind how far you send for it so long as you get it.

(h) I am very anxious that the Battalion shall reap full benefit both from the rest, comfort and training point of view, so please do your utmost in conjunction with Major X., Lieutenant T., and the Padre to see that everything that can be done is done.

(i) I particularly wish the Sergeants of the Battalion to have a room set aside as a Canteen and Reading Room. If this is not possible for the whole of them, then arrange that each Company has its own room for Sergeants and full Corporals to mess in, etc.

(j) See that Battalion notice boards are put up on various institutes, shops, etc.

The Transport Officer.

(a) I want you to let your men know that I shall inspect them on the 29th (afternoon), and that I will give small prizes for the Competitions which I wish you to arrange and hold in conjunction with this inspection. See the Officer Commanding Train, and ask him if it will be convenient for him to attend and to assist me in the Inspection and Competition on that date. If it is not, arrange with him the date, place and hour when he can be present. I prefer the afternoon, and any day, except Tuesday, the 28th.

(b) Let me know by Friday morning, the 24th, what facilities for training there are in or near the billets, with special reference to ground both for manœuvre and parade movements, its extent and proximity; ranges, position and accommodation of; Bayonet Courses, Trenches.

The Sports Committee.

I want you to arrange a good series of games and competitions for the men whilst in billets. I suggest the following :—Football, Bayonet, Bombing and Rifle Competitions—all on the knock-out system.

The Padre.

(a) I want you to assist Major X. actively in arranging Battalion Concerts, and also Lieutenant T. in the Battalion Sports and Games Competitions; also, if there are no Divisional and Brigade Canteens, I wish you, in consultation with Major X. and Lieutenant Q., to start a Regimental Canteen, and to arrange a room for the men, where they can obtain papers to read and material for writing purposes.

(b) I wish you 'to identify yourself with the lives of my men in every way.

The Medical Officer.

(a) On arrival go very carefully into the sanitary state of the billets. Let me have your suggestions *re* improving them from your point of view.

(b) Arrange with your sanitary men for their duties to be told off daily. Pay particular attention to the water supply, and let me have a full report on the whole sanitary situation by Orderly-room hour on the day of our arrival.

(c) Report to me *re* the condition of the men after the march.

(d) Visit the men during the bathing hours, so that you can have an opportunity of seeing them stripped and questioning them and examining them regarding their condition.

(e) Let me know daily the general state of health of the Battalion, and draw my attention to any improvements you consider necessary for ensuring the welfare of the men.

The Regimental Sergeant-Major.

(a) You will proceed with the Second-in-Command to CRECY on Friday, the 24th, at 6 p.m., and assist him in any way you can. He will tell you what he wishes you to do. In addition, you will find out from the outgoing Sergeant-Major or, if he has left, from some Warrant Officer or non-commissioned officer of the Battalion we are relieving, the best place for a Canteen for the men, a Sergeants' Mess for the Sergeants, and a Drill-field for young non-commissioned officers. You will tell the Second-in-Command all you have found out, so that he can fit in with his arrangements.

(b) You will look out for a good place for the Guard-room (Headquarters) and the Provost Staff; also some central place for parade, where working parties, etc., can assemble. Look out for a billet for Orderlies near the Orderly-room, and arrange with the Second-in-Command for a place for kits, etc., to be stacked when off-loaded. Meet the Adjutant on arrival, and have all details ready to tell him regarding the village, the duties to be found, and the position of Signallers, Orderlies, etc.

PAPER "B" (Typed Instructions).

The detailed arrangements mentioned in the Table below will be made by those Officers referred to in Column 2, as soon as orders are received that the Battalion is to come out of the line and will proceed to billets.

Nature of Arrangement.	By whom made	Remarks and Points to be attended to.
(1) **BATHS** — Always 1st day—	2nd in Command or Qr.-Mr.	(a) Accommodation per hour. (b) Plenty of clean things in stock, for which apply to Staff Captain or D.A.A. & Q.M.G.
(2) **PAY** — Always 1st day—	2nd in Command. T.O.	Amounts from Company's C.Q.M.S. N.B.—Fd. Cashier only pays money certain days.
(3) **PROGRAMME OF TRAINING**—	Adjutant.	See programme of training for one week in billets.
(4) **CONCERTS**— (a) Divisional Troupe. (b) Divisional Band. (c) Battalion Band. (d) Any other Divisional Troupe.	2nd in Command. Padre. T.O.	(a) Apply to Officer i/c Divisional Band to play at Officers' Mess. When billets scattered. (b) Battalion Band evenly distributed.
(5) **PLACES OF INTEREST**— to be visited by Officers, N.C.Os. and men.	2nd in Command, or T.O.	Lorries from Staff-Capt. for D.A.Q.M.G.
(6) **LEAVE**— Officers, N.C.Os. and Men to Paris, Amiens, St. Omer, etc.	2nd in Command.	Lorries.
(7) **BEER**—	2nd in Command, T.O., or Qr.-Mr.	Estaminets. Limber or lorry to fetch.

Nature of Arrangement.	By whom made.	Remarks and Points to be attended to.
(8) **CANTEEN — RECREATION ROOM — N.C.O.'s ROOM —**	2nd in Command. Padre. Qr.-Mr. R. Sergt.-Major.	(a) Divisional Canteen. (b) Brigade Canteen. Plenty of stock, food, cigarettes, writing materials; suppers, potato chips. N.C.Os'. Mess—If possible, special estaminet for N.C.Os.
(9) **OFFICERS' COMFORT —**	2nd in Command. Qr.-Mr. Padre.	(a) A meal on arrival. (b) A Mess as a Battalion if possible, or, failing this, 2 or 3 Companies together. (c) Good billets. (d) Beds for all, and Pioneers to help.
(10) **TRAINING FACILITIES —**	2nd in Command. T.O. R.S.M. to help.	(a) Ground for drill and manœuvre. (b) Bombing trenches. (c) Ranges, targets, etc. (d) Bayonet Course. (e) Map of area from Bde.
(11) **CLOTHING AND BOOTS —**	Quarter-Master.	(a) Have a good stock ready, and get rough estimate from Companies coming out. (b) Visit your friend D.A.D.O.S. (c) Surplus always with bootmakers.
(12) **BILLETS — CANDLES AND STRAW —**	Quarter-Master.	Arrange straw with outgoing Bde. Pioneers mark and improve billets. Material from R.E. Drying room.
(13) **RUM — OXO — TEA —** On arrival out of trenches.	2nd in Command. Qr.-Mr.	(a) Make sure of the Rum. The men appreciate this more than anything else. (b) Regimental funds can help here.
(14) **INSPECTION OF TRANSPORT & 1st LINE DETAILS —**	Your instructions to the T.O.	(a) Will be carried out 1st afternoon, and will take the form of Competition with prizes, etc.

Nature of Arrangements.	By whom made.	Remarks and Points to be attended to.
		(b) Ask O.C. Train to judge himself, or detail an Officer to do so from the Train.
		(c) Long rest ; organise horse and transport show.
(15) **GAMES — COMPETITIONS —** During Rest.	Sports Committee. 2nd in Command.	(a) Six-a-side Football. (b) Bombing Competition. (c) Rifle Competition. N.B.—All on the "knock-out" system.
(16) **SANITATION —**	M.O.	(a) Look into state of Billets, Incinerators, Latrines, Refuse Pits and Men's Rest. (b) Inspection of condition at Baths. (c) Health in Tenements. (d) Private Baths. (e) Barber's Shop. (f) Chiropody.
(17) **GUARD ROOM — ASSEMBLY GROUND** working parties. **BILLETS FOR H.Q.** details. **DUTIES** in Village.	R.S.M.	The R.S.M. generally helps 2nd in Command.

CHAPTER XIII.

FIELD ENGINEERING.

I.—The Rôle of the Commanding Officer in His Relations with the Royal Engineers and the Pioneers.
II.—Notes on Consolidation.
III.—Notes on Working Parties.
IV.—Notes on Compass Work.

(*For Wiring, see S.S. 177.*)

Part I, by Brigadier-General R. J. Kentish, D.S.O.
Parts II, III, and IV by Lieut.-Colonel H. C. McNeile, M.C., R.E.

PART I.

INTRODUCTION.

It is a libel on the British soldier to state, as many so often do, that he cannot work as the German soldier can. The British soldier can work just as well and better even than the German, if and when those over him know the first principles of defence and of work organisation, and knowing and understanding those principles set him to work on sound, practical, and common-sense lines. What those principles are, or at any rate what some of them are, I propose to discuss here with you to-night, and I hope and trust that my address to you, and the discussion that will follow it, will be of help to you all when you return to your regiments.

Let me speak to you first on what is perhaps the first of the principles, viz., The correct attitude of the Commanding Officer towards the officers of the Royal Engineers and of the Pioneer Battalion in his Division, and then we can discuss the bearing and rôle of the latter towards the officers of the Infantry later.

THE GENERAL ATTITUDE OF THE COMMANDING OFFICER.

Co-operation between the officers of the different arms of the Service can only be secured provided the Commanding Officers of those arms take an active part themselves in securing it. What that active part between the two arms in question should be I propose to suggest to you now. Every one of you must first of all get to know the officers of the Royal Engineers and Pioneers almost as well as you know your own officers, and you must let them see that you are all out to help them in their work at all times, and that you look to them for, and expect from them, their help and co-operation in return. In some Divisions the C.R.E. is known to every Commanding Officer, and to a great many other officers as well. This, however, depends a great deal on the personality and type of officer filling that position, and concerning this particular point I shall have more to say to you later. Here I merely state that every Commanding Officer should systematically get to know every single officer of the Divisional Staff well, and if he does he is bound to make the close acquaintanceship of the C.R.E., and so gain the first part of his objective. The simplest and easiest way to commence the task is by inviting that officer and his Adjutant to dinner and getting as many of your officers as possible to dine or come in after dinner, and then to introduce them to your guests. If you do this you will have made a good start, and if you continue to keep up his acquaintance by a periodical invitation of this kind, and he in his turn does his duty in this respect and invites you and your Adjutant and your Second-in-Command from time to time to have a meal with him, there is no doubt whatever that a close entente will spring up that will make itself felt right throughout the Battalion and with the best possible results. To co-operate without personal knowledge of those with whom you are co-operating is at all times a difficult undertaking; whereas to co-operate knowing them is comparatively a simple matter.

And so, if you will apply the same methods to the officers of the Field Companies and of your Pioneer Battalion, you will soon ensure a close and intimate knowledge of them, and if, in addition, you give your officers very clear direction as to their duty in this respect, then you have secured the whole of your objective, and the results of such action on your part will be very manifest in all the operations in which you and your Battalion and the Royal Engineers and the Pioneers may be subsequently engaged. I know from personal experience how true this is, and I therefore very strongly advise you, first of all, to act on the lines indicated, and to get to know—really get to know—the Royal Engineer and Pioneer Officers, and to see that all your officers do likewise.

OPERATIONS.

I now propose to show you how, after having made a real good start on the lines indicated, you can follow up your initial success by further well-thought-out and concerted action when actively engaged in combined operations with the Royal Engineers and Pioneers.

Operations may be either of a stationary or of a moving nature, viz., trench warfare or open warfare. I first propose to discuss the former, as this has become, owing to the force of circumstances, a form of warfare which consumes our time and energy for the greater part of the year in France.

(A) TRENCH WARFARE.

(i) The System To-day.

I do not propose to enter here into discussion regarding the system of defence prevailing in the British Armies in the Field in France. I know that to all of us, who have commanded everything, from a Company up to a Brigade, and who therefore know the situation very intimately from our own point of view, the situation which obtains is an enigma to many of us. But, then, there may be some very good and clear reasons for not establishing the system we all of us so strongly advocate, e.g., the permanent allocation of the different sectors of the line to permanent Sector Officers, having under them a number of equally permanent officers, each one of whom has a perfect and intimate knowledge of the whole of the sector apportioned to him, and each of whom is charged with the transmitting of that knowledge to the Regiments, Field Companies, and Pioneers of the incoming and relieving Division the moment the Division arrives in the line. I have no time here to discuss the advantages and disadvantages of the two systems; all we are concerned with here is the system we have in front of us, and which we have to support, and I propose to see how we can best overcome the many disadvantages it most certainly has.

(ii) The Disposition of the Battalion in its Sector.

First and foremost we come to the system by means of which the Commanding Officer decides to carry on the defence of his sector and how he will dispose his Battalion in the line and apportion to each company its own particular rôle and piece of the line to look after. Of course, the situation varies very considerably, according to the conditions prevailing, but if we decide to deal with the most common of the situations confronting us, I think we shall be able to pick up much that is of the greatest value to us.

The Diagram attached to this paper shows a more or less normal system of holding a Battalion sector, and the distribution of the Companies over that sector. The notes at the bottom denote the system of allocating different defined areas to each unit, and fixing the responsibility of the upkeep of each sector on to different individuals. The system makes it perfectly clear which Company is responsible for the upkeep of any part of the line, and the Commanding Officer can at any time apportion praise or blame to any individual or Company concerned.

(iii) The General Plan of Work in the Sector.

Next we come to the drawing up of the general plan of work for the sector, and it is here that we so often fail, because there is no real system of ensuring continuity of construction, with the result that in the absence of that system many Commanding Officers coming into the line for the first time invariably break out into constructing some entirely new work which they consider of primary importance, whilst all the time there are other partly finished works left behind by the outgoing unit which are even of greater importance than that on which he has just embarked, but which, in the absence of the Permanent Sector Officer, they are entirely ignorant of. To avoid the possibility of such a state of things happening, my advice to you is to take no action until you have definitely ascertained the situation in the sector allotted to you in your new line. You can only definitely ascertain the situation by a systematic piece by piece inspection of that sector, during which, with the Defence Map in your hand, you are able to take in the tactical features of the ground, and note the state of the work that has been undertaken by your predecessor handed over by him to you. Having got the situation well in your head, you then take action, and as the action you take depends so much for its success on your having in your Battalion a really sound and well organised system, I propose to define to you what my opinion of such a system is.

*A diagram showing w
of holding a Battalion S*

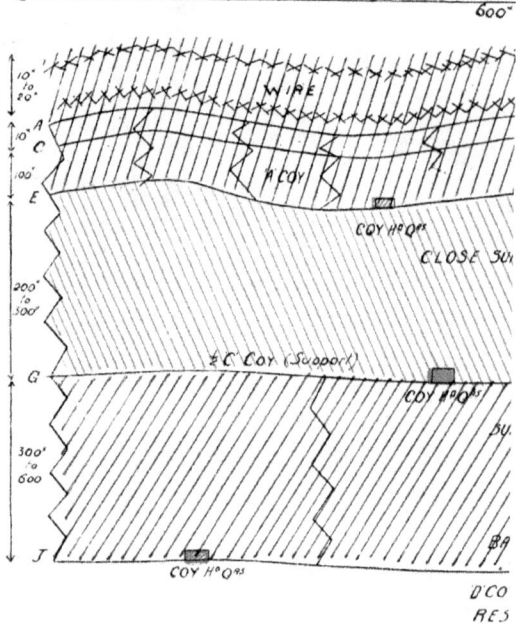

NOTES O

(i) The Officer Commanding a Battalion who is hc work over the whole of that Sector, from

He is assisted in this duty by his WORKS C Commanding the detachment of Royal EN

(ii) Officers Commanding Companies in the front MAN'S LAND back to the CLOSE SUPI

(iii) Officers Commanding Companies in the SUI CLOSE SUPPORT LINE exclusive to the

(iv) The Officer Commanding the detachment of R charge of the work from the SUPPORT I clusive.

hot is perhaps a normal method
Sector in Trench Warfare

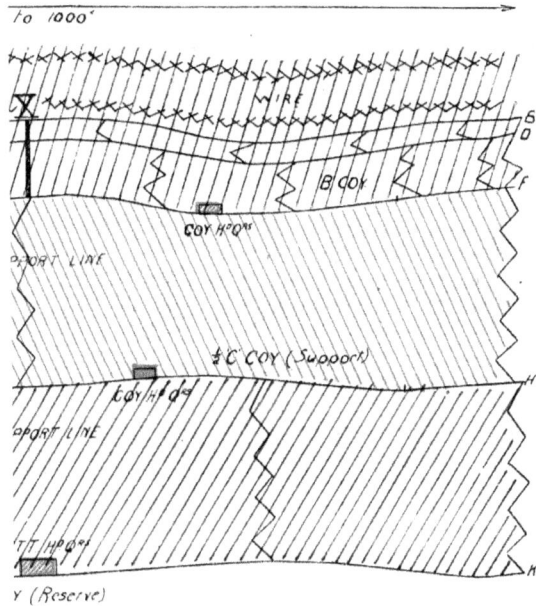

N ABOVE.

olding a Sector exercises general control as regards
NO MAN'S LAND back to the Reserve line.

OFFICER, who acts in close liaison with the Officer
IGINEERS attached to that particular SECTOR.

line supervise the whole of their Sectors from NO
'ORT LINE (E F on sketch).

'PORT LINE supervise their SECTORS from the
: SUPPORT LINE (G H on sketch) inclusive.

loyal Engineers attached to the SECTOR has special
.INE exclusive back to the RESERVE LINE in-

(iv) The Battalion Works Officer.

First and foremost you must have in your Battalion an officer whose principal rôle is to act as liaison Officer between your Battalion and the Royal Engineers; the officer best suited for this duty is your Second-in-Command. To fill the rôle with advantage he must make himself acquainted with the whole of your sector and with every defence work in course of construction, and, knowing what is in progress and, therefore, what is required, he must see to it that the working parties are properly told off and supervised, and at the same time he must keep in the closest touch with the Royal Engineers and Pioneers throughout the period of the Battalion's stay in the sector. This officer will make it his special business to see that any Working Parties ordered by the Brigade or by the Battalion Commander for a specific purpose are at their rendezvous and engaged on their task as soon as possible after their arrival. He will pay constant visits to them whilst the work is in progress, and to assist both officers and men with his advice and words of encouragement, and he will often be present at the termination of the work. By this means he will be able to ascertain, both by personal observation or by inquiry of the Royal Engineer Officer supervising the work, whether the parties have arrived in the numbers asked for, whether they have been at the rendezvous at the appointed time, and whether they have worked well or badly. He will lose no opportunity of bringing good or indifferent work to the notice of his Commanding Officer, and the latter will take the necessary action in either case.

I finish this part of my address to you by telling you that in the two Battalions I commanded in France my Second-in-Command was appointed Works Officer, and the results were most satisfactory.

(v) The Working Party.

We now have the Battalion disposed in the line, with its officers in close touch with the Royal Engineers and

Pioneers, and we have everything ready to carry on the general plan of defence in the sector, and let us now discuss those who are going to do the actual work, i.e., the Working Parties. There is no doubt that the Working Party plays a big and important part in all Royal Engineer work, and it can safely be said that when the Working Parties are properly detailed, told off to the work, supervised, and the men composing them encouraged, the work in hand is in 90 cases out of 100 completed expeditiously and well. The Commanding Officer, however, must play his rôle in this respect, and it is a most important one. I here intend to suggest to you how, by your own personal action in the matter, your Battalion can earn either an evil reputation with the Royal Engineers or else it will be spoken of by them as a Battalion composed of officers and men with splendid working qualities. I personally maintain that in a good Regiment the officers and men turn out and enter into the spirit of the work in hand with the same zest as they would turn out for a ceremonial parade, or for anything else they might be called upon by their Commander to undertake.

But in a bad Regiment, or, rather, in a Regiment that is not so good, there will be no willingness on the part of either officers or men to do the work apportioned to them, with the result that that Regiment will gain an unenviable reputation throughout the Brigade, Division, Corps, and Army, and will be spoken of as a Regiment lacking those most essential qualities that are indissolubly bound to the really good Regiment. And as none of us here, gentlemen, desire to be connected with such Regiments, I propose to put to you a certain line which you, by adopting, will ensure for all time that your Battalion is, when engaged on trench construction or on other defence works, carrying on the task allotted to it in a manner that is in keeping with the rest of its work.

First and foremost comes the composition of the Working Party. A golden rule to work on is never to detail a scratch party of officers and men to form the party. If the Brigade orders you to send 200 men and a proportion of Officers and Non-commissioned Officers, then send one complete Company; and if this is not sufficient—and it never will be—then send two or three Platoons of another Company, but also quite complete. And by the word complete I mean the Company Commander, his Subalterns, the Company Sergeant-Major, and the Non-commissioned Officers. If the numbers approach what is half the strength of the Battalion, then see that your Second-in-Command goes in command; and should the whole Battalion be required, then, of course, you, the Battalion Commander, will go with it. This is true leadership.

I remember so well being ordered in the winter of 1914-15 to find from my Company 100 men, and a proportion of Officers and Non-commissioned Officers, to dig with other men, and I remember equally well that the order did not, as it should have done, detail my Company and other Companies for the work. We were merely to form part of a pack of 400 men, with a proportion of Officers. I insisted to my Commanding Officer the right that I considered to be mine to take my Company out with every officer and non-commissioned officer composing it, and I remember how I was told that it was not proposed to make any alteration in the form of the order detailing the officers and men for that particular Working Party, but I could, of course, go on with my men if I so desired—and I remember going. I also remember that the four other Company Commanders interpreted the order as I did, and took their Companies out complete.

The detail of what happened on that night I remember well, but I have no time to relate this to you here. All I can tell you is that the presence of the four Company Commanders, with their Companies complete, saved many casualties, and, incidentally, very materially helped the young Royal Engineer Officer to dispose them in the most expeditious manner; and the work in hand was grappled with in real workmanlike manner. But this was entirely because the 400 men consisted of properly formed units of the Battalion, viz., four complete Companies organised as Companies with their own officers and non-commissioned officers. Therefore, never permit a scratch lot of men to be taken for Working Parties, and keep your organisation, when your men are called upon to dig, etc., as you would when they are called upon to fight.

The next point of importance is what the individual Commanding Officer should do, and what his rôle is when his men are digging. I think that here, again, the solution is a simple one. If the Commanding Officer permits his officers and men to be marched out from their billets to work at night in all kinds of weather, what time he and his Second-in-Command and his Adjutant remain cuddled up before a nice bright fire, drinking rum punch or other equally exhilarating beverages, he and his Staff will certainly spend their night in warmth and comfort, but the men will not; and if they never see their Commanding Officer whilst they are at work, they begin to realise very quickly that he does not attach the same importance to digging and trench construction as he does to fighting and other important duties. And if he has gone out of his way to impress on his officers and men that digging and trench construction are just as important as fighting, and then never visits them when engaged on their work with the Royal Engineers and Pioneers, he will earn the reputation of being an officer who does not practise what he preaches, and, as such, will quickly lose the confidence of his command.

I am not suggesting that a Commanding Officer should live at night with his Working Parties, but I am suggesting that he should take a real live interest in their work. The best plan to ensure this is as follows :—

> (a) If the number of men he is ordered to furnish approximates to the strength of his whole Battalion, then he and every officer should accompany it.

(b) If to half the Battalion, then he and the Second-in-Command should take it in turns to be present during the night.

(c) If small parties, e.g., one or one and a half Companies or less, then his Second-in-Command or Adjutant, and occasionally himself, should visit them.

This was the rule I observed in my Battalion, and it worked well.

Next in importance of the points connected with the Working Party comes the important question of the arrangement beforehand, if possible, of the details of the work to be carried out, distribution of party, rendezvous, etc.

The Second-in-Command of your Battalion, or whatever officer is acting as Works Officer, should, in conjunction with your Adjutant, and in close liaison with the Royal Engineers, supervise the whole of these arrangements, and every means should be taken to prevent the men being unnecessarily harassed by being taken out either too soon or by wrong and unsafe routes, or by being kept waiting at dangerous rendezvous huddled up in masses, with no one in authority to direct them to their work. This experience has been, and is to-day, the experience of so many Working Parties, and every time I hear of such experiences I attribute the cause always and at once to the incompetency on the part of the Commanding Officer, and to a failure on his part to realise the responsibility that is his to make such arrangements as will preclude the possibility of such untoward incident occurring to his officers and men. And I maintain that such things would never happen if you insisted on the Royal Engineer Officer coming to see you or your Second-in-Command, in order that every detail of the work might be first of all discussed and worked out beforehand; and it is, I submit to you, a duty you owe to your men to observe this excellent rule.

My final word to you regarding Working Parties generally and the work your men are called upon to do is this : There is nothing like a word of praise, both on the actual scene of operations, when the men are all out digging for all they are worth, and also afterwards on their return. If you never go yourself to see your men at work, you can never be in the position to apportion praise. You will certainly hear all about it from the Division if your men have not accomplished their task or have worked badly. It is just as well, therefore, that you should either go yourself from time to time and see them at work, and, when you do, get hold of the Royal Engineer Officer to accompany you when you reach the ground, and ascertain from him how your men are working, and, if his report is favourable, give them a word of praise and encouragement on the spot. It is astonishing what an effect the presence of the Commanding Officer, when his men are digging on a real foul night, has on their Moral if he knows what to do when he gets there. If you cannot go yourself, see to it that your Second-in-Command or the Senior Officer present invariably acts on these lines, and also have a standing order in your Battalion that this Senior Officer always makes a point of personally ascertaining from the Royal Engineer Officer whether he is satisfied or dissatisfied. If the former, then a suggestion to him that he should send a report into the Division, thereby ensuring a word of praise to them from the Divisional Commander, and this, if the men have really worked like Trojans, will not come amiss; and if the latter, let your Senior Officer go into the matter on the spot and rectify it.

I firmly believe, and I state this as a result of my own experience as a Company and Battalion Commander, that our work on our trenches, both back and front, and on our lines behind, would be twice as expeditiously carried out if the human touch and the personal interest from the top was a little more in evidence than it is to-day.

You Commanding Officers therefore see to it that you never fail yourselves in this respect, and your officers and men will bless you for your interest, and the encouragement that such interest gives to every officer, non-commissioned officer, and private working magnificently under the worst possible conditions for you and the honour of their Regiment.

There is another very important side to this question, and that is the part the Commanding Officer or his Second-in-Command can play in seeing that his men, when ordered out to work, are really required in the numbers demanded. Without wishing for a moment to say a single uncomplimentary word about our friends of the other arms, I do remind both you and them that there are such numbers as 15, 25, 35, etc., as well as 20, 30, 40, etc., and also other numbers such as 80 and 90 and 120 and 130, as well as the " stock " numbers 100 and 150. Officers of the Royal Engineers, Army Service Corps, and Army Ordnance Corps, who have to deal with Working and other Parties of Infantry, never quite seem to realise what the furnishing of that extra 5, 10, 20, or 30 men may mean to the Infantry Battalion, and they often call for parties in what I term their stock numbers, e.g., 100, 150, 200, 250, etc. Never do they call for parties of 80 or 90, or 130 or 140, or 180 or 190; no, it must be as stated. If, however, you give your Works Officer clear directions to report to you every time he considers men have been demanded in excess, and if you also act on the lines indicated, and frequently appear on the scenes, you may hit on a night when the numbers at work are obviously in excess of those required, and then you can represent the matter unofficially to your friends the Sappers, and ask them not in future to call for 150 or 200 men, when 130 or 180 would have done equally well.

(vi) A Few General Remarks.

There are in almost every sector of the line certain Royal Engineer and Pioneer Units and individuals of those units who are not under the Officer Commanding the Battalion holding that sector, but who at the same time may, in the case of attack, be either a hindrance or a help to the Commanding Officer. I especially refer to the Tunnelling Companies, and it is my intention here to outline quite briefly what I suggest should be the Commanding Officer's attitude regarding them. As a Commanding Officer I used to regard my Battalion sector as I would regard the barracks occupied by my Battalion in times of peace. That is to say, I regarded my sector as my home, so to speak, and the safeguarding of which was my one and only consideration. To provide adequately for its safeguard, I considered it my duty to be in touch with every individual engaged on work in my line, and no matter how great the secrecy or how confidential the nature of the work on which the Tunnelling Companies were engaged, I insisted on being informed as to the nature of the work, and what their rôle was in case of the line being attacked. To have mining operations going on in the sector for which you are responsible, and to know nothing about those operations, I considered then, and consider still, to be an act of criminal lunacy on the part of the Commanding Officer. It is due to your men that you should get in touch with the Royal Engineer Officer in charge of the mining operations, and that they should learn from him what the chances are of the enemy blowing up any part of your front. Having got this information, you can then dispose your men accordingly. This is from your own point of view. With regard to the actual Tunnellers or Miners, you can assist them in many ways as Battalion Commanders, if you know the nature of the work on which they are engaged, and they will appreciate your efforts on their behalf very much.

In some sectors the Tunnelling Companies have their orders regarding their rôle in case of attack given them by their Officer Commanding Companies. What those orders are should and must be known to you. It will therefore be necessary for you to get into touch immediately with the Tunnelling Officer, and ascertain his general dispositions in case of attack, and see that they fit in and do not clash with yours.

Again, with regard to Signal Companies, it has happened that Corps Signal Officers have entered sectors held by Battalions, and neither with or by your leave they have commenced to lay cables along the trenches, both fire and communication, without any reference to the Officer Commanding the sector, and I have known cases where I have, as a Brigadier, found a whole width of fire trench completely put out of action by a Signal Company entering my trenches, and without a word either to me or to the Officer Commanding the Battalion holding that sector, digging up the trench from end to end, and making it impossible for the garrison to use it as a fire trench. This happened in the 14 Bis sector in the Loos trenches, and in the same sector a Signal Company laid a cable in an inch pipe along the floor of a long communication trench, leaving the pipe unburied, and at least in places a foot above the level of the trench, rendering the latter entirely unserviceable as a communication trench. This could never have happened had there been close liaison with the Corps Signal Officer, and if the Commanding Officer of the Battalion in whose sector these operations occurred had declined to permit any work to be undertaken in his sector without the whole plan having been first of all disclosed to him.

And this is the point I am trying to make and to impress on you, e.g., That you are the king, so to speak, of your sector, and that as king you should never permit your kingdom to be violated, or any part of it dug up without your knowledge; and I make this further point, and that is this: — If outside units will have the civility and common sense to tell you of their plans, and to invite your co-operation, their task will be very appreciably lightened, and the work will be very much more expeditiously carried out.

The last point I would like to emphasise is the importance of the Commanding Officer knowing how to inspect work carried out by his Battalion or by the Royal Engineers or Pioneers. It is absolutely essential that he shall be able to judge when the work has been well or badly executed. He cannot do this, neither will his daily walk round the trenches be of the slightest use, if he comes to a part of the line in which a Company or a Platoon has been at work on, say, a traverse or a revetment, or a dugout, and he is unable to place his finger on both the bad and the good spots in that work. He can only do this provided he has knowledge, and he can only acquire the knowledge by private study and practical experience, and it is his duty to acquire this knowledge at once. I have been able to inspect my line, and to call up an officer or a non-commissioned officer and to apportion praise and blame for the work done, and all my officers and men have known that I was able to discern the good from the bad. The effect of this was very manifest right throughout the work of the Battalion at all times. I therefore strongly urge you to get knowledge of the first principles of drainage, revetments of all kinds, wiring traverses, trench construction, etc., so that you may always appear in front of your men as their true leader.

I conclude this part of my address by saying that it will repay you over and over again to have the Officer of the Royal Engineers and the Pioneers at work on your sector into a meal in your dugout, and to see that your Company Officers are equally hospitable. And if you can, when a section of Royal Engineers has carried out some especially nasty piece of work under very adverse conditions, arrange to give them a drink of coffee or a tot of rum before they leave your line; the entente between you and your Sappers and Pioneers will be established for ever. In my Battalion, in the winter of 1914-15, we used to look after our Sappers in this manner down on the River Souve, and I knew what it meant both to them and to us.

I had said that I had made my last point to you under the heading of "General Remarks," but I have not. There is one still remaining, and one that is perhaps the most important of all. Make it a golden rule never to call for Sappers or Pioneers to come and help you on work which you really ought to be able to carry out unaided.

I know of Battalions whose reputation was well known for calling out for Sappers and Pioneers at all times and places to come and do work which really they ought to have done themselves. But it was not an enviable reputation. I know that in good Regiments Commanding Officers will do anything rather than call on the hard-worked Sappers to come and do something which he knows is a difficult job, but which he is determined to attempt himself, rather than appeal to others. Such Regiments will always stand high in the estimation of the Field Companies and the Pioneer Battalions, and my advice to you is: "Range yourselves rather on the side of this type of Battalion than with the other."

(B) OPEN WARFARE.

There is very little to say regarding the Commanding Officer and his relations with the Royal Engineers in open warfare. The Field Companies may not be so much in evidence during an advance or an attack as they are in trench warfare, attack or defence, but this will not absolve the Commanding Officer from getting to know exactly what the rôle of the Sappers in open warfare is, and so of being able to co-operate in the truest sense of the word with them if and when the occasion presents itself. Beyond this I have nothing to say.

IN BILLETS.

I now propose to finish my address by suggesting to you what benefits and advantages a close entente will bring to your Battalion, when resting either for long or short periods behind the line. If you know your Field Company or your Pioneers well, you will in the event of your deciding to put your companies or certain selected officers and men through a short course of Field Engineering, be able to obtain quite unofficially and without fuss of any kind the services of one or two Sappers to assist you, and they, of course, will be of the greatest assistance to you. If in addition the Officer Commanding the Field Company or the

Pioneer Battalion will either come himself, or occasionally send an officer over to see your classes at work, so much the better. But this officer will not come, neither will the two Sappers be available, unless you have definitely and designedly established a proper feeling in your Battalion towards the Royal Engineers and Pioneers.

Again, a series of inter-Company or inter-Platoon Competitions in rapid wiring, digging, revetting, with the Sappers arranging the details of the competition and judging in it, proves an excellent means of cementing the friendship between the two arms, and certainly adds to the proficiency of the men. But here again it must be the Commanding Officer who must set the ball rolling.

And finally there is the benefit to your whole Battalion to be derived from getting the C.R.E. or other Royal Engineer Officer to give your men a series of addresses on the rôle of the Royal Engineers and the Pioneers, and introducing into the subject the many ways open to the two arms to co-operate to attain their end.

I can say no more, except perhaps to ask you to take to heart every word I have said to you, and to act on the lines indicated all through this address; and I know that if you do, your relations with those splendid and gallant officers and men of the Royal Engineers will always be of the most cordial description; and not only will this be the case, but because of the happy state of things prevailing you will achieve results which, under any other circumstances, would be impossible of achievement, and all the time you will be rendering your side a real service and adding much to the reputation of your Regiments.

PART II.

PRÉCIS OF LECTURE ON CONSOLIDATION.

1. Consolidation consists merely of the improvement of an existing position, or the construction of a new one. Since this improvement or construction depends entirely for its quality and extent on the use of engineer material and tools, it follows that the crux of the whole matter is the question of carrying parties.

It is therefore proposed to consider the question with the carrying party as the governing factor, and to divide it into three main divisions.

First Division—Construction or Repair of a Normal Fire, Communication, or Assembly Trench.

N.B.—The assumption is that carrying parties are available, with sufficiency of engineer materials. It is not suggested for an instant that the plans and sections given are in any sense a standard design which should always be worked to; they are merely *one type*.

(a) *First Task.*—Soil left standing at natural slope, which has been taken as 4/1. This will be dealt with more fully later.

Eleven men to 13 yards.

N.B.—Berm at least 2 feet.

PLAN.

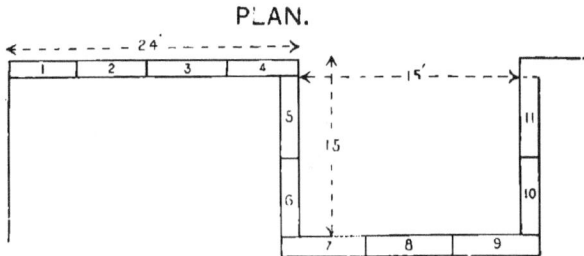

SECTION.

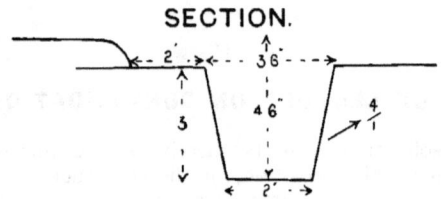

(b) Second Task.—Earth thrown on parados—berm 2 feet, same number of men.

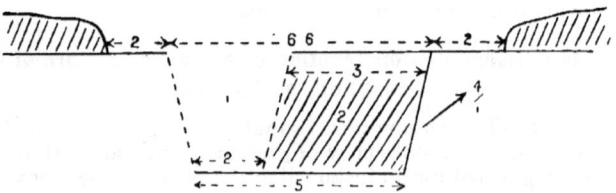

(c) Third Task.—Same number of men. Double throw may be necessary.

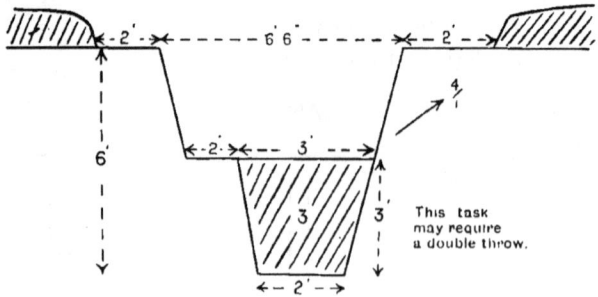

(d) *Round Traverse.*

    (1) Trench may be of same type.

    (2) A narrower trench may be dug, of a type suitable for communication or assembly trenches.

    First task as in (a) above.

(e) *Second Task.*

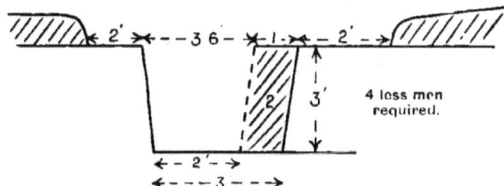

(f) *Third Task.*—As in (c) opposite.

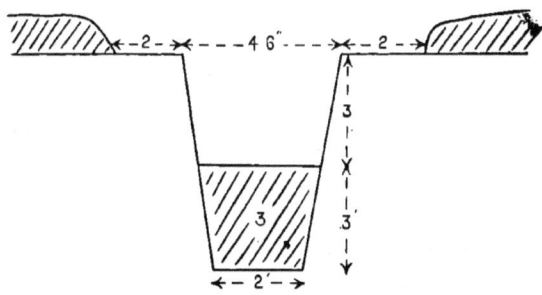

(g) *Revetment.*—The governing principle is that the bottom of any trench should be revetted with heavy material, and that the top should be unrevetted, the soil standing at its natural slope.

Short "A" frames, 3 feet high, placed at 3 feet to 4 feet centres, with corrugated iron, form perhaps the best revetting material for the lower part of the trench. (If corrugated iron is not available, expanded metal, rabbit wire, or hurdle work may be used.)

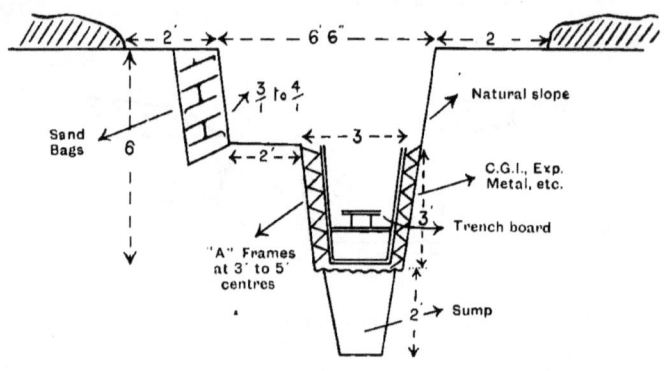

N.B.—(1) Corrugated iron, placed right at bottom of trench.

(2) If "A" frames are not available, 5 feet 6 inch angle irons can be driven into the ground until flush with edge of fire step in front of corrugated iron.

For Upper Part of Trench.

(1) If possible, unrevetted at natural slope.

(2) Sandbagged. This need only be done when natural slope too flat. The disadvantages of sandbags are that they rot easily, but if the trench is blown about they are not difficult to clear.

Points on Sandbagging.

(1) Laid at slope of 3/1 to 4/1.

(2) Laid perpendicular to slope, *not* horizontal.

(3) Bottom row headers on prepared bed, and alternate rows, headers, and stretchers.

(4) Always work from one flank to the other—not inwards from two flanks.

Thus—

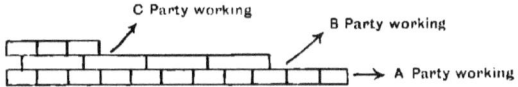

(5) Seam inside.

(6) Choke not sticking out.

(7) Well beaten down.

(8) *Break joint.*

Drainage.

Make each section of trench self-draining by digging deep sumps under trench boards.

If the bottom of the sump is above water-level, if it is kept clear of refuse, tins, etc., and occasionally picked over with a pick, any average rainfall will soak away.

Sumps should be at least 2 feet deep.

The principal factor in all drainage is that water flows downhill, and if that flow is dammed by tins, putties, etc., whether in a sump under a trench board, or in a duct leading to a big sump off the trench, that flow is stopped.

A Few Points for Platoon Commander.

(1) Never allow undercutting.
(2) Berm at least 2 feet.
(3) Clear all falls as soon as possible.
(4) If "A" frames are not available, see that trench boards rest on piles.
(5) *Dig deep sumps and keep them clear.*

Second Division—Forward Shell-Hole Line after an Attack.

2. (a) The objective has been obtained, the assaulting troops are scattered in shell-holes.

It is only in the rarest circumstances that a carrying party is available. Any consolidation, therefore, will depend on what engineer material and tools can be carried forward by assaulting troops themselves.

At the maximum the stores available will be a shovel per man, an odd pick or two, and half a dozen sandbags per man.

Consolidation Possible.

(1) A recess dug above water-level in front lip of crump-hole.
(2) The linking up by means of a rough trench two adjacent crump-holes to establish communication between a section and escape sniping.

N.B.—(a) Sandbags are practically useless when the soil filling them is wet.

(b) The linking up of two shell-holes gives information to those behind, by means of aeroplane photographs, as to position of front line.

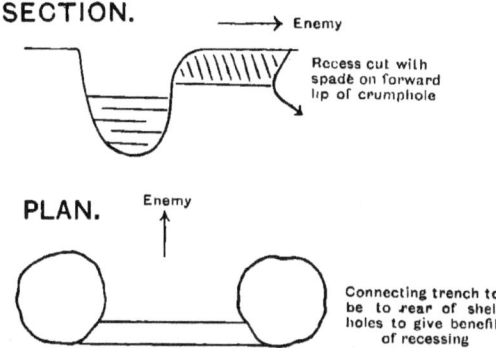

(*b*) Trench to trench attack. Old German trench held.

Consolidation Possible.

(1) Converting old parados into parapet, *i.e.*, making rough fire step.

(2) Blocking forward communication trenches.

(3) Making forward bombing straight.

(*c*) When old German trench is not held, but new one dug.

Owing to the going being fairly good, tools at the rate of one shovel and a few sandbags per man can be got up into the forward line; also the ground has not been very badly "strafed."

The consolidation in this case will consist of the rapid digging of short lengths of trench—section approximately the same as the first task in Division 1. These lengths can ultimately be joined up by sapping if required.

The point which must be borne in mind is the danger of getting long lengths of untraversed and unrecessed trench. To obviate this, the following system might be considered.

Each short length of trench, instead of being straight, should have 5 feet wings turned back at 120 degrees.

Thus AB, CD, etc., are each 5 feet—a one-man task.

B—C, F—G are of such a length as to give the remaining men a 5-feet task.

Thus if section is six strong, B—C will be 20 feet.

The distance D—E would be 15 feet—20 feet long.

During the day sapping along line D—E is carried out from both ends.

Third Division—Support Shell-hole Line after an Attack.

3. This may be broadly defined as the strong point line, lying 200 yards—500 yards behind forward line.

Again, the whole question depends on how much material can be brought up. It will certainly be limited if the going is at all bad, and any carrying party available will in all probability be exhausted in bringing wiring material alone.

(a) *Type of Strong Points.*—No standard type. In diagram cruciform and Z-shape shown.

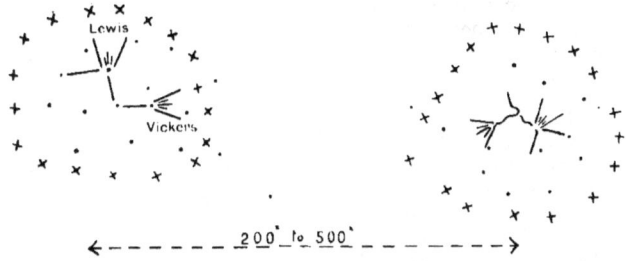

Each point capable of all-round defence.

(*b*) *Object.*—Particularly to support one another by flanking fire in event of counter-attack driving in front line. Therefore, field of fire to flank even more important than to the front.

(*c*) *How Made.*—By specially detailed parties of pioneers, or infantry working under R.E. supervision. These parties should not be sent forward until it is definitely ascertained that the places where they have to work are in our hands, and that covering parties are beyond them.

(*d*) *Siting.*—In the primary instance often by aeroplane photograph, but personal reconnaissance must be made where possible. Noticeable landmarks, such as cross-roads, etc., to be avoided.

(*e*) *Consolidation Possible.*—Entirely dependent on material available. Whatever the size, whether a cruciform strong point for a Company, or a shell-hole for a Lewis gun, the main principle is that enough work must be done the first night to admit of it being held during the following day. Wire becomes, therefore, one of the first considerations. (Drill, 3, S.S. 177, G.H.Q. instructions in wiring: low wire—for concealment—35 yards to 50 yards from post.)

The actual consolidation will consist of the linking-up of shell-holes by trenches, designed to give covered communication between different parts of the work. These trenches and holes will be revetted in time as material becomes available, tending towards some such pattern as is outlined under Division 1 above.

If the post is being constructed by infantry under Royal Engineers' supervision, the working party will remain in the position and hold it the following day, or until relieved. If the post is being constructed by Royal Engineers or Pioneers, close liaison should exist between the Officer in charge of the working party and the Battalion Commander, whose duty it is to take over the strong point at dawn or whenever the working party finish. Cases have occurred where the working party have left before being relieved by the holding troops, and the work has therefore been thrown away.

(*f*) *Special Case of Woods and Villages.*

  (1) It is laid down that after the successful capture of a wood or village, the front line (Division 2) should be pushed forward, if possible, 200 yards to 300 yards on the enemy side, to escape shell-fire.

  (2) That strong points should be constructed (Division 3) on the same principle as outlined above, in the wood by special parties—say, 150 yards to 200 yards from front edge of the wood, and at suitable points inside the village.

  In the case of the village, the strong point will probably be merely a Vickers or Lewis gun concealed in the ruins of a house and covering the road.

  (3) That in the case of villages only, further strong points should be constructed 100 yards or so from the rear edge covering roads leading out of the village.

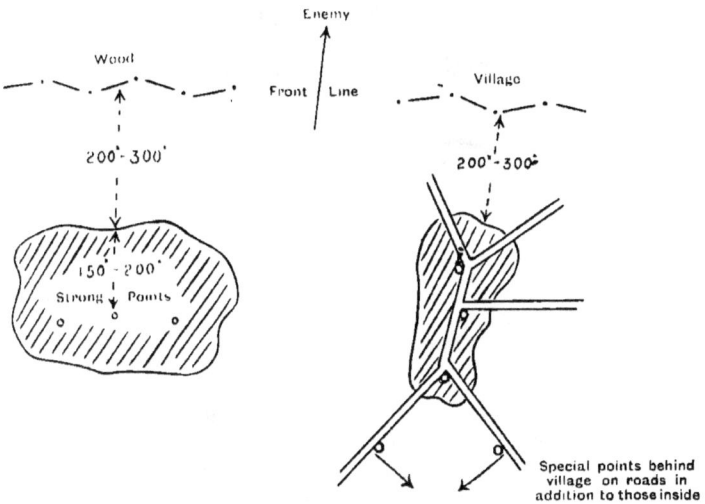

N.B.—*The principle of all consolidation is obtaining a position from which a rifle may be used in the shortest possible time, and it cannot be too strongly insisted on that consolidation is not the job of special parties, but is the job of every man.*

PART III.

WORKING PARTIES.

1. Method of Putting on to Work.

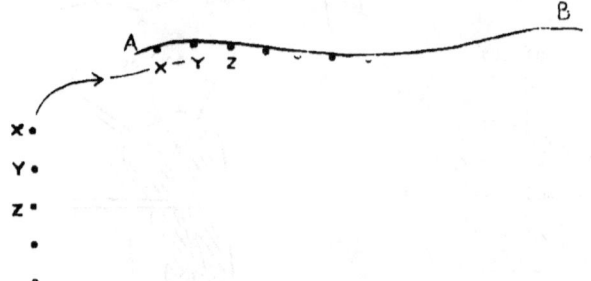

Let us assume AB is the trace of work, and X, Y, Z the three leading men of working party.

The men can be led on either from left to right or from right to left. In this case assume the first: i.e., men led to A first. (The main principle is that X should NOT be led along the tape until he comes to B, with the working party following behind him.)

    (a) X is placed by N.C.O. or Officer in charge at point A, Y next to him, and Z next as shown, the distance between them being the length of the task—say two paces.

    (b) Men lay their tools down, showing direction of their task; and they kneel down in front of the tape with their rifles until the whole party has passed them.

    (c) When last man has passed X gets up, lays his rifle *behind* the work, takes off his equipment —if so ordered—and commences his task, if he knows what to do. If he does not know, he lies down *behind* his task and waits to be told.

(d) The question of whether bayonets should be fixed and equipment taken off is one for Infantry Officer in charge to decide.

N.B.—With large working parties good discipline is essential if delay is to be avoided, and the men must have it impressed on them that under no circumstances are they to wander from the tape.

General Points.

1. *New Work.*—When new work is to be dug at night, the Royal Engineer Officer in charge of the work must reconnoitre the site during daylight and tape out the work before it is quite dark. He should then return and meet his working party at some previously selected rendezvous and lead them to the work.

2. *Guides.*—Guides who know the way must be distributed along the length of the column, otherwise touch is generally lost in the dark and a large part of the column fails to reach the work. Sufficient time is not usually allowed for working parties to reach the site of the work; it is not safe to reckon that large parties will move faster than *one mile per hour* at night.

3. *Reconnaissance.*—If possible, it is a great advantage for the Infantry Officers who are with the working party to go over the ground by daylight with the Royal Engineer Officer. This entails their preceding the Working Party by possibly an hour or more.

4. The Royal Engineer Officer is responsible for seeing that the Infantry Officer knows exactly what to do, but the Infantry Officer is responsible for seeing that it is done.

PART IV.

COMPASS NOTES.

There are two sorts of bearing—True and Compass. True concern Map and Protractor; Compass concern Ground and Compass.

All bearings are measured CLOCKWISE. In the case of True, from the True North; in the case of Compass, from the Compass North.

Thus, True Bearing of B from A is shown in black; the Compass Bearing in red.

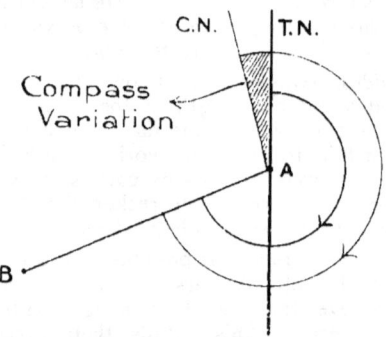

In England and France the C.B. is always greater than the T.B., since the Magnetic Pole at which the compass points lies to the west of the North Pole.

In England the difference is 15°; in France 12°.

But since no compass is quite accurate, no compass differs exactly by 15° or 12°, as the case may be.

It is necessary, therefore, before using any compass, to find the exact difference for that compass.

This is known as the Compass Variation or Deviation, and is the shaded angle in above diagram.

Let us first consider how to find a True Bearing, *i.e.*, the black angle.

I. To Find True Bearing.

(a) We wish to find the True Bearing of Church A from cross-roads B.

[*N.B.*—This is MAP and PROTRACTOR only.]

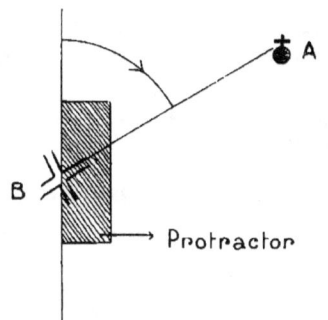

1. Through B draw North Line.
2. Join AB.
3. Place protractor (with arrow at 22 on 2 inches to a mile scale) at point B, with long side N. and S., as shown, and on same side of N. and S. Line as A.
4. Read Bearing on OUTER scale.

(b) When church is other side of N. and S. line through B.

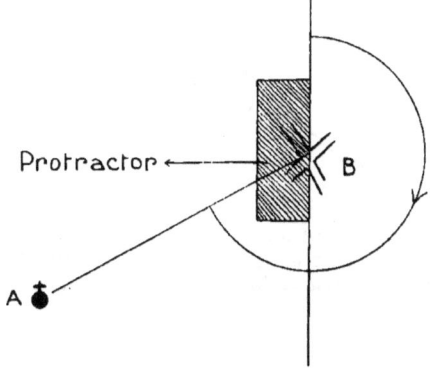

Procedure exactly the same, except that protractor is placed on other side of N. and S. line, and bearing is read on INNER scale.

N.B.—Whenever protractor is used bearings are read on—

> OUTER scale, if on right of North Line.
> INNER scale, if on left of North Line.

In laying off true bearings :—

> If under 180°, placed on right of North Line.
> If over 180°, placed on left of North Line.

II. To Find Compass Variation.

1. Locate two places on ground *and* map, A and B.

2. Go to A on ground and take compass bearing on B, 243 say.

3. Find True Bearing of B from A (as in I), 227° say.

4. Then 243 —227°, i.e., 16° = C.V.

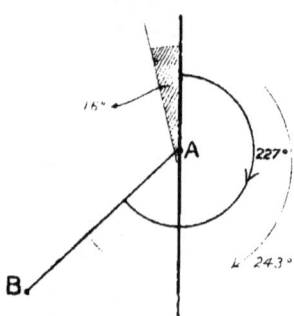

This is a constant angle for any given map and any given compass. It is *not the same* in England as it is in France, and must be found afresh in each case.

Both in England and France, however, it must be subtracted from C.B. to find T.B.

N.B.—The Grid North Line on a gridded map may be used to determine true bearings.

We have now found a certain angle which for any given map must always be subtracted from C.B. before that bearing can be used on a map.

Let us now consider the two daylight compass problems.

III. Spotting a Flash and Putting it on the Map.

(*a*) Assume a machine gun has been spotted in German front line; it is desired to put it on a Trench Map.

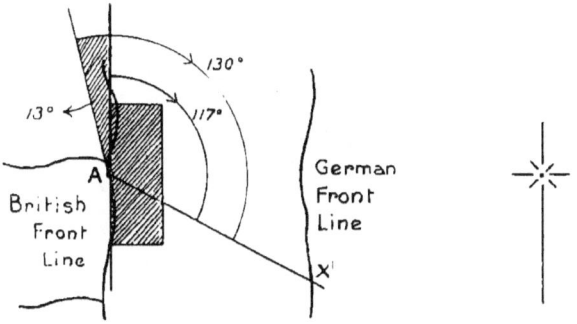

(1) Go to a point A, which can be spotted on map (possibly near a C.T.).
(2) Take a C.B. on machine gun position (say 130°).
(3) Subtract Compass Variation (say, 13°, found as in II), which gives us true bearing, 117°
(4) Through A on the map draw North Line.
(5) Place protractor on right of this line, as angle is less than 180°.

(6) Lay off angle of 117°.

(7) Machine gun is in this line, and also in front trench. Therefore where they meet is position X.

(b) Where machine gun is not located in German front line.

It is still necessary to obtain an intersection, and therefore a bearing must be taken from two points in our own front line, A and B. Assume figures for A as above.

(1) Assume C.B. from B 30° with same compass.

(2) Then T.B. = 30° − 13° = 17°.

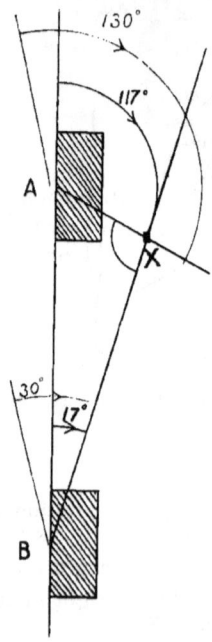

(3) Lay off angle as before.
(4) Intersection X is machine gun.

N.B.—The angle AXB should be a "fat" one, somewhere between 60° and 120° if possible.

IV. Resection of Position.

It is assumed that you are lost, but have been able to locate two places on the ground and on the map—Church A and Windmill B.

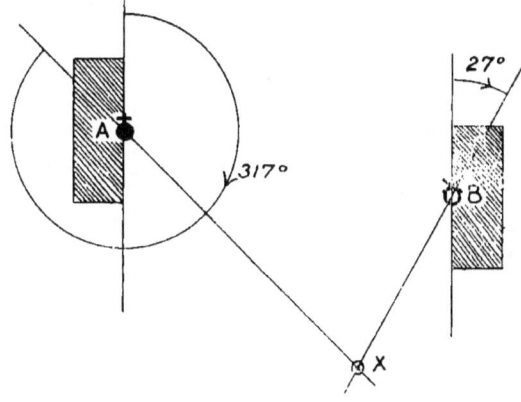

(1) Take Compass bearing to each, say 330° to Church, and 40 to Windmill.

(2) Subtract Compass Variation (say 13°) from each to obtain **True Bearings**, viz., 317° and 27°.

(3) Through A and B draw North Lines.

(4) Set off bearing of 317° from A and produce *backwards*.

(5) Set off bearing of 27° from B and produce *backwards*.

(6) Where these lines meet at X is your position.

V. Night Work.

It is required to march from A to B—two points known on the map—and at B to lay out an assembly trench BC.

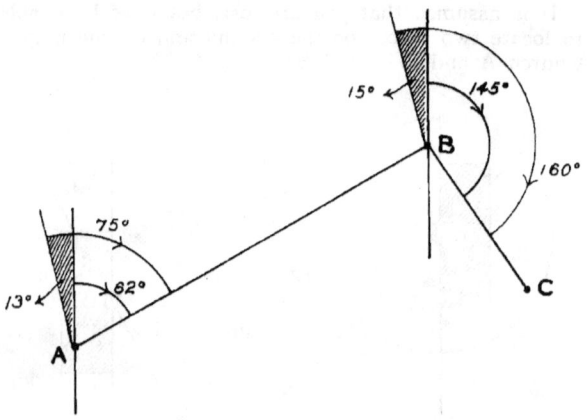

(1) From map find T.B. of B from A, say 62°

(2) Measure AB, say 1,000 yards.

(3) *On First Compass.*—Add C.V., say 13°, and set compass for 75°.

(4) Find T.B. of C from B, say 145°.

(5) Measure C.B., say 400 yards.

(6) *On Second Compass.*—Add C.V., say 15°, and set compass for 160°.

(7) The march can now be carried out from A to B on bearing 75° and distance 1,000 yards, and tape can be laid down from B to C on bearing 160° and distance 400 yards.

Notes.—(1) A different compass for every leg of march.

(2) A pebble in the pocket for every hundred paces.

(3) March by stars if possible; if not, by a bush, or something outlined against horizon.

Marching through woods or fog, or on night when no stars or marks can be picked up.

Three men, A, B, C, are lined on bearing by D, the compass bearer. E paces.

A moves forward to point A1, and aligns himself backwards on B and C, carrying on the bearing. B and C do the same at B1 and C1.

The method of aligning will depend on local conditions, viz., an electric torch inside the coat, luminous paint, a piece of paper, or the luminosity of the compass.

At every third leapfrog D rechecks bearing. E paces.

This method is very slow, and should only be used as a last resource.

Where double bearing has to be taken.

If march is from A to B, and it is seen on the map that a big obstacle intervenes.

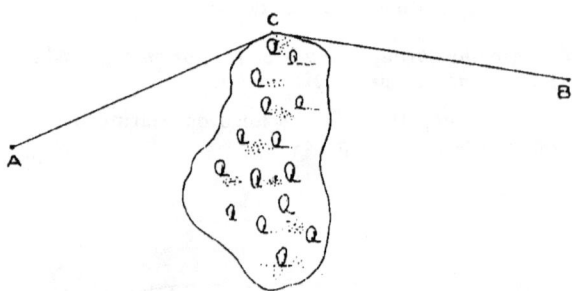

Two bearings must be taken and two compasses used. Each bearing AC, CB must be measured.

Where a sudden, unexpected obstacle is met with.

It is to be assumed that it is small, since it is not shown on the map.

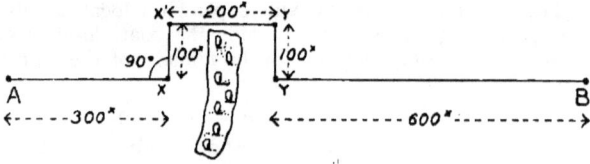

Assume march is from A to B on bearing of 110°, distance being 1,100^x.

At X an obstacle appears in the nature of a copse, with dense undergrowth—AX being 300^x.

(1) Swing compass needle to an angle of 90°, with

direction mark on lid, and strike off on new bearing XX' till clear of obstacle, say 100^x.

(2) Go back to old bearing 110° along line X' Y' till again clear of obstacle, say 200^x.

(3) Swing compass needle to an angle of 90° *the other side* of direction mark on lid, and strike off on new bearing YY' for 100^x.

(4) Go back to old bearing 110° along line YB for 500^x.

N.B.—It is important to strike off at right angles, as a right angle is an easy one to judge.

General Notes.—Every Officer should know how many paces he takes to the 100^x.

Never take a bearing with iron or steel close by, viz., a machine gun.

Steel helmet and small box respirator cause sufficient deviation to prevent an accurate bearing being taken, but NOT ENOUGH inaccuracy to prevent the general direction being ascertained if one is lost. However, to be on the safe side, they should, if possible, be removed, and if an accurate bearing is required they must be removed.

CHAPTER XIV.

PART I.

LECTURE BY
LIEUTENANT-COLONEL T. C. DALBY, D.S.O.,
on
BATTALION ORGANISATION.

(In this connection see S.S. 143, pages 29, 30, 31, of this book. Where this lecture, as originally given, is at variance with recent publications, it has been revised.)

1. I must necessarily deal with numbers and discussion of those numbers—dry stuff to listen to. As against that, it is a subject a great many of you have strong ideas upon, especially as regards employ and experts, their numbers and use. You can compare what is suggested here with what holds good in your own Battalions; think over the points and discuss them.

Why has Battalion Organisation presented difficulties? These are some of the reasons :—

(1) Heavy casualties, succeeded by uneven and scanty distribution of drafts.
(2) Extraction of men for outside work—Trench Mortars, Tunnelling Companies, etc., etc.
(3) Training going on all the time.
(4) Inexperience of some Officers as regards organisation.
(5) No help from higher authorities till as late as February, 1917, when the difficulty was realised, and O.B./1919 was produced by G.H.Q.

2. Main points showing importance of good organisation :—

(a) **Tactics** and **Organisation** must hang together.

It is impossible to work out details of attack or any operation unless you, as Commanding Officers, know your numbers and whereabouts of those numbers. You as Commanding Officers must have details of your machinery at your fingers' ends, and the machine taken into action must be in perfect order. You ORGANISE to FIGHT—the only important thing. Before fighting you must train, and before training, ORGANISE.

(b) **Suitable blending of weapons** with which the infantry are armed. To quote S.S. 143, Section I, para. 6 (a): " The platoon should constitute a unit for fighting and training, and should contain all the weapons with which the infantry is now armed."

The composition of the sections will normally be :—

3 Sections Riflemen.
1 Section Lewis Gunners.

(c) **Man power,** or competing as well as possible with SHORTAGE of men. Need for ECONOMY.

It is not my business to go into the real reason of insufficient reinforcements. It is not the Army's fault your Battalion is short and remains short. As a matter of interest, REINFORCEMENTS are of necessity pooled round the battle area, i.e., only those units who have been depleted in that battle area or elsewhere, and are withdrawn to another part of the line, get the available reinforcements, and only when they are going back to the battle area.

We must be economical.

(d) To obtain **Flexibility,** i.e., the capacity of any unit to increase or decrease, without destroying its organisation, G.H.Q. have given a guide, which, though allowing certain latitude, has standarised organisation.

The platoon—now the fighting unit—will not normally exceed 40, and should not be allowed to fall below 24.

Take away 4 for platoon headquarters, gives you

36 highest,
20 lowest.

That is 9 men maximum and 5 men minimum per section.

Latter is the lowest number of men who can combine in the use of their weapons effectively. With less, the homogeneous idea ceases to exist.

3. Now for the remedy when you get below your numbers.

What does G.H.Q. say? During active operations, should casualties be such as to reduce the strength of platoons below the minimum figure given, the necessary numbers will be obtained by the temporary amalgamation of companies in the Battalion, or platoons or sections in the company, as best meets the exigencies of the case.

No one likes amalgamation or breaking up a unit. There is a SPIRIT which runs through every unit, big or small, or should do in a good Battalion; but you *must* make this rule.

IF IN YOUR REDUCED CONDITION **there is a probability of your being required to take part in active trench operations, you must organise, so as to have not less than 5 per section, plus leader.**

Remember, if you amalgamate platoons, it means economy of platoon leaders, probably necessary under the circumstances.

If you amalgamate sections it affects fewer men.

On the other hand, if reinforcements can reasonably be expected to come along, and it is improbable that you are for Active Operations, do not be in a hurry to amalgamate.

Take as an example of amalgamation :—

" A " and " B " Companies have had a rough time and average 12 or 13 men a platoon. Keep " A " and

" B " as Companies of two platoons each, but leave out of the line for a time two or three of the men from the platoons which have temporarily disappeared—men of the right sort—and when the platoons get going again, after reinforcements, they will be there to put the right spirit back again.

As examples of Battalions amalgamating :—

My own Battalion (4th/60th) and P.P.C.L.I. formed one Battalion after Second Battle of Ypres.

In my Brigade at Suvla two Battalions amalgamated after the blizzard in November, 1915. In both cases the Battalions benefited by the temporary amalgamation.

NOTES ON APPENDIX I.
(S.S. 143, pages 30 and 31 of this book.)

1. The idea of this Appendix is that it gives you a suggested number of ALL employ and experts in the Battalion in the first column, and their distribution is shown in the other four columns.

If you subtract the 1st column from your Battalion strength, and divide by 16, it will give you the average number per platoon.

(N.B.—See page 73, S.S. 135, " The Training and Employment of Divisions, 1918," dealing with the percentage of Officers and specialists left out of the line, which must be learnt and remembered.)

One thing G.H.Q. has not allowed for is a band. We must have bands. They are worth anything, and more than pull their weight as employ and experts. We must take care of them. Call them Reserve Stretcher Bearers. Anyone who wishes can have a copy of " Suggested band of 19 or 23, sergeant included " (23 is far better). I can also give you suggested additions to ordinary drums and fifes—instruments required, where obtainable, etc.

2. Reference, S.S. 143, Section I, para. 3.

There is no difficulty in carrying out the instructions in this paragraph.

Sections can be composed as convenient. For instance, at Battalion Headquarters' fighting portion :—

> Signallers form a section;
> M.O.'s group form another;
> Scouts and snipers and runners form two more, and so on.

The same applies to Battalion Headquarters administrative portion and Company Headquarters.

It is strongly recommended that every employ and expert should not merely belong to a **company,** but should belong to a **platoon.**

Each platoon can then have one or more reserve sections—really, " paper " sections—composed of employ and experts.

3. Orderly-room.

1 and 1. Suggest also a third, i.e., shorthand-typist; if all are shorthand-typists, so much the better.

4. Platoon Sergeants.

They are now part of Platoon Headquarters.

5. Storemen.

Regimental Quartermaster's Clerk and Storeman. Quartermaster GATHERS A CROWD OF MEN. Beware of him! This allowance is enough.

One per Company at Company Headquarters. Important men. (See note on Gas Non-Commissioned Officer.)

6. Pioneers.

Same as War Establishment. Under this subject train an *Armourer*. Armourer-Sergeants in some Divisions are pooled, so you lose him, but you want a substitute.

Tradesmen much easier to find in some Battalions than others.

They make gas precautions on dug-outs, transport repairs, stables and floors, targets and falling plates, boxing stage, crosses, beds for Officers, and the thousand and one things one wants.

7. Transport and Grooms.

That number will do it if they are good men. Non-commissioned officers wanted, and good ones. Have a non-commissioned officer in charge farriers. Farriers look after spare animals.

8. Shoemakers.

Can do about 30 pairs a day. Sometimes D.A.D.O.S. very close, and only allows a certain number of boots per month; 70 pairs quite enough if your shoemakers do their job; in fact, 1 and 3 can manage it.

9. Tailors.

Enough if hard workers.

10. Butcher.

He is an expert and required.

11. Postman.

If he is keen and thorough he makes a great difference to Battalion's welfare.

12. Cooks.

The numbers shown appear excessive, but those numbers are intended to include two cooks per Company under training. It is suggested that one of the cooks in each Company should be a Lance-Corporal. Of the remainder the two non-commissioned officers at Battalion Headquarters are the Sergeant and Corporal-Cooks, who should be employed to the best advantage and help Officers Commanding Companies. If they are kept up to the mark they are invaluable in this way.

13. A **Signalling Instructor** is not included, and he may be added as required.

Signallers, i.e., personnel as apart from instructors, are trained at Army Schools. The only actual personnel that are so trained. But do not depend on getting all your requirements trained outside—whether Signallers or others.

14. A book similar to A.B./70 can be bought at Gale & Polden's. Any well-bound, large, ruled notebook can be cross-ruled to suit. (See Appendix A.)

Duplicate books must be kept in the Orderly-room, and checked at same time as Conduct Sheets.

15. A Few Notes on the Absorption of a Draft.

Get Employ and Experts filled up first, i.e., Band, Lewis Gunners, Transport, Pioneers, Signallers, etc., etc.

Then equalise Companies and post non-commissioned officers according to requirements.

When men are keen to go to a Company in which they have served before, see that they get what they wish, whenever possible.

16. Courses.

Officers, non-commissioned officers and men should be carefully chosen, and do not put off selection till names have to be submitted.

Keep careful record in Course File and A.B./70, or its equivalent.

Insist on all ranks being properly fitted and well turned out before leaving for a course.

See all ranks before they go and when they return, and point out the opportunity they have of being a credit to their Regiment and Battalion.

Appendix B.

Shows suggested index for Battalion files.

Appendix C.

This shows in diagrammatic form how the duties in a Battalion are sub-divided and the chain of responsibility.

APPENDIX B.

SUGGESTED INDEX FOR BATTALION FILES.

No. File.
1. Honours ⎫
2. Officers ⎬ Confidential—Kept by C.O.
3. Secret Operations ⎭
4. Waiting.
5. Court-Martial or Discipline.
6. Training.
7. Open Warfare.
8. Trench Warfare.
9. Engineering—Wiring.
10. Courses.
11. Bombing.
12. Lewis Gun.
13. Leave.
14. Defence Schemes.
15. Raids.
16. Past Operations.
17. Intelligence.
18. Current Work.
19. Miscellaneous.
20. Battalion Standing Orders.
21. Brigade Orders.
22. Signalling.
23. Gas.
24. Transport.
25. War Diary.
26. Roll of N.C.Os.
27. Regimental Orders.
28. G.R.O.

Note.—(a) These may be combined in some cases, according to circumstances, and kept as few as possible.

(b) A good " Zip " File can be bought for a few pence at Map House, Sifton Præd, St. James's Street.

(c) Of course, mostly left with First Line whilst in the trenches.

(d) In spare time these files should be sifted and unnecessary *"paper" burnt.*

(e) The Bombing, Lewis Gun, and Signalling Files, although kept in the Orderly-room, should always be available for inspection by the expert Officers concerned.

They should initial documents in their file to indicate that the subject of the correspondence has been read and noted.

APPENDIX A.

Regimental Number	RANK	NAME	Date of Enlistment or from which service counts	Age on Enlistment	Date of Joining Battalion	Terms of engagement on which serving		Class, Service or Proficiency Pay	Allotment	COURSES PASSED DATE					
						Colours	Reserve			Musketry	Lewis Gun	Machine Gun	Signalling		
5846	L/cpl	Roy Geo Arthur	8-8-11	19.6	1-1-16	7	5	4	6'		196				

Lance Corporal	Corporal	Lcel Sergeant	Sergeant	Further Promotion	Reversion	HOW EMPLOYED IN THE BATTALION	Religious Denomination	Married or Single	Children	Trade or Calling	ADDRESS OF NEXT OF KIN	Killed	Died of Wounds	Missing	Sick	Transferred	Wounded	HONOURS REWARDS. WOUNDS REMARKS
	17.10	1.9.10	1.9.13	C.S.M 1.1.18		Super Corpl L.G. Sergt Instr L.G. C.S.M	RC	M	2	Cabinet Maker	Mr Geo Arthur Roy WIFE 7 Penhurst St Winchester						1.1.19	W Sept 14 · Jan. 15 DCM June 14 Bar to DCM Jan 15

APPENDIX C.

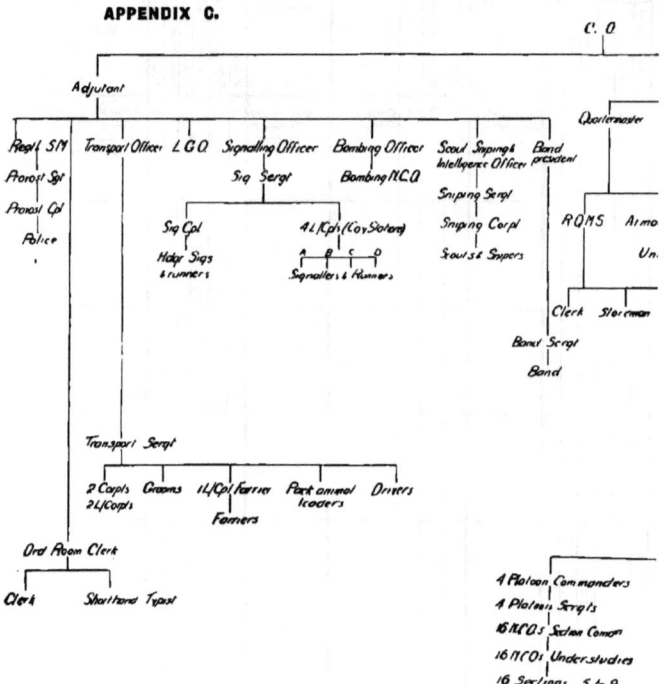

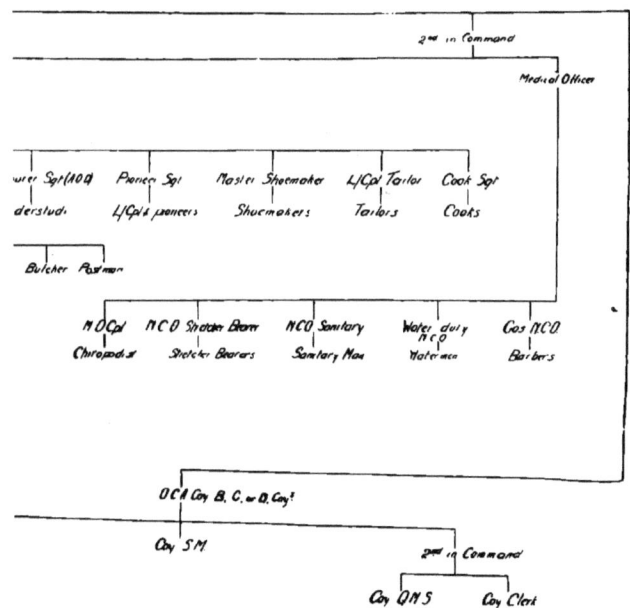

PART II.

INTERIOR ECONOMY AND ADMINISTRATION.
By Lieut.-Colonel J. F. R. HOPE, D.S.O., K.R.R.C.

Interior Economy may be defined as a system by which the duties of all ranks are co-ordinated so as to maintain the efficiency and well-being of a unit. The duties of all ranks, from a Section Commander to a Commanding Officer, were discussed at the Senior Officers' School, and the following table of duties were considered such as should be carried out by the various Commanders concerned.

Duties of Section Commander.

1. To look after his section at all times—in billets, in trenches, and on the march.
2. To inspect his men on all parades, including "Stand to," and to report to his Platoon Commander.
3. To know the characters of his men, their names, previous employment, good points, and limitations; he must know his section roll by heart, and be able to identify any man by the sound of his voice.
4. It is his duty to look after the food, water, clothing, arms, equipment, necessaries, and fuel of his section.
5. He must understand (a) the platoon roster of duties, and be acquainted with the allotment of tasks; (b) the duties of a sentry, and post them when on platoon duty; (c) his duties when employed on carrying or digging parties.
6. He will at all times set an example to his section in drill, smartness, cheerfulness, and allow no grousing.

Duties of Platoon Commander.

1. He commands his sections, and therefore must know thoroughly all the duties and difficulties of his Section Commanders.

2. It is his duty to inculcate discipline, and train his Section Commanders and their understudies in their duties.

3. He is responsible for knowing and promulgating all orders, including defence schemes, etc.

4. He must at all times keep a platoon roster of duties, and have a platoon parade state in his possession. He will also keep a platoon roll book on the lines of A.B. 70.

5. He sees that kits of all men killed, missing, or absentees in his platoon are properly handed in to Company Headquarters, and that the kits of men wounded go with them to hospital.

6. He renders a casualty report to the Officer Commanding the Company daily.

7. He will always acquaint the relatives of any men killed, wounded, or missing belonging to his section.

8. He must pay great attention to the fitting of boots, clothing, and state of the men's feet in his platoon.

9. He inspects the arms of his platoon daily under all circumstances, and must see that oil bottles are filled.

10. He ensures that all blankets are thoroughly aired and beaten at least once a week, and always after a tour of duty in the trenches (should blankets have been taken in).

Platoon Sergeant.

He understudies and assists his Commander in every way, and, additionally, is responsible that all non-commissioned officers and men get up punctually at Réveillé, and that the billets, etc., are clean and tidy.

Duties of Orderly-Sergeant.

1. He takes over the detail and order book from his predecessor.

2. He collects the platoon absentee reports at "Rouse" and "Tattoo," and reports to the Battalion Orderly-Sergeant.

3. He attends all parades of his company, including guard mounting.

4. He sees all lights out, and reports to Battalion Orderly-Sergeant.

5. He parades all men for Company orderly-room, and if necessary parades them for Battalion orderly room 15 minutes before the hour given.

6. He receives the detail from the Company Sergeant-Major, and enters it in his detail and order book.

7. He warns all non-commissioned officers for duty.

8. He makes out the Company sick report.

9. He attends the issue of meals and goes round with the Company Orderly Officer.

10. He supervises the duties of the Company Orderly-Corporal.

11. He will not leave his Company billets except on duty.

12. He collects platoon states and makes out a Company Parade State from them, for signature of Officer Commanding Company.

13. On the march he makes out a " Falling out state," for Officer Commanding Company's signature, and hands it in to the orderly-room.

14. He sees that all fire buckets are kept ready for instant use.

15. When in camp he sees the flies of all tents are rolled up at " Rouse," and that all kits are neatly placed in line in the open.

Duties of Company Orderly-Corporal.

1. He assists the Company Orderly-Sergeant and reports to him at " Rouse."

2. He is responsible for handing over the rations of men confined to the guard-room and prisoners to the non-commissioned officer in charge of the guard.

3. He hands over the kits of men confined on their **arrest.**

4. He takes over the sick report from the Orderly-Sergeant and marches the sick to the parade. He will bring back the completed duplicate copy of the report.

5. He will not leave his Company Quarters during his tour of duty, except on duty.

6. He is responsible that urine tubs are removed and replaced in accordance with instructions issued on the subject.

Duties of Orderly Officer (Battalion or Company).

1. He visits the breakfasts and dinners of his Company and attends the issue of meals from the cooker.

2. He visits the cooker and sees that it is clean.

3. He visits the incinerators, refuse pits, latrines, and washing places of his Company.

4. He will see to the cleanliness of the Officers' Mess kitchens and utensils.

5. He inspects all guards before Battalion Guard Mounting Parade.

*6. He visits the wet and dry canteens.

*7. He turns out all guards and visits the sentries once by day and once by night. This should include the stable piquet if within a reasonable distance of billets.

*8. He visits the men confined to the guard-room.

*9. He collects reports at "Tattoo" parade and reports to Officer Commanding.

10. He reports to his Officer Commanding at Company Office on the succeeding day.

11. His duties commence and end at "Rouse."

Note.—Duties marked * can be performed by Company Orderly Officers in rotation and report to the Adjutant.

Duties of Company Quartermaster-Sergeant.

1. He takes over the Company rations in bulk from the Quartermaster and issues them as required to Com-

panies in the trenches, reporting to Officer Commanding.

2. He ascertains the wants of Platoon Commanders and prepares requisitions for articles of clothing, equipment, necessaries, arms and ammunition for the signature of Officer Commanding Company.

3. He prepares acquittance rolls and keeps duplicates.

4. He is responsible that the Company is supplied with books, message forms, papers, Army Forms, as required.

5. He is responsible for the upkeep of A.B. 70, and that all casualties are at once entered up.

6. He prepares returns when out of the trenches for signature of Officer Commanding Company.

7. He is responsible that all casualties affecting, and forfeitures of, pay are entered at once in A.B. 64.

8. He enters the quarterly state of accounts in A.B. 64.

9. He is directly responsible to the Second-in-Command of the Company for all matters affecting the men's pay, clothing, comfort and general well-being.

Duties of Company Storeman or Clerk.

1. He assists the Company Quartermaster-Sergeant in all clerical duties.

2. He makes out all routine returns in the trenches for the signature of the Officer Commanding Company.

3. He is responsible for the liaison of the Company Quartermaster and Transport Officer whilst the Company is in the trenches.

Duties of Company Sergeant-Major.

1. He is responsible for the tone and general deportment of the non-commissioned officers of his Company.

2. He must possess a perfect knowledge of drill and set a personal example of punctuality and smartness at all times.

3. It is his duty to observe constantly the conduct and character of the non-commissioned officers of his Company, and be their adviser at all times.

4. He is responsible for the proper conduct of the Company Sergeants' Mess.

5. He attends Company guard mounting parades and the parades of piquets and other Company duties.

6. He attends all Company Parades and Company and Battalion orderly-room.

7. He details all Company duties.

8. He is responsible (subject to an Officer) for the taking over, custody, and handing over of trench stores.

9. He submits all A. and G. returns to his Company Commander for signature.

Duties of Officer Commanding Company.

1. He is primarily responsible for the interior management of his Company, for the clean and soldierly appearance, for the discipline and general well-being.

2. He is responsible for the training of his Officers and men.

3. He must encourage and promote games and amusements among his men and keep them always in good heart.

4. He is responsible that his subordinates know the exact state of their commands at all times.

5. He must observe and know the characteristics of all his subordinate leaders, and constantly look out for suitable understudies.

6. He keeps the leave roster of his Company, and submits names when called for. He must personally see that it is equitably administered.

7. He is responsible that the kits of all his Officers and men killed and missing are handed in to Battalion Headquarters.

8. He must write to the relatives of Officers and non-commissioned officers killed, wounded or missing in his Company.

9. He is responsible for the proper conduct of the Company Officers' Mess, and that all mess accounts are punctually paid.

10. He is personally responsible for the correctness of entries in the soldier's pay book (A.B. 64), and for all money drawn on behalf of his Company.

11. He is personally responsible for all Company accounts.

Duties of Company Officer Second-in-Command.

1. He assists and supports his Company Commander at all times.

2. He undertakes the duties of pay, clothing, equipment, arms and necessaries of the Company.

3. His special function is to interest himself in all that relates to the comfort of his men.

4. He supervises the instruction and training in musketry of his Company.

5. He is responsible for the " Q " Branch of the Company generally.

BATTALION DUTIES.

The Provost-Sergeant.

1. He is responsible for the discipline of the Regimental Police, and for the efficient performance of their duties.

2. He is responsible for the carrying out of field punishment in a proper manner, according to his orders and the regulations. Those orders must be in writing. (N.B.—The non-commissioned officer in charge of the guard is responsible for custody of all men placed under his charge.)

3. He is responsible for carrying out defaulters' parade and punishment drill.

4. He invariably attends Battalion orderly-room and notes all punishments in a book.

5. He visits the wet canteen frequently, supervises the non-commissioned officer on canteen duty, and sees that rules are enforced.

6. He visits drinking places and places of public resort near billets and reports any irregularities.

7. He assists and supports the Battalion Sergeant-Major.

8. He marches with the Regimental Police in rear of Battalion.

N.B.—**The duties of this non-commissioned officer are those that require of the individual both tact, common sense and discretion, if the life in a Battalion is to run smoothly.**

The Pioneer-Sergeant.

1. He is under the orders of the Quartermaster or Second-in-Command.

2. He is responsible at all times for the discipline of the pioneers.

3. He will ascertain particulars of casualties and make crosses for those killed.

4. He supervises generally the work of the pioneers, and constantly endeavours to further the comfort of Officers and men by making beds, tables, forms, washing places, latrines, repairs to billets, etc.

5. He is responsible, under the Transport Officer, for the correct markings being painted on the regimental transport, and for the smartness and repair of all vehicles.

6. He is responsible for the stock of tools being kept up in a serviceable state and for indenting for material on Battalion Headquarters.

7. On the march he follows the wagon on which his tools are.

8. He may be responsible for the drawing and issue of R.E. material.

The Shoemaker-Sergeant.
1. He is under the orders of the Quartermaster.
2. It is his duty to keep in close touch with Companies, and to know what repairs are needed.
3. He must be careful to mark each pair of boots for repair, so that they can be re-issued to the owner.
4. He supervises the repair of harness and all leather equipment of the Battalion.
5. He is responsible that he is in possession of a sufficient quantity of tools and equipment for repairs.
6. On the march he follows the wagon in which his tools are, and must be prepared to execute repairs at short notice.
7. He is responsible for the discipline of the shoemakers.

The Armourer-Sergeant.
1. He is a member of the Army Ordnance Corps, and is attached to the Battalion. He works under the Quartermaster.
2. He inspects the arms of all units in the Battalion at least once a month.
3. He is responsible for the repair of all arms. He must report any injury to, or tampering with, arms to the Quartermaster.
4. He trains any assistant he may be given.
5. He will frequently overhaul all Lewis Guns.
6. He is responsible for the repair of the bicycles.

The Orderly-room-Clerk (Sergeant).
1. He works under the orders of the Adjutant.
2. He is responsible for the regularity of the orderly-room in general.

3. He should prepare punctually all returns for signature.

4. He is responsible, in conjunction with the signallers, for the punctual despatch of all correspondence.

5. He is responsible that all urgent letters and telegrams should at once be brought to the notice of the Adjutant, or Officer answering for him.

6. He is responsible for the letter-book and correspondence register being kept up to date, and that letters are correctly filed.

7. He should prepare lists, with dates, etc., of all returns required.

8. He is responsible for the discipline of the clerks.

9. He must maintain the strictest secrecy on all matters which come to his knowledge in the course of his duties, and impress this on the clerks.

10. He is responsible that requisitions are made at the proper time for all paper, books and forms, etc., and that the office is always well equipped. He is also responsible for the issue of stationery to Companies.

11. He must see that no one loiters round his office, and that no unauthorised person is permitted to enter in.

12. Remember that the " Orderly-Room Sergeant " (Staff Sergeant) is with G.H.Q. 3rd Echelon, Base.

The Regimental Quartermaster-Sergeant.

1. He is under the immediate orders of the Quartermaster.

2. He attends the issue of rations to the Battalion in the absence of the Quartermaster.

3. He attends all issues of stores, superintends all parties receiving or collecting stores, clothing, equipment, etc.

4. He inspects daily the incinerator, refuse bins or pits, latrines, ditches, drains, etc., in the vicinity of the regimental transport duties.

5. He reports any irregularities to the Quartermaster.

6. He supervises the work of the Company Quartermaster-Sergeants when with the Quartermaster's Department.

7. He is responsible for the good conduct of the Sergeants' Mess (second echelon), and generally maintains the discipline and smartness of the Quartermaster's Department.

8. He prepares all indents for rations and fuel on A.F. B 55, and all indents for articles of ordnance stores, arms, equipment, clothing and necessaries, etc., for the Quartermaster's signature on A.F. G 994.

9. He attends Battalion orderly-room in the absence of the Quartermaster.

Regimental Sergeant-Major.

1. He will be an example to all warrant officers and non-commissioned officers of the Battalion in all things and at all times.

2. He acts as the connecting link between the Adjutant and the non-commissioned officers of the Battalion.

3. He must observe closely the character and demeanour of all subordinates, and bring to the notice of the Adjutant any breach or dereliction of duty.

4. He gives out the detail of Battalion duties.

5. He acts for Battalion Headquarters as a Company Sergeant-Major does for a Company.

6. He parades guards, piquets and Battalion duties. He should be present at Réveillé, Retreat and Tattoo at least twice a week.

7. He is responsible for the proper routine of the regimental orderly-room as regards accused, witnesses, recommendations, and interviews. He will also see that the Field Offence Report is correct in every particular.

8. He is responsible for the Battalion ammunition reserve when in the trenches.

9. He supervises the work of the Provost-Sergeant.

10. He is responsible for the proper conduct of the Sergeants' Mess.

The Adjutant.

1. He is the Staff Officer to the Commanding Officer.
2. He must be a pattern of dress, drill, discipline and smartness.
3. He is responsible for warning Officers for duty and courses of instruction.
4. He inspects Battalion duties at guard mounting.
5. He keeps—
   (a) The Officers' Book, giving particulars of age, services, next-of-kin, address, honours, courses, wounds, promotions, appointments, with dates and authorities, etc.
   (b) The non-commissioned officers' book, seniority roster by ranks, with dates of promotion and appointment, honours, wounds, courses, etc.
   (c) Lists of specialists, men on regimental employment, and those that have qualified at courses.
6. He is responsible for correctness and punctuality of all returns. Officers Commanding Companies should be furnished with *pro formas* of all returns required. The more important returns are Field States (A.F. B 231), Field Return (A.F. B 213), Fighting Strengths, Casualty Report.
7. He must be firm and respectful in his dealings with Officers Commanding Companies, and try to carry out the routine of the Battalion with the least friction.
8. He is responsible for reporting all irregularities and departures from the rules and customs of the Service to the Commanding Officer.
9. He keeps up a complete and up-to-date list of all regulations, etc., required.

10. He is responsible for the Battalion imprest accounts.

11. He is responsible particularly for the discipline and smartness of Battalion Headquarters, including the Band, and makes them an example to the Battalion; he should inspect them daily.

12. He is responsible for the issue and observance of all Regimental and Battalion Standing Orders, and for the Battalion Routine Orders.

13. He should, subject to the discretion of the Commanding Officer, deal with and sort all the kits of killed and missing Officers, sending in the necessary statement of accounts, signed by the Commanding Officer, to the Base Paymaster. The Quartermaster does this if the Battalion is in action.

14. The following books and files are in his keeping, and he is responsible for their correctness :—

> (1) Defence Scheme; (2) War Diary, A.F. C 2118 (in duplicate); (3) Historical Records; (4) Casualty Book; and all files except those kept by the Commanding Officer or Officers' Confidential File and Honours and Rewards File.

15. He takes summaries of evidence for Courts-Martial.

16. He keeps the Officers' leave roster and duty roster.

17. He is responsible for the drill and instruction of drafts, both Officers and other ranks; the Regimental Sergeant-Major will assist him in these duties.

18. He must not sign papers intended for the Higher Command. Should the matter be urgent, he may sign " For " the Commanding Officer, and in such cases the Commanding Officer must be informed at the earliest opportunity.

19. Whenever a non-commiss'oned officer leaves the battalion owing to wounds, sickness or other causes, the

Adjutant sees that a record as to the fitness for promotion or otherwise and any special act of gallantry of that non-commissioned officer accompanies his documents.

It is recommended that a form on the lines indicated below, filled in by the Commanding Officer, should be attached to the non-commissioned officer's A.F. B 122 when that document is sent to the Base.

No.	Rank	Name	Regiment	Recommended for Promotion.	Recommended for Accelerated Promotion.	Not Recommended for promotion and reason	Any Special Acts of Gallantry
5067	Corporal	Brown, A	10/Bn. Rifle Brigade	Yes—a good sound N.C.O. who always does his duty well.	No !	—	

Place   *In the Field*   *A. H. JONES,* Lieut.-Colonel,
Date   *6th May, 1917*   Comdg. *10/Bn. Rifle Brigade.*

The Quartermaster.

1. He acts as a Staff Officer to the Commanding Officer.
2. He is generally responsible for the provision of the correct rations of food, forage, fuel, arms, clothing, boots, equipment and necessaries and all articles of ordnance stores.
3. He attends the refilling point.
4. He should keep the closest touch with D.A.D.O.S. of the Division, and work in with him and with the Brigade Supply Officer.
5. He should constantly inspect the cooks and cooking arrangements, and with the Medical Officer the sanitary arrangements.
6. He should attend orderly-room daily, and when in the trenches either he or the Transport Officer should report daily to Battalion Headquarters.
7. He is primarily responsible for the accuracy of his ration indents, and must keep himself constantly in

touch with the Adjutant to check Company Quartermaster-Sergeants' indents.

8. He should be present when stores are drawn and issued.

9. He keeps a letter book and files of all receipts, duplicate indents, etc.

10. He arranges for the washing and exchange of shirts, drawers, socks, when possible.

11. He must ensure a sufficient supply at all times of spare parts for rifles and Lewis guns.

12. He carefully inspects and disposes of the kits of men killed in action or missing, or absentees, in accordance with General Routine Orders.

13. He is in charge of all details left at the Administrative portion of Battalion Headquarters. This also includes the Postman.

14. He is in charge of the Battalion mails.

The Second-in-Command.

1. He is an understudy to the Commanding Officer.

2. He assists and supports the Commanding Officer in every way.

3. He instructs the younger Officers in their duties, and gives them advice whenever necessary.

4. He takes charge of the Regimental accounts, and undertakes the running of canteens and recreation rooms for the benefit of the men. (N.B.—The Padre will assist.)

5. He checks the Field Conduct Sheets with the Offence Reports and the entries in A.B. 70 with Battalion Route Orders (as corrected by A.F. O. 1800 from base).

6. He brings to the notice of the Commanding Officer any irregularity.

7. He attends to all matters affecting the comfort of the men in billets and trenches, such as provision of baths, beds, ovens, latrines, good washing arrangements, etc.

8. He supervises the food and cooking arrangements of the men, and tries to improve them by allowing grants for extra groceries from the Regimental funds, etc.

9. He acts as Works Officer, keeping in close touch with the R.E.

10. He is in general charge of the Regimental workshops.

11. He is responsible for organising an efficient system of salvage within the Battalion.

The Commanding Officer.

1. Although the Commanding Officer is responsible for everybody and everything in his Battalion, he is primarily responsible for—
    (a) Fighting efficiency,
    (b) Training,
    (c) Discipline
        in the Battalion.

2. It is his duty to see all drafts on arrival, and to talk to them on the history and reputation of the Regiment. He will explain to them their responsibilities, pointing out especially the difference that exists between irregularities committed at home and those committed with the Expeditionary Force on active service in France.

3. It is his duty to see all Officers, whatever their rank, on joining the Battalion.

4. The Commanding Officer will write to, and, if possible, see, the relations of all Officers killed, wounded, or missing.

Similarly he will write to the relatives of Warrant Officers, senior non-commissioned officers, and any particularly gallant non-commissioned officers or men who are killed or missing.

5. The Commanding Officer will hold orderly-room daily (Sundays excepted). This duty will not be dele-

gated to another Officer except under exceptional circumstances.

At orderly-room the following duties will be dealt with :—
- (a) Disposal of offences.
- (b) Interview of men released from field punishment.
- (c) Interview of non-commissioned officers for promotion or appointment; also non-commissioned officers and men proceeding for employ, on command, on courses, etc.
- (d) Interview of any Officers or men who wish to see the Commanding Officer.
- (e) Quartermaster's correspondence.
- (f) Adjutant's correspondence.

6. All correspondence intended for higher authority has to be signed by the Commanding Officer personally. When this is not possible, it may be signed by another Officer " ' for ' the Commanding Officer."

7. The Commanding Officer is responsible that the War Diary is written up to date, and initials entries to it daily. In addition, it is his duty to see that a full and detailed record of the Battalion is kept, in order that it may later on form the basis for the historical records of the Battalion.

8. The Commanding Officer is responsible that the various accounts in the Battalion are audited from time to time—if possible, once a quarter—as laid down in King's Regulations.

EXPERTS.

The Transport Officer and Transport Sergeant.

1. He is responsible for the whole discipline and interior economy of his command, including pay.

2. He is responsible for the condition of the animals and vehicles.

Note. A chaff-cutter and a portable forge are essential for this purpose.

3. He must constantly inspect and supervise the shoeing.

4. He should be present at two feeds daily, and either he or his Sergeant must be present at all times. Feeds should be mixed behind the animals and all fed together by whistle.

5. He is responsible for the proper conduct of watering, which must be done as a parade before feeding.

6. He must see that every wagon and cart is provided with its proper complement of tools, and that grease-boxes are full.

7. He inspects the harness and pack saddlery, and sees that all is systematically arranged, ready for immediate use.

8. He is responsible for the drill, mounted and dismounted, of his unit; for their horsemanship and driving abilities.

9. He inspects the grooming of the animals after Morning Stables.

10. Officers' grooms are under the Transport Officer for discipline.

11. On the march he orders " Dismount " at every halt of five minutes and upwards, when all drivers, must inspect their harness. At long halts all girths should be loosened and saddles eased.

12. He must see that no man ever rides in the wagons.

13. Either he or the Quartermaster will always report to the Commanding Officer on bringing rations up to the trenches.

14. He is responsible for the allotments of loads.

15. He will see that all brakesmen are present.

16. He inspects the arms of the transport daily.

17. He keeps—
    (a) A transport book, giving details of all animals in his charge and casualties affecting them.
    (b) A book showing all harness, stores, etc., in his charge.
    (c) A duty roster book, both as regards men and animals.
18. Detail all animals and teams for duty.
19. He is responsible that the Battalion reserve S.A.A. and bombs is always correct (in reserve at second echelon).

The Medical Officer (R.A.M.C., attached).

1. He must regard himself as an Officer of the Battalion.
2. He is responsible to the Commanding Officer for the health of the Battalion.
3. He will inform the Officer Commanding Battalion of all orders received from the A.D.M.S.
4. He controls and constantly inspects the sanitary arrangements of the Battalion, including incinerators, refuse pits or bins, and latrines.
5. He attends the bathing of the Companies, and properly administers these parades. The chiropodist and barbers also attend. He assists the Second-in-Command in creating a good system of baths whenever possible.
6. He assists in the instruction in gas duties of all ranks and for the upkeep of vermoral sprayers and flappers.
7. He is responsible to the Commanding Officer that all hygienic measures are taken to prevent sore feet and trench feet.
8. When possible, he visits the trenches daily, and takes measures to alleviate the evils resulting from exposure.
9. He must make himself acquainted with the characteristics and idiosyncracies of all ranks,

10. He is responsible for the training of stretcher-bearers and sanitary men. These can be interchangeable. At least 32 should be available.

11. In conjunction with the Quartermaster, he is responsible for making conditions comfortable for the sick and wounded whilst in his charge, i.e., provision of Oxo, hot tea, spirits, etc.

12. On the march he will ride in rear of the Battalion, and be able at any time to acquaint the Commanding Officer of the numbers of men who have fallen out on the line of march and the reasons, etc., why they have fallen out.

The Signalling Officer and Signalling Sergeant.

1. He is responsible for the training and efficiency of the signallers at Headquarters and with the Companies.

2. He forms classes when out of the line, and is responsible, in conjunction with the Divisional and Brigade Signalling Officer, for arranging for tests.

3. He takes over signals in the line before the Battalion enters the trenches, and must be thoroughly acquainted with the system, of which he must have a plan.

4. He arranges for communication by telephone, visual, and runners by night and day.

5. He is responsible that the equipment is complete and serviceable, including bicycles, indenting on the Quartermaster when necessary.

6. He has access to the Signallers' File, which is kept at Battalion Headquarters, and must keep himself fully acquainted with all correspondence relating thereto.

7. He is responsible that all offices have their proper complement of signallers, are gas proof, and have sufficient message forms, also that an in and out message register is kept.

8. He will keep touch with the Brigade, and see that touch is obtained on both flanks.

9. He should, if at Battalion Headquarters, assist and learn the Adjutant's work.

The Lewis Gun Officer.

1. He is responsible for the constant training of Lewis gunners, and that all detachments are correct and up to strength.

2. He advises Officers Commanding Companies and the Commanding Officer as to the tactical handling and dispositions of the guns.

3. He trains classes whenever possible out of the trenches.

4. He sees that all items of equipment, carts, etc., are complete and in good order, and that a supply of spare parts is available.

5. He is responsible that ranges are taken and range carts are available for each gun.

6. He is responsible for drawing up and issuing " Standing Orders " for Lewis gunners, and that each team is in possession of a copy, and is thoroughly conversant with them.

7. Prior to the Battalion going into the line he will go on ahead and thoroughly investigate the system in force and arrange details for relief.

8. He controls supply of ammunition in action, and takes charge of and fights any reserve guns given him by his Commanding Officer.

9. He visits gun detachments constantly, and advises Officers Commanding Companies as to work to be performed and stores required.

10. He assists the Adjutant and acquires a knowledge of his duties.

11. He keeps in touch with the Brigade Machine Gun Company.

12. He has access to the Lewis Gun File, which is kept at Battalion Headquarters, and must keep himself fully acquainted with all correspondence relating thereto.

13. He erects and manages rifle batteries, etc., and is responsible that full particulars of objectives, angles, etc., are clearly painted on a board.

The Bombing Officer and Bombing Sergeant.

1. He advises the Commanding Officer and Officers Commanding Companies as to the handling of bombers.

2. He takes over and organises the system of supply before entering a new line.

3. He keeps in touch with the Brigade Bombing Officer, if there is one.

4. He tests and helps to instruct all Company bombers when out of the line, if possible with live grenades.

5. He is responsible for the erection of rifle grenade batteries, catapult bombs, etc.

6. He has access to the Bombing File, which is kept at Battalion Headquarters, and must keep himself fully acquainted with all correspondence relating thereto.

The Intelligence Officer and Sergeant.

1. This Officer is responsible for information; he acts as eyes to the Commanding Officer, and keeps him informed of all changes and movement.

2. He maintains the closest liaison with F.O.Os.

3. He trains his scouts and snipers in all their duties, and also assists Officers Commanding Companies with the training of their scouts and snipers.

4. He assists in the preparation of the Battalion Intelligence Report.

5. He co-ordinates his work with the Battalions on his flanks.

6. He is responsible for the condition and testing of telescopic rifles, telescopes, etc. He should be an expert in the use of the Marindin Range Finder.

GENERAL REMARKS.
Officers.

1. Every Officer must learn the history of his Regiment and endeavour to make history for it. He must inspire his men with the desire to emulate the deeds of their predecessors.
2. Officers must be careful as to the smartness and correctness of their dress. Spurs are only worn dismounted by Field Officers and Adjutants.
3. Gambling is prohibited.
4. Standing drinks in mess is not allowed.
5. Practical joking leads to trouble, and is therefore forbidden.
6. Officers unable to perform their duties through sickness must report at once to their Officer Commanding Company, and the Adjutant must be informed.
7. Officers must be present when the Commanding Officer or Second-in-Command inspects a unit under their command.
8. An Officer may not change duty with another without permission of the Adjutant.
9. Officers must consider duty first, amusement after; they must obtain a thorough knowledge of all their duties if they wish to command the respect and confidence of their men.
10. An Officer, by putting his signature to a paper, renders himself responsible for the correctness of facts or figures stated in that paper.
11. Only the Officer ordering a parade can give leave from it.
12. Officers must be acquainted with all orders; absence on leave or sickness is no excuse for ignorance of orders.

13. All Officers joining or returning from leave of absence, or from command, must report personally to the Commanding Officer.

14. Officers must invariably check or take notice of any slackness or improper behaviour on the part of officers or of soldiers, either of their own or other Regiments, whenever met with.

15. Officers may not leave the Battalion area without leave.

16. All Officers must pull together and support their Commanding Officer at all times and in all places.

17. An Officer who misses a duty by inadvertence should at once report the fact personally to his superior or the Adjutant, if it is a Battalion duty.

18. An Officer, except the Second-in-Command, who wishes to speak to the Commanding Officer, should first ask the Adjutant and explain to him the circumstances shortly.

19. Officers should be courteous at all times to all ranks, and must return salutes in a soldierly manner.

Non-Commissioned Officers.

1. Non-commissioned officers must not walk out with private soldiers, or associate with them in a familiar way. Their friends must be non-commissioned officers.

2. A non-commissioned officer returning from leave of absence or command should report himself to the Adjutant or the Regimental Quartermaster.

3. Non-commissioned officers must never lend to or borrow money from private soldiers.

4. Sergeants must not enter the men's canteen except on duty. (N.B.—If possible, a place should be arranged for non-commissioned officers, and if no canteen is available, an estaminet should be reserved for them.)

5. Non-commissioned officers must never use harsh or intemperate, and, more particularly, obscene, language to the men.

6. Non-commissioned officers must back up their officers always, and pull together for the honour of their Regiment.

7. In walking out, non-commissioned officers must give an example of dress and smartness. Sergeants wear belt and side-arms; other ranks belt only.

8. They must be examples at all times to their men, and endeavour constantly to increase their military knowledge.

Private Soldiers.

1. Every soldier must remember that he may by his individual bearing and actions either enhance or injure the reputation of his Regiment.

2. By good behaviour and civility to strangers, cleanliness and smartness in dress and turn-out and drill, gallantry and devotion in the field, he increases the reputation of his Regiment, he increases the respect for the Army, and creates self-respect in himself.

3. *Instant obedience is the root of discipline.* A command must be obeyed cheerfully and quickly, whether given by a Colonel or a lance-corporal.

4. Any soldier wishing to speak to an Officer must be accompanied by a non-commissioned officer. If the soldier then wishes to speak to the Officer on a private matter, the non-commissioned officer can, for the time, fall out.

5. Employed men must show by their smartness that they are worthy of their employment.

6. Dress in walking out must be carefully studied, and belts must always be worn.

7. Soldiers on guard must remember that it is often from them only that a Regiment may be judged.

8. Every soldier must think he belongs to the best section in the best Platoon, Company, Battalion and Regiment in the Army.

9. Every soldier will address a warrant officer (including Classes I. and II.) in the same manner as when addressing a Commissioned Officer, but they will not salute.

Guard Duties.

1. The Commander of a guard will make himself thoroughly acquainted with the orders of his guards and sentries. The orders of the guard will be read to them before the guard dismisses and those of sentries on posting. (*Note.*—Orders for a guard must invariably be in writing.)

2. He or his Second-in-Command will inspect all reliefs of sentries before going on duty and on return.

3. Clothing and accoutrements are not to be taken off except for purposes of cleaning and washing; only one-third may remove them at a time.

4. Guards will turn out at Rouse, Retreat and Tattoo and Fire Alarm sounding.

5. Commanders of guards must not leave their guards except on duty, nor will they allow any member of their guard to do so.

6. Soldiers in arrest will be searched, and unauthorised articles taken from them. The boots of drunken soldiers will be removed.

7. If violent, soldiers may be handcuffed, but if so, they must be visited every hour.

8. If doubt exists as to a soldier's drunkenness, the Regimental Sergeant-Major will be summoned. If doubt still exists, the Medical Officer will be summoned.

9. Non-commissioned officers must be careful to avoid personal contact with violent or drunken soldiers.

10. Sentries will present arms to Field Officers and ranks above; they will slope or shoulder to other ranks and tap the small or sling of the rifle. After Retreat they will stand to attention.

11. Guards turn out and present arms to all armed corps, to all General Officers, and Battalion guards once by day to the Officer Commanding Battalion.

12. Guards turn out, but do not present arms, to all armed parties.

13. Between Retreat and Rouse guards will not turn out except to Grand and Visiting Rounds; to the former they present arms.

14. Guards, on dismounting, will be marched to their Battalion parade ground, and will be dismissed *by an Officer* after they have been inspected.

15. Only a third of a guard may be absent for any purpose at the same time.

RATION STATE 1st Bn THE BUFFS 10.3.17

Distribution	Ration Strength	Bread	Meat	Bacon	Milk	Tea	Sugar	Rum	Cheese	Jam	Pork & Beans	Candles	Coal	Coke	Hay	Oats	Signature
Bn H.d Q.rs																	
Adm																	
Officers																	
Officers A																	
A. Coy																	
Officers																	
B. Coy																	
Officers																	
C. Coy																	
Officers																	
D. Coy																	
Officers																	
TRANSPORT Detachment Fact. A																	
Dump F																	
ISSUED																	
IN HAND																	
RECEIVED																	Lieut & Q.r 1st Buffs

Trench Roster No 1. Platoon B. Coy. 1st BUFFS 10.3.17

Names	Noon 12	1	2	3	4	5	6	7	8	9	10	11	12	1	2	3	4	5	6	7	8	9	10	11	Remarks
Pte HORNE	S		W	W	S				W	W	W	R	R	R	R	R	R			S					No 1 SP
PLUMER		S	W	W	W	S			W	W	W	R	R	R	R	R	R		S					S	work on post 8pm-6pm
ALLANBY			S	W	W				W	W	W	R	R	R	R	R	R	S						S	
RAWLINSON			W	S	W				W	W	W	R	R	R	R	R	S						S		
GOUGH	R	R	R	R	R			LP	LP	LP	LP	LP	LP	LP	R	R				W	W	W	W		Listening Post
HOLLAND	R		R	R	R			LP	LP	LP	LP	LP	LP	LP	LP	R	R				W	W	W	W	under Cpl BOLS
JACOBS	R		R	R	R			LP	LP	LP	LP	LP	LP	LP	LP	R	R				W	W	W	W	Teas after
PULTENEY	R		R	R	R			LP	LP	LP	LP	LP	LP	LP	LP-R	R					W	W	W	W	STAND DOWN
WOOLCOMBE	R		R	R	R		S		W	S	W	W	S		S						R	R	W	W	
FANSHAWE	R		R	R	R			W	S	W	W	S		S							R	R	W	W	Work on post
HALDANE	R		R	R	R		S	W	W	S	W			S		S					R	R	W	W	8-12 mn
SNOW	R		R	R	R		S	W	W	S	W		S			S					R	R	W	W	
WESTON	R		R	R	R		.	S	W	W	S			S			S				R	R	W	W	
GORDON	R		R	R	R	STAND TO		S	W	W	S			S			S	STAND TO			R	R	W	W	
MORLAND		DINNER	R	R	R	TEAS		P	P	P	P	P	R	R	R	R	STAND	BREAKFAST	W	W	W	W			Patrol under
HAKING			R	R	R		STAND	P	P	P	P	P	R	R	R	R			W	W	W	W	W		Lieut SMITH
CONGREVE	R		R	R	R		TO	P	P	P	P	P	R	R	R	R			W	W	W	W			
CAVAN			R	R	R			R	R	R	R	R	P	P	P	P			W	W	W	W			Patrol under
QUEENS			R	R	R			R	R	R	R	R	P	P	P	P			W	W	W	W			Cpl MALCOMB
FERGUSSON			R	R	R			R	R	R	R	R	P	P	P	P			W	W	W	W			
L.G. Section																									
Pte BENN	S	S	R	R			R	R	S	W	W	W		S								W	W		
BUGG	R		S	S	R			R	R	R	S	W	W	W			S					W	W		
BUTCHER	R		R	R	S	S		R	R	R	W	S	W	W				S				W	W		
BAKER	R		R	R	R		S	R	R	R	W	W	S	W				S	S			W	W		
BROWN	R		R	R	R				S	R	R	W	W	W	S					S	S	W	W		
GOW	R		R	R	R					R	S	R	W	W	W	S						S	S		

Duties 2 hrs Sentry by day, 1 hr by night. when the next for duty must sleep at the gun within reach of the Sentry.

N.C.O's Duties & Platoon Hd Q's

Sergt Haig   Company Duty.   12 Noon - 6 p.m.   12 mn - 6 am

L/Cpl Horrington. No 4. Section (L.G) Platoon Duty 12. mn - 6 am & when section working

Cpl Malcomb   No 3 Section   ———"———   12 mn - 6pm & takes 2nd patrol

L/Cpl Montgomery No 2 Section ———"———   6 pm 12mn 6am 12 Noon

Cpl Bols   No 1 section (Bombers) Listening Post & when section working.

Pte Jones. servant to Lt Smith. work in platoon commanders Dug-out. 8-12 noon. 8-12 mn

" Brown. Platoon Cook.   build small oven in own time

" Smith - Sanitaryman. Dig new refuse pit, collect & clean all scattered ammunition & hand in to Coy Sgt Major

N.B. Half Rum Ration will be issued by me at Breakfast & half at Teas.

Water & Rations are brought up by Support Coy.

Sd J.A.Smith.   Lieut
10/3/17   O.C. No.1. Platoon

Trench Roster.

1. The roster (p. 373) for trench duties is given as an example of one that can be kept by every Platoon Commander in A.B. 152. It shows a platoon finding two sentry posts (one found by Lewis Gunners), a listening post (in good weather), and two reconnoitring patrols.

2. Unless a roster is kept it is impossible to see, either, that the men do the proper amount of work, or that they are not asked to do too much.

3. After the roster is completed, the roster can be restarted either from the bottom or section duties changed about, so that all duties may be apportioned on a fair basis.

4. The work of a front-line platoon cannot be very ambitious, but a lot can be done by sound allotment of tasks. New constructive work can be done by platoons sent up from the supporting company, who are in this case also bringing up rations, water, R.E. material, etc. If Companies relieve each other, and work together on the same system, it leads to greatly increased efficiency.

PART III.
INTERIOR ECONOMY.

LECTURE by
LIEUTENANT AND QUARTERMASTER H. NAYLOR, EAST LANCASHIRE REGIMENT, ON THE DUTIES OF A QUARTERMASTER TO A BATTALION IN FRANCE.

Delivered 12th December, 1916.

The Quartermaster must first realise what an important factor he is in the comfort, welfare, well-being, and consequently in no small degree, in the efficiency of his Regiment. To be successful he must have the whole-hearted support of his Commanding Officer. Without the support of his Commanding Officer he can do very little and his Regiment suffers, but with the support of his Commanding Officer he knows he can go " all out "; that any mistake, any error of judgment, etc., provided he makes it in good faith and on behalf of his Regiment, he knows he will come to no harm over it. I suggest that it is not only necessary for the Quartermaster to know that he has the support of his Commanding Officer, but he should be told so. I attach great importance to that point, because a Quartermaster sometimes feels and knows that he has the support of his Commanding Officer, but he has never been told so. On every change of Commanding Officer he should be told to go " all out ": " whatever you do, right or wrong, I am behind you."

The duties of a Quartermaster are pretty clearly laid down. He is responsible to his Colonel—and to his Colonel alone—for rations, clothing, equipment, arms, and billets of his Regiment. He is not in any way or any degree responsible for the supply of ammunition or grenades. I am going into the question of the method of supply. We have Railhead columns, Divisional columns, and Brigade columns. We will assume it is 6 p.m. At 6 o'clock every evening we have a day's rations in hand on the 1st line Transport at the Brigade Supply Column, and we have a day's rations in hand at Railhead. Rations are supplied through Brigade arrangements. The ammunition is supplied direct under Divisional arrangements with the nearest Divisional Ammunition column. The duties of a Quartermaster are what he cares to make them; they vary with every changing situation.

First: To Establish and Maintain Friendly Relations with the Staff.—By that I mean the Ordnance and Army Service Corps. It may be thought that is not necessary. People may say that if you indent for a thing and are entitled to it you will get it, and if not you won't get it, but I consider it to be a necessary duty. Then he must pay frequent visits to his Brigade Headquarters and keep in constant touch with his Staff Captain, who, after all, has the most to do with him. In our Division we have a Staff who are all "out to help." The Assistant-Quartermaster-General is all out to help us, and where in peace-time various references had to be made through the ordinary routine of the Orderly Room, we can now go to Brigade Headquarters and make our enquiries direct. We have frequent conferences which are very helpful. Various points are raised, and we confer on them, and we come to certain decisions; but every Quartermaster should, before he goes to these Conferences, see his Commanding Officer and ask him if he has any points he would like to raise; but it is no good going to these Conferences unless he knows exactly what he is talking about.

The next point is the **Organisation of the Quartermaster's Staff.**—A great deal depends on this point. It must be properly organised. He must have a system; must encourage initiative, and give his Staff a free hand, but the moment a member of his Staff proves himself unfitted or unworthy he must report to his Company Commander that night for duty with his Company. The Quartermaster's work should go on as well in his absence as when he is there. The Quartermaster must make himself useful outside his own sphere; he must co-operate with his Company and Platoon Commanders, and I know from experience that they are very grateful for any help or advice you can give them. The Quartermaster should be looked upon as a friend, and not, as sometimes is the case, as one who must be approached with fear and trembling. He must work with the Platoon Commanders, and must not be in a water-tight compartment; he must be all out to help. He is responsible for the training of the Company Quartermaster-Sergeant, and on each occasion as casualty arises he must train a fresh one. If necessary he must be prepared to accept anyone, and if he cannot by help, patience, tact, and good teaching, make a good Company Quartermaster-Sergeant, he is not a good Quartermaster himself. He must not go in for red tape. The Quartermaster frequently does. . . . He must be conversant with the conditions under which the men live in the front line Theoretically the Quartermaster's duties cease with the 1st line Transport; he has no official duty which takes him beyond there, but in my opinion he must be conversant with what men are doing in the front line, and to do that he must visit the front line. From information he gains there—his own powers of observation will help him—he can form an opinion as to what can be done; whether it is possible to do cooking on the line, and 101 things besides. He must visit the line by day as well as by night; things appear very different by day to what they would by night. The Quartermaster should see his Commanding Officer every 24 hours; many things to talk about. He should see his Company Commanders at least twice during one turn of the trenches; he can do more in half an hour with them than he could with all the memos. they can send him or he could send them.

A Company Quartermaster-Sergeant must report to his Company Commander every night. A system was instituted by the present Commandant in my Regiment, and is now almost universal. Everything going up to a Company, whether rations, or whatever it is, must be enumerated in duplicate, and be checked and signed by the Quartermaster and receipted by the Company Commander.

Relief Nights.—I am dealing with them under two headings: First, *From Trenches*: Men must know, and they must look forward to coming back, as it were, to a warm, bright billet. Certainly it is possible to give them a fire every time they come back; there should be a blazing fire, rum, tea; no effort should be spared to give those men a warm time; you cannot do too much for them. Again, while in rest billets we find working parties; no working parties should ever return to quarters unless they are sure of a meal or a hot drink. In this connection I would go into the question of Officers. Rightly we think of the men first, but it is quite a small thing to remember that Officers should be considered. Have a small fire in each Officer's billet. Secondly, Relief Night *To Trenches* : A most important night, and although we have been fitting up through the week a hundred and one things have to be done at the last moment, and the Quartermaster should see the Company Commander during the day, and certainly during the last two or three hours as to any points which might want attention. Several of the Subalterns have probably used their rounds in seeing how many Bass bottles they can shoot down for practice, and sometimes they forget to replace their ammunition. In my Regiment at present the Company Commanders are all Second-Lieutenants, and, although doing well, they may forget certain details, and without interfering in the least with the management of the Company you can often fill in the gap.

Co-operation with the Medical Officer.—A very important point; requires great attention both in and out of the trenches. I am assuming that the Quartermaster goes up every night, as he should do. Some people say it is not necessary for two Officers to go up together and risk both being knocked out; but I submit that the Quartermaster does not finish his duties by placing rations on board and then saying "Goodnight"; his duty does not end until they have moved down to the line. I submit that every night the Quartermaster should see the Medical Officer and talk over what has to be done. It may happen that he wants certain things which he can supply. In our own Battalion last winter we kept 150 shirts and 250 pairs of socks up at the Dressing Station, and any man coming in ill or wet could have a change.

Regimental Hospital.—This has only recently been started, and is very successful. The Medical Officer has been able to keep men by sending them down to the Hospital, where they would otherwise be sent to the Field Ambulance and then be evacuated.

Regimental Workshops.—If these workshops are properly organised, they are very useful in a hundred and one ways, particularly the shoemaker's shop, when it is very difficult to get new boots; but at the same time have regard to the question of economy, which I shall deal with later on. Keep your shoemakers' shops properly going, and going strong, and keep a record of your work, and you can get a good deal of work done. It is not wise to let your shoemaker's establishment run below four men in addition to the Sergeant-Shoemaker; if it should run below this you should take steps to apply for men from another Regiment. Four men and the Sergeant can turn out 50 boots in a day, i.e., 25 pairs.

Examination of Arms.—A thing which is sometimes overlooked, but it should be a fixed principle that every time a Battalion goes up the line, whether for close support or for rest, every rifle should be examined, and you cannot attach too much importance to this point. It often happens that the men's rifles are out of order and they do not know it. Some Regiments have not got an Armourer. We pool the Armourers in our Division, but every Regiment has an Armourer, whether he is with a Divisional Armoury or not, and his services are always available. The Quartermaster should make a point of seeing that the rifles are overhauled on the first available opportunity.

Cleaning of Ammunition.—This is very important, and each inspection should show that not only is the man in possession of the necessary number of rounds, but that *each round* is absolutely *clean* and fit for use. As the men are often in possession of their ammunition for quite a long time, it often happens that it gets dusty or rusty, and consequently unfit for use. The Quartermaster will issue paraffin oil for this purpose.

Co-operation with Transport Officer.—It frequently happens that the Transport Officer has just joined up for the War. Sometimes—more or less latterly—he has not the faintest idea of discipline or organisation; he is out to help the Regiment, but he has been no time with the Regiment; he is merely " doing his bit." It is up to the Quartermaster to give him a friendly eye and to advise him, and it is to his interest to do so. I can tell you of one Regiment where this want of harmony existed, where if the Quartermaster wanted to do anything with the Transport Officer it had to go Officially through the Adjutant, although he was perhaps billeted within a few yards of him. The Quartermaster should make himself conversant with everything connected with the transport, and to do that he need not know anything about horses. He should go in for co-operation with Quartermasters of other units. He should remember that his job does not begin and end with the duties to his own Regiment. They should co-operate with one another and help one another, but if you meet a " number-oner " (a man all out for himself) drop him.

Reception of Reinforcements.—Two kinds, the old hands and the fresh arrivals. It is just as well when they arrive at the first line, and before you send them on, to have a talk with them; but before you talk to them it is as well to separate them. . . . You have the opportunity of giving them advice; you can talk about the Corps; about the splendid traditions of the Regiment, and appeal to them to play the game. The question of talking to the men on *esprit de corps* is very difficult. Once we got a draft of 300 men of the North Staffordshire Regiment, several of whom had served in Gallipoli. I talked to the other 250; told them about the Regiment. The men had already been at home nine months, and had been frequently told, and rightly so, that they were the finest Regiment going. Later on the Colonel saw them, and, being a big draft, the Divisional Commander also saw them, and they were simply left to decide who was the biggest liar of the three. In my own Battalion we have a system, which was instituted by the Commandant, of giving the men on a printed slip an address by General Prowse, and every private soldier is in possession of his Trench Orders. At this time of the year it is very necessary to talk about frostbite and trench feet, but don't waste time on the old hands; they know more about it than you do, and so far as frostbite is concerned they now know how to produce it.

Frostbite and Trench Feet.—They may be considered by some as not one of the departments of the Quartermaster, but it is. The Commander-in-Chief recently sent out a memo. that he considered the question of frostbite or trench feet was due to neglect of discipline, as well as faulty interior economy, and that he intended to hold Officers personally responsible. . . . If the Quartermaster does not do all he can to prevent frostbite he must take responsibility; he must do all that is humanly possible. He must make sure that a constant and sufficient supply of whale oil is supplied. It can be got, and must be sent up, and he must ask when he visits the line whether they want any more, or things like that. Here again co-operation with the Medical Officer comes in. By keeping in touch with the Medical Officer and Company Commanders, by supplying, and making sure that he is in a position to supply, what is wanted, he is doing all he can. It is only a question of hours; delay is fatal. One Regiment had 200 cases within a week. In my own Regiment we did not have one case last winter, and up till 10 days ago no case this winter. We are up against the problem of some men who are not only not anxious to avoid it, but who actually wish to get it. We do not allow men to wear putties in the trenches, and we are to be allowed 12 pairs of socks per man and two pairs of boots to prevent trench feet. (The Lecturer explained, in reply to questions at this point, that the socks would probably be six pairs Regimental and six pairs reserve.)

Economy.—It has become necessary to issue a very drastic order. Up to a year ago it was simply appalling the waste which went on, and it is now merely colossal. It is the duty of the Quartermaster to let the Commanding Officer know at once which Company is showing evidence of waste. He must have no sentiment about it. If he sees evidence of neglect or waste in any Company it is up to him to at once tell his Colonel. We must for ever get rid of that pernicious idea that *" There is more where that came from."* The need for economy is very real and very necessary, and

Platoon Commanders, if they have close support and co-operation with the Quartermaster, can help to a large degree to cut down this enormous waste. It is to be very much regretted that there is no real inducement to economise in the question of rations. The contract price of the preserved beef is about 1s. 3d. per tin. . . . There is no Officer present here who can deny that he has seen a great deal of waste going on in bully beef. . . . Under the head of Economy comes the issue of clothing. At the commencement of the War they decided to do away with the kit allowance and to provide free issues. It would pay the Government to bring into use again the pre-War conditions; if, instead of the 2d. a day, they would give the men 6d. per day kit allowance, the Government would save many thousands of pounds in every Division. The waste of ammunition is another very serious item. It is not so bad as it was, but it can only be prevented by a frequent and constant checking of ammunition. There is a difference between waste and saving. We are constantly being exhorted to save and to prevent waste, but there is no inducement to save in the ration line, and you cannot save. In fact, it takes you all your time to get what you want for your "Relief Night," but the Quartermaster is able to do a great deal to prevent waste. The orders for clothing to replace unserviceable articles are usually not worth the paper they are written on. It is a good plan every time the men return from the rest billet for the Quartermaster to inspect every Company, and decide what is serviceable and what is not. He is better able to judge from his experience and he knows how far he can go, and what his resources are. . . .
The system of making men pay is very successful. We make men pay for things about which they cannot satisfy their Company Commander, and he alone decides whether he should pay or not if he loses a thing. Recently we have got another system introduced: we

get 200 iron rations per fortnight to turn over. If you issue them to the Commanders, say 50 each, they are simply used up, but if they are issued in the evening after the evening meal the Company Commander is able to give every man from whom an old one was taken a fresh iron ration. Waste has an effect on the units, especially when the troops are on the move. Equipment is difficult to replace and very often impossible. Where Battalions show the greatest evidence of waste, there is want of discipline and interior economy.

Bathing.—This is usually done by Divisions, but as Divisions are moving about now, they seldom have time to carry out bathing properly; but every Quartermaster should have a scheme cut and dried whilst waiting for the Division Baths to open, and, anticipating that they will not open, make arrangements whereby the men have a bath every week.

Laundry.—Whilst Divisions staying in one sector may have a laundry working successfully, it often happens when moving that the Divisions cannot establish a laundry, or—as recently happened—the ladies of the laundry at Amiens went on strike; they wanted higher pay, and, of course, we could not give it. Again, the Quartermaster should have his scheme ready. It is possible to give every man a bath and fresh clothing once a week, and all he wants is a staff of about eight or nine old soldiers not in the line.

Institutes.—It should be possible for a man to purchase everything he wants in the front line that he could purchase while at rest. This is really the job of the President Regimental Institutes, but as he is often up at the Headquarters he must rely upon the one person who can help him, and that is the Quartermaster. By keeping in touch with the men, and ascertaining what they most require, he can keep his show going in the front line. That, if I may say so, depends very largely on the Commanding Officer. (The Lecturer made reference to the price of Woodbine Cigarettes, and said that a case had been referred to the Commander-in-Chief by the Commanding Officer of the 4th King's Own Regiment, as the result of which the price was reduced from 1d. per packet to two packets for 1½d.)

Trench Stores.—This is really a Staff Captain's job, but it often happens that the trench stores are nobody's chickens. You simply take over the amount, so many so-and-so; no one cares; many things unserviceable. I submit that if the Quartermaster would walk round and see things and then talk over the matter with the Staff Captain, he would remedy it.

Continuity of Work.—It is necessary that Quartermasters of various units should have continuity of work in rest billets. If you work together with harmony—you are all out to make your Brigade comfortable—what one Quartermaster has started another one should continue with a view to making the billets as comfortable as possible.

Comforts.—The Quartermaster is charged with the fair and equitable distribution of comforts, and there should be a permanent record kept of what arrives, what number, and from whom. His great task is to see that they are acknowledged by the Commanding Officer. The Regiment where the Commanding Officer acknowledges the gifts—and acknowledges them quickly—generally gets a greater number than those Regiments where the Commanding Officer does not acknowledge the gifts.

Deceased and Wounded Officers' Kits.—I cannot understand how, with the regulations now in force and the means at our disposal, any Officers' kits can go astray. Cox & Co. have issued very large sacks, printed outside **"Cox & Co."** The deceased or wounded Officer's kit is brought into the store—in some cases it is there already—and then listed. Some units do not trouble about an inventory, but I submit that the Quartermaster should make a list in quadruplicate; one should be sent with the Memo. to the person to whom it is being sent; one with the kit; the third copy for the President of the Committee of Adjustment, and the fourth copy should be kept as a record. The kit is then placed in the bag and sealed. Every unit has a stamp to seal their Officers' kits with. It is then handed over to the Supply Officer, who has to hand it over to the Railhead, who will not accept any kit unless sealed every two inches. The most important things in the kit are the field glasses and revolver, and if the Quartermaster does not get these articles it is up to him to notify the Adjutant that the field glasses and revolver of any Officer becoming a casualty are not forthcoming.

CHAPTER XV.

LECTURE
by
MAJOR-GENERAL C. H. HARRINGTON, C.B., D.S.O., General Staff, Second Army,
on
THE RELATIONS OF THE STAFF TO COMMANDING OFFICERS, AND VICE VERSA, THAT OF COMMANDING OFFICERS TO THE STAFF.

Delivered 13th February, 1917.

I need not say how glad I feel at being asked to come and see this School of Instruction. For a long time I have wanted to see it, and I knew that when I came I should be impressed, as I have been to-day, with what I have seen.

I am going to speak to you about what many of us think rather a difficult subject, viz., the relationship between the Staff and the Regimental Officer. It is a subject in which I am very interested, and I know there is room for a great improvement, and I am going to tell you how I think that improvement can be brought about.

I am not going to burden you in any way with details about the duties of Staff Officers. . . . I will explain to you presently some of the reasons which have caused a gap between the Staff and the Regimental Officer, chiefly owing to the great number of what are called untrained officers in this enormous army. This gap has got to be closed, and it can only be closed by the co-operation of both sides, Regimental and Staff Officers, and that is why I have come to ask you, who form a great number of Regimental Officers, for your assistance.

This School forms a big reserve, and it is a reserve

we badly want. We want you out there to draw from as future commanding officers. I can only talk to you about this subject from my own personal point of view. I think I know to a great extent the difficulties from the point of view both as a Regimental and Staff Officer. When this war broke out I was commanding a company in Talavera Barracks, Aldershot, and so I know the difficulties from a Battalion point of view. Since then I have held a number of Staff appointments, and I know the difficulties from the Staff point of view. In order to close this gap I have adopted two methods. (a) I assembled the whole of the Staff Officers in the Second Army and spoke to them very strongly on certain points in order to try and improve matters from the Staff point of view; and (b) I have also, during the last few months, held conferences at the Second Army Headquarters of twelve Infantry Commanding Officers a week. We have them there for a week at a time and show them all we know of the army and the instruction and training which goes on in such an army. We are also able to talk freely about their difficulties. Commanding Officers are hampered by certain things which they feel very acutely, and possibly very often they do not understand the reason for those difficulties. We have to a great extent been able to explain that. So I have had these talks with Commanding Officers, and I know pretty well their point of view, and the object I have in talking to you is to try and put both points of view before you. It is quite certain that, if I can do that, we shall get some improvement. There are undoubtedly a lot of difficulties on both sides, and I think the principal difficulties may be summarised as follows :— (i) Want of training. (ii) Want of closer relations between the Staff and the Regimental Officer. They ought to know each other as friends, and that in many cases is not so at present. That is really the crux of the whole matter. And (iii) a closer study of human nature. Another difficulty is the fact that there is far too much writing in the Army, and I will presently put forward a proposal which I think can reduce it.

Another evil is that Commanding Officers are not told enough. They are very big men; they command a thousand men, a position we all respect, and holding that position they should be told a great deal more than is usually the case. I don't refer to secret things or plans, but I mean all the general operations and things which happen. We want to broaden out the Commanding Officer's necessarily confined horizon. There is sometimes a failure on the part of the Staff to realise the Regimental Officer's position, and the result is that all bad work re-acts directly on the troops themselves. They are the people who suffer from bad Staff work. I am not here to make excuses for the Staff. We have got our troubles, and it is our business to settle them; but I am quite certain that if both sides realise and explain each other's difficulties we can improve things. It is necessary to realise what the size of the army in France is, and that is why I have brought you down this map (The lecturer here explained the enormous growth of the Army in men and personnel.)

In the army I am connected with I never lose an opportunity, when R.E. material is short, of explaining and rubbing in how necessary it is that the troops down South should have the preference, for the conditions down there are much harder than they are up North, and that explains to Commanding Officers a very good reason why they are not able at times to get all they require.

The Lecturer then referred to the question of transport, and explained that in order to compete with the enormous difficulties the management of transport had been handed over to one man, who had taken over the railways, light railways, docks, roads, etc., and everything up as far as the motor lorries can go. He is helped by the ablest assistants, and all the restrictions in this country as to increased fares, fewer trains, etc., have been introduced so that whatever is saved may go to France. Every day the French railways which had got broken down are being gradually replaced by British railway stock. In about six weeks or a couple of months we shall, no doubt, feel the enormous benefit from this new organisation.

I now come to difficulties of the Staff. At first a corps had as a Staff one Brigadier-General, General Staff; a first grade General Staff Officer, a second grade General Staff Officer, and a third grade General Staff Officer. At the present moment a corps has exactly one fully qualified Staff Officer, and an army has two. Everything else has had to be improvised since the war started, which, of course, is no mean achievement.

I don't say that our training as Staff Officers was good, but it was constantly rubbed in to us that we only existed for one purpose, viz., to help the troops, and that is a lesson which is not easy to rub in to-day to officers who have not had the same initial training. Of course, short courses are held both at home and in France for the training of Staff Officers, but they are not enough. What I am always preaching is that we have a very heavy year in front of us. No one imagines that this army has been put together for nothing. Everything has been done to help troops in their training: musketry, bayonet work, physical training. What I am always asking Staff Officers is, whether we are doing all we can to help troops to reap the benefit of that training, because it must be a point of honour with all Staff Officers that they do not let down the side, and if they are not sufficiently trained, and do not know their duties sufficiently, the troops are bound to suffer. I tell Staff Officers there are two ways of ensuring that they shall not let down their side :—(1) Knowing their own work and doing it, and (2) helping the troops. We should remember we are all Regimental Officers ; we were Regimental Officers first. There is hardly an officer on the Staff now who is not a Regimental Officer. It is very helpful for all Staff Officers to remember that. Another thing to remember is that the Regimental Officer has a harder and rougher time than a Staff Officer. It is the Regimental Officer who feels the pinch when Staff Officers make mistakes. The remedy, or the greater part of it, is to tell the Regimental

Officer more. He is the first person to realise the difficulties, and if you only tell him your difficulties and the reasons, he is the first to appreciate them. The impression I have formed from talking with many Commanding Officers is that in many cases the Staff do not know enough of the actual conditions of the trenches and the trench life, and the Commanding Officers feel that they do not know the Staff sufficiently as friends, and think that the latter come down to criticise.

In my opinion no Staff Officer, whether he belongs to the "G" or the "Q" side, is fit for his position unless he knows the actual condition of the trenches and the troops. Perhaps this failing is brought about by the fault of trench warfare and its monotony. The worse the conditions and the worse the weather, the more must the Staff be there to discuss and help the Regimental Officer, and the more will they be appreciated for doing so. Staff Officers have always got to be full of energy and tact, and be always cheerful. There is no room for anybody who is not cheerful; he had much better be somewhere else.

Now I come to the question of writing. It is perfectly ridiculous the amount of writing that goes on. When I went, some nine months ago, to the Second Army I asked the Army Commander if I could stop at once the writing of all these reports. I know what a nuisance and how inaccurate they are, and how much eyewash was in them. I asked if they would trust me to carry out a plan I adopted in Aldershot, and I would guarantee to send them any information that was wanted. From that time to this a report was sent only once a month. Everything else was obtained by visiting. I adopted that system while I was there. I got every Commanding Officer or Adjutant to keep my name on his desk, and anything which occurred to him during the day that he wanted to ask me about was written down. He knew that I could be found at 8.30 a.m., or again in the evening, and I could then give him an answer; or if he was wrong, could put it right at once.

That enabled me to be out training all the day. I have continued that system ever since. I got the next highest Staff Officer to pursue that principle, and I have asked all Corps and Divisional Commanders and all Staff Officers to try that system. If all Brigade Majors and Staff Captains will go down and talk over things with the Regimental Officers, and hear from them what is required, it will save seventy-five per cent. of the writing in the Army. I know it can be done. I know there are Adjutants who practically never get out of their office. If Regimental Officers are lumbered up with this constant correspondence, they cannot think of their proper business, which is fighting and beating the Boche, and if Staff Officers are lumbered up with the same stuff, they cannot think of their special duties, which is to assist the troops. In my own regiment I never allowed more than one man to be in the office. Very few Staff Officers of to-day have any experience of what is before them, because they have had no experience of moving warfare. It is a very different thing from the problem they have been confronted with up to date. The next time this enormous army moves it won't be a question of the army being exhausted; it will move quickly, but it cannot do this if the Staff work is bad. Almost a different brain is required in a Staff Officer for this moving warfare. No time for drafting and submitting orders to a Senior Staff Officer. If a Staff Officer is told to do a thing, he has got to make his arrangements and do it. If he makes a mistake, the troops suffer, and that is a lesson to put to Staff Officers. Are they doing all they can to fit themselves to accept this responsibility when the time comes? There must be unity. The "G" Staff, "Q" and "A" branch, gunner, sapper, etc., must all be one, and the onus for that must be placed on the "G" branch. That branch has the first information of what is required, and what is going to happen, and the onus is on them to tell other branches, because it is quite impossible for the latter to look after troops unless they know what is required, and the only people to tell them is the "G" branch. If there is anybody on the Staff who throws sand on the wheels of the machine he must go, and if the machine does not work properly there is only one person responsible, and that is the Senior Staff Officer.

Another thing I always impress on Staff Officers is that they often do not realise—and that applies to the Commanding Officers as well—the importance of the Signal Service. Success or failure depends to a very large extent on the Signals. The Signals are a most magnificent branch. There are a great number of people who do not quite realise what the Signals mean. The Staff can also assist you greatly in the organisation of work. There has been throughout an enormous wastage of energy. In the same way relations between Infantry and Engineers are, in many cases, not properly understood. Sometimes the reasons are good; sometimes bad. Nothing has improved more in France than the relations between the Infantry and the Field Artillery. The co-operation between the two branches is now quite first-class, and this must mean an enormous increase in efficiency, and we are trying to get a better feeling between the Infantry and the Heavy Artillery. We are carrying out an interchange of Officers with the Heavy Artillery.

In talking with Commanding Officers I have found that a great deal of the energy which is being put into the formation of Schools has, I am sorry to say, in some cases been wasted. These Schools are the very greatest value to the Army. We have your School here, and the big Army Schools in France, Corps Schools, Divisional School; courses of various kinds to assist Regimental Officers. It is no good getting away from the fact that the Battalions have been very short of officers Commanding Officers have not realised the value of the courses. They have told me openly that they have not selected the officers they would have done if they had known more about the courses. It comes back to what I said before: Commanding Officers have not been told enough. They have sent men who are not the best. The Schools exist simply to help them. In many cases their idea of the Schools is they are an infernal nuisance ; just as they are going into the trenches they get a wire, " Send an officer here and there."

I tell people that in issuing an order it should be issued with consideration. It is a very great help to anybody who issues an order to put themselves in the position of the person who receives it. If you do this, it will very often save stupid orders being issued.

INTELLIGENCE.—Many Commanding Officers have very little idea of what use intelligence is put to, and how valuable often quite little things may be. I have maps which show what has been located, and what deductions can be made from information gained from the front line supplied by observers, Flying Corps pilots, and I have found them intensely interesting. I have also impressed on them the necessity for accuracy in those reports ; you cannot be too careful, when sending in information, about the accuracy of it. If you cannot see things with your own eyes, be quite certain of the eyes of the person who has seen it for you

Another lesson for Commanding Officers and a lesson for the Staff, too, is the necessity for looking after the men ; extra comfort in the Camp ; an extra hut here and there ; extra arrangements for warming, etc.—they all help. People say this cannot be done, but a man of sufficient energy will get it done. The Staff and Regimental Officers can help each other.

Another point which bothers Commanding Officers is, why it should be necessary to use Infantry for making roads, etc.? I can tell you perfectly straight that there is no man who more resents Infantry being taken away from training to work on railways than the Commander-in-Chief himself, and large gangs of labourers are on their way over now to relieve this work. There is a reason for these things. They are not done without thought. Commanding Officers have said to me, " Why is not this done by German prisoners?" Well, it wants a good lot. All the available prisoners are being used. There is a reason for everything, and I impress on

Staff Officers that it is their business to let the Regimental Officers know the reason, so that they are not bothered by these things. By these methods the Staff Officer gains confidence, and when he goes down to help the lower formations he will know whether he is resented or accepted. It is the little things that matter. I think it was Baden-Powell who invented the Boy Scout's badge to remind the boy to do at least one good turn a day. It is the duty of the Staff Officer to help both those above and below ; to think a little ahead, and to have things ready. It makes all the difference if you know the people you are working with. A word with regard to clerks : remember, they are not machines. I am very glad to have a good clerk. Treat them with consideration.

A Staff Officer should make it a point of honour not to have to be told to do a thing twice. Nothing annoys a Commanding Officer more than to ask a fellow to do a thing, and then to find days afterwards that he has not done it. No necessity for it, because if you cannot remember things, put it down in your notebook.

The thing to do is to make a point of driving your work, and not let your work drive you. If you are going to allow yourself to be snowed up with work, you will not get out to visit your troops, and in so doing you are letting your work drive you. You also want to get system in your work ; the whole thing is a matter of organisation and system. Personally I give each Staff Officer a typed list when he joins showing what his duties are in this kind of warfare, and in moving warfare, so that he will not forget them. What we want, of course, here is a body of enthusiasts. You all know the Army Gymnastic Staff. Major Campbell frequently comes out to visit our Armies. They simply breathe enthusiasm into everybody and everything. Another point, do all you can to encourage the men. We cannot do too much for them. In the Second Army we have the South Irish Division next to the Ulster Division. Nothing pleased me more than to know that the South Irish Division has given a Cup for competition in the Ulster Division.

Another point : insist on giving lower formations early warning of what is going to happen. It helps more than we can say if you know a little of what is going to happen. Nothing is so worrying as to think that this has been known by people higher up, and not passed on to lower formations.

When orders are issued they should be stuck to. If they have to be altered, it should be explained to the people who are affected by the alteration, why it has been necessary to do it. I find that a great number of orders that have been issued do not get down to the troops. There must be some system.

Commanding Officers, in many cases, do not know what they are entitled to in the way of stores and how to get them. It is generally the fault of the Quartermaster, but of, course, not in some cases. A good Quartermaster will always know what to get. I found a Commanding Officer only last week who did not know he was entitled to any magnetic compasses, but if the Staff would come down and talk with them they will find these things out.

Another difficulty Commanding Officers have to contend with is the sudden call, often when in reserve, for working parties. These cannot be evaded, but it is up to the Staff to let Commanding Officers know the situation. We hope to get the musketry training on the same lines as the Army Gymnastics. Assistance is also required in teaching the tactical use of the Lewis gun

TO SUMMARISE.—There should be a closer sympathy between the Staff and the Regimental Officer. We want to save writing by visiting, and this applies equally to Administrative Staffs, by talking direct with Commanding Officers and by means of conferences. The system we work on is that the Army Commander is out all day, and so am I. Each of the Staff carries a notebook, and anything we come across in our visits we put down ; also anything anyone asks us to do. At six o'clock every evening we meet, and everything is attended to at once. If Corps, Division, and Brigade Commanders pursue that system, I think that we shall save a lot of writing. You Regimental Officers can help a very great deal. You cannot get away from the fact that in many cases Staff Officers are rather resented by Regimental Officers. It may be in many cases their fault, but not in all. We want to put that by the board; we have got a big job on hand. We send them down to try and make friends with you; we want your help as well. It just occurs to me this moment how Commanding Officers can help. I remember an instance of taking over some trenches from your Commandant in not too pleasant a place. I remember the assistance he rendered to those going in to hold it; he told us what to do; how to hold it, and what was in his mind. That is how outgoing troops can help incoming troops. When you come to this course, it is your Commandant's wish and our wish that we should get you to Army Headquarters, and I hope those coming from the Second Army will meet there so that we can show you what we are showing Commanding Officers, and hear your views of how you think things can be improved from the knowledge you have gained here We only want to know, and to get what is required for the Regimental Officer. It is these Schools which have got to set the standard of thought and training. This is the premier School, the one for Commanding Officers, and then we have the Army Schools for Company Commanders, Platoon Sergeants. Whatever is evolved from lessons of recent fighting and training must be started at these Schools, and it is by going through this course, and the Officers of other Schools going through their courses, that they can be put on the right lines; and when you go from these Schools you are in a position to act as agents to disseminate that information.

CHAPTER XVI.

The following points, which have been compiled by Brigadier-General R. J. Kentish, D.S.O., with the assistance of Lieut.-Colonel J. F. R. Hope, D.S.O., K.R.R.C., may assist Officers who find themselves promoted to the Command of Battalions in France.

A Part II. has been written by Brigadier-General R. J. Kentish, D.S.O., entitled " Some of the things that please a Commanding Officer," but as all the points refer to the Brigadier and his relations with his Commanding Officers, it is not proposed to print them in this book. If, however, any student Officer should be promoted to the Command of a Brigade, a copy of Part II. will be forwarded on application in writing to the Commandant.

PART I.

SOME OF THE THINGS THAT PLEASE AN INFANTRY BRIGADIER,
By a BRIGADIER.

1. A Commanding Officer who has knowledge, and who knows how to impart his knowledge to those under him.

2. A Commanding Officer who salutes and turns out well himself, and insists on all his Officers doing the same.

3. A Commanding Officer who does not get rattled directly the Brigadier or the Divisional Commander or any other General hoves in sight.

4. A Commanding Officer who insists on a good Headquarter Mess and good Company Messes for every one of his Companies.

5. A Commanding Officer who trains his Battalion sensibly and in moderation.

6. A Commanding Officer who does not permit his men to be pulled out of their beds before 7 a.m. either in summer or winter.

7. A Commanding Officer who does not allow parades of any kind on an empty stomach before breakfast.

8. A Commanding Officer with a cheerful manner.

9. A Commanding Officer who can answer any reasonable question put to him regarding his own Battalion.

10. A Commanding Officer who insists on keeping up a good corps of drummers, buglers, or pipers.

11. A Commanding Officer in whose Battalion crime is practically non-existent, and yet in which the Officers and men work hard and fight well.

12. A Commanding Officer who is always thinking of, and encouraging by day and night, *esprit de corps* in his Battalion.

13. A Commanding Officer who reads his orders and correspondence with care, and deals with both in a sensible and systematic manner. Also, one who, when called upon to give his opinion on some point, keeps to the matter in hand, and does not break off into some extraneous subject.

14. A Commanding Officer who insists on his Adjutant getting away from his office and being a fighting soldier rather than an officer's clerk, which a good many Adjutants prefer and think it their duty to be.

15. A Commanding Officer who will not permit his Officers to wear freak garments (e.g., snow white

gloves, collars, ties, and breeches, pudding caps, etc.) or to grow Charlie Chaplin moustaches.

16. A Commanding Officer who realises the importance of keeping for ever in front of his men the cause for which they are fighting.

17. A Commanding Officer who is human and a man of the world, and who therefore sympathises with his Officers and men in their desire to enjoy whatever the opportunity permits (e.g., when the Battalion is billeted near towns or other places of interest, one who allows them to enjoy the amenities of life in those towns, provided the necessary leave is forthcoming).

18. A Commanding Officer who says what he thinks in a tactful, yet determined, manner, and not what he thinks will please the Brigadier.

19. A Commanding Officer who, in a tactful manner, will bring to the notice of the Brigadier any order issued from the Brigade, which may be unworkable and so unsound.

20. A Commanding Officer who puts his Battalion into action only after thorough reconnaissance of the ground, and after pointing out to his Company Officers **on the ground** exactly what he wishes done.

21. A Commanding Officer who in action really commands his Battalion, and keeps the Brigadier accurately informed of the situation.

22. A Commanding Officer whose men are playing games in the afternoon, or otherwise enjoying themselves and keeping fit.

23. A Commanding Officer who plays himself and can lead his Battalion in games as well as in action.

24. A Commanding Officer who knows his Officers and non-commissioned officers intimately, and who can address many of the private soldiers by name.

25. A Commanding Officer who has the interests of his Officers and men at heart when alive, and when dead

honours them by decent burial, and who thinks of their relatives.

26. A Commanding Officer whose Officers, non-commissioned officers and men know the history of their regiment, and who are bent on making history for it.

27. A Commanding Officer who knows when a gallant action has been performed, and sees that the right man is rewarded.

28. A Commanding Officer who is respected and trusted by every member of his Battalion.

29. A Commanding Officer whose Battalion is clean, smart at drill, well fed, and on the march does not straggle. Whose Battalion can move off as a compact unit at very short notice, and for any purpose, cheerfully and in good heart.

30. A Commanding Officer who has a good canteen, wet and dry, under all circumstances possible, a recreation-room properly equipped, and always a separate room or mess for his Warrant Officers and non-commissioned officers.

31. A Commanding Officer who, if in the trenches, knows his line from end to end, not only as regards the actual trenches, but is also thoroughly acquainted with the actual ground in and in front of his sector.

32. A Commanding Officer whose Officers, non-commissioned officers and specialists are the best in the Brigade—thoroughly trained and thoroughly reliable.

33. A Commanding Officer who never forgets to praise when praise is due, but who allows no slackness or dereliction of duty of any kind whatever.

34. A Commanding Officer who is not content with telling his non-commissioned officers that they are the backbone of the Army, but who, by taking an active part in their training, assists them to improve their knowledge, and who, by insisting on them living properly and under conditions in keeping with their rank

and position, enables them to preserve their status in the eyes of their men.

35. A Commanding Officer who has knowledge and because of this knowledge can handle his Battalion at all times in action in such a manner as to inspire his men with the utmost confidence.

36. A Commanding Officer who personally sets every single Officer, non-commissioned officer and private in his Battalion the finest example in everything he calls on them to undertake.

CHAPTER XVII.

PRÉCIS OF A LECTURE
By MAJOR P. O. L. JORDAN, R.E.,
on
TRANSPORT (HORSEMASTERSHIP).

Any Officer in charge of horseflesh is responsible that all possible means are taken to ensure (1) freedom from disease; (2) working condition.

Skin Disease (Mange, Ringworm, Lice).

Given conditions of overwork and underfeeding, the intense irritation caused by skin disease may just make the difference, and cause a heavy mortality amongst horses in the field.

A Transport Officer must therefore endeavour to—

(1) Prevent introduction of disease from outside sources, i.e., segregate remounts, etc., until perfectly satisfied as to cleanliness.

(2) Make conditions unfavourable for an outbreak by good grooming, etc.

(3) Detect the slightest suspicion of disease at once by thorough daily examination of every animal (insist upon the " passing " of every horse after grooming once a day by the N.C.O. in charge).

(4) Segregate suspects at once and take full precautions to prevent any spread of disease. (Isolation of suspect and contacts; separate watering arrangements; disinfection of harness, rugs, grooming kit, standings; destruction of bedding, clippings.)

Glanders and Farcy.

Glanders and farcy may lay dormant, but the carrier can infect other animals. The Mallein test gives a reaction in infected animals and should be applied to remounts.

Cracked Heels and Thrushy Feet.

Cracked heels and thrushy feet, if prevalent under normal conditions, are discreditable to the stable management and the farriery.

Condition.

A uniformly good average is the result to be aimed at. Success lies in the study of the individual horse. Generous workers and delicate feeders may have to be fed at the expense of the lazy workers and good doers.

A harsh, staring coat and hidebound condition of skin may indicate digestive trouble. Look out for sharp teeth and worms. Try crushed oats, linseed, boiled food, etc.

Condition and Work.

Condition cannot be forced by fast work. Nothing tells on a horse's condition so much as fast work unless the feeding is on a higher scale than is general in the service.

A fit horse requires two hours exercise daily to keep him fit. Walking and trotting; the " hound jog " is the best of paces when exercising at the trot. Keep on the " soft " whenever possible; more horses are broken down from " hard going " than from any other cause. Dismount whenever possible.

Watering.

Water as often as possible.

Nothing tells on a horse's condition so much as lack of water. Don't lose sight of the fact that on a cold morning horses will often refuse to drink and therefore on the march may require watering early in the day. Never allow trotting to and from water. Horses can be watered when hot, provided there is no chance of their becoming chilled afterwards—for example, when on the march. Water before, never immediately after, feeding with corn.

Feeding.

The guiding principle is to feed " little and often."

It is better to give five feeds a day if practicable than to give only three.

Avoid long intervals between feeding, *e.g.*, from 5 p.m. to 7 a.m.

Bulk food in hay or other form is essential for a horse's digestive organs to work properly, especially important in the case of heavy draught horses.

When horses are accustomed to regular grazing, they take no harm from large amounts even if the grass is wet, but at first go carefully.

A hot bran and linseed mash once a week is a beneficial and laxative change of diet.

Chaff with corn feeds induces mastication and prevents whole undigested oats being passed through the animal and wasted.

Sick horses should have their oats cut down and should be placed on soft (laxative) food.

Horses appreciate and benefit from salt.

A Transport Officer should always keep a roll of poor conditioned horses which are (perhaps only temporarily) " on extra feed."

Grooming.

Grooming greatly influences an animal's condition, fitness, and appearance, and keeps him free from skin disease.

Grooming is quite distinct from cleaning or quartering, such as is done in the morning to make the horse presentable, and consists in getting through the hair to the actual surface of the skin with the body brush or dandy brush.

The way the grooming is done in a troop stable is a sure sign of the state of the stable discipline.

The best time is after the day's work, and all men, when possible, should be at work on their horses at the same time.

The "passing" of every horse when groomed by the Officer or N.C.O. in charge is the only way of ensuring good and quick work, and thorough daily examination for injuries and disease.

Except for hasty rubbing over of wet steelwork with an oily rag, harness should never be touched until the horse is passed clean.

Washing either legs or bodies is forbidden, as tending to produce cracked heels and mud fever.

The articles of grooming kit used, as a rule, in the Service, are the body brush, the currycomb, and the stable rubber.

The currycomb is not allowed to be used for cleaning the horse, and is intended for cleaning the brush.

The stable rubber is for giving the final polish to the coat. It is also useful rolled up for "banging" the horse when wisps are not available.

Wisps of hay or straw rope are most useful; ten minutes hard banging with a wisp is a most beneficial form of massage, especially on winter evenings.

When horses come in hot and their backs are wet, the back and loins should always be covered until they can be dried.

Standings.

Much can be done in the way of filling in bad standings with sand, rubble, brushwood, etc.

Clipping.

Various orders are issued from time to time about the difficult question of clipping. Whilst a "clipped out" horse may suffer from exposure, on the other hand working in a heavy coat takes a great deal off a horse's condition, drying becomes a matter of great difficulty and chills are taken, and the proper cleaning of the skin becomes an impossibility. It is best always to leave the legs unclipped as horses suffer from cold in their extremities. A rug is generally reckoned as worth 2 pounds of corn.

Transport Officers.

Transport Officers should be constantly in their horse lines; always during the normal midday stable hour and frequently at other times, both during the regular stable hours and also when the men are not in the horse lines.

Shoeing Rolls.

Shoeing Rolls showing date of last shoeing should be kept in every stable, so that the Commanding Officer can ascertain that no horse has been allowed to go more than a month without the necessary attention at the forge.

Pack Loads.

Every effort should be made to get the loads on each side of the same weight.

Keep the loads as high as possible, *i.e.*, over the top of the ribs and as little as possible over the sides of them.

The girths and surcingle must be tight.

It is of advantage to cross the girths.

Injuries are remedied by extra stuffing to the panels if thin or by chambering, *i.e.*, removing the stuffing where the injurious pressure occurs.

Horses and mules require accustoming to pack.

It is advisable to break in riding horses to draught against emergencies and to have all draught horses interchangeable as regards their places in pairs or teams.

Mules.

All general rules as to care of horses may be applied to mules.

Mules are more fastidious than horses in the matter of their water, but less so as regards food.

Mules have strong feet, but are inclined to grow high at the heels; this point needs attention.

March Discipline Notes.

A first halt should be made for a few minutes after one or two miles to allow horses to stale.

Whenever a vehicle is halted the driver should dismount.

At regular halts girths should be loosened and drivers should " look round " their horses, *i.e.*, look under breast collars, collar shields, girths and breechings for galls and examine feet for loose shoes or stones.

A small square of sheepskin with tapes attached is a useful first aid for galls and should be carried by every transport N.C.O.

When opportunity offers raise saddles off horses' backs for a few seconds.

If off-saddling is possible hand massage or slap backs well to relieve congestion caused by pressure.

On a dusty march it is a relief to animals to have eyes and nostrils sponged.

A driver with a trace down or leg over can usually pull out of the column and avoid causing a check.

A mounted man off his horse should under no circumstances leave his rifle on the saddle.

A farrier can usefully carry in his tool wallet a set of thin old shoes, which can be bent cold to an extemporised fit for any horse whose spare shoes have been mislaid.

On the picket line bad rope galls are avoided by seeing that the head ropes are not too long and are attached by some form of quick release knot to the picket line.

Notes on Harness, Etc.

The harness in general use in the Service is known as P.D.G.S. (pole draught G.S.) harness.

When used with a limbered vehicle, the "neck piece" supports the pole bar which carries the weight of the pole.

When used with a vehicle which has a fixed pole, the "neck-piece" is connected to the pole chains by a small piece of harness known as the "neck-piece tug."

For shaft draught a "luggage saddle" is required for the off-horse. For a four-horse team, short traces are required to connect leaders to wheeler.

Breast Collar.—When inspecting, look at the inside of the breast collar. It is most important that the surface next the horse should not be hard or caked with sweat and dirt. Dubbin or grease should be used occasionally in moderation between the inner and outer linings. The surface next the horse should always be sponged clean and dressed with soap.

See that the breast collar is not too low. If low, the play of the shoulder is in contact with it, and a gall is probably caused. Adjust the height by the "neck strap," which often stretches. Within reason the breast collar cannot be too high.

Backing Rings.—These are the big rings on the breast collar which enable the horse to "take" the breeching.

The links on the end of the "neck-piece" must pass down through the backing rings correctly. Mistakes are often made in this connection, and a sore neck or even an accident may be the result.

Pole Bar.—The pole bar must be level, or a sawing motion on the horse's neck may be caused and produce a gall. The ring on the pole bar through which the pole passes should incline forward. If the pole bar is put on wrong, the ring will incline back and jam when the horse goes up to his collar. The horse may then lean on the pole bar and get a sore breast-bone.

The Pole.—If a limbered vehicle is properly packed and balanced there will only be a few pounds' weight on the pole. A heavy pole means weight on the horse's neck, and is the cause of one of the commonest and most serious galls.

Neck Piece.—Supporting the pole bar. The buckle should be on the near side, bringing the raw edges of this double strap and the tongues of the attachments to the front and not to the rear.

Quick Release Attachments.—The tongues of these attachments should be free and not wrongly tucked away for appearance sake. For example, the ends of the tongues of the attachments connecting the traces to the draught tugs are sometimes passed through the big D's on the breast collar. If a horse is down, it is necessary to release the attachments quickly; they are then found jammed and the object of the attachment is defeated.

Hip Strap.—The hip straps pass over the croup and support the traces by means of long "tugs" or "buckling pieces" in front, and support the breeching by means of short tugs or buckling pieces in rear. In careless harnessing, sometimes short tugs are in front and long tugs in rear. Then when the traces are taut, they will not be in a straight line, and there will be a pull on the croup.

Traces.—In teams or pairs a straight line of draught is the ideal, though not always practicable.

Breechings.—Should lie under and not over the traces, and admit a hand's breadth between breeching and horse when the horse is up to his collar. They should be about 16 inches below the upper part of the dock.

Trace Carriers.—Are intended to support the traces, and should be used unless the pattern of harness is one that does not then permit a straight trace.

Saddles.—One should be able to see daylight through, from back of the saddle to front, *i.e.*, the saddle must on no account be down on the horse's backbone.

Neither the burrs nor the fans (the front and rear points of the side bars) should press on the horse's back.

The saddle blanket should be raised well into the front of the saddle, and by altering the folding of it a saddle which does not fit a horse by reason of loss of back muscle can usually be made to fit correctly. The blanket takes the place of the stuffed panel in the civilian saddle.

The Throat Lash.—Should be visibly loose, and only tight enough to prevent the headstall slipping over the horse's ears.

Before a March.—Be satisfied that every horse has spare shoes and nails available, nosebags are clean, in repair, and filled with corn (not grooming kit), buckets are carried for watering whenever opportunity offers, and that axles have been properly greased.

On the March.—See that every horse is taking his fair share of work, an alteration in pairing or teaming will often defeat the lazy horse that lies back in his breeching, and give the generous puller a chance. Dismount the drivers on every possible opportunity, and see they frequently "look round" their horses and loose the girths.

Cleaning Harness.—The inner surface of the leather work is really of more practical importance than the outside.

If leather is very greasy or dirty, it may be necessary to scrub with cold water and yellow soap. Never use hot water or soft soap, as both are most injurious.

Scrubbing is not good for harness, and should be seldom necessary.

Harness should always have the dirt and sweat sponged off, and may then be put in soap and oil or in polish.

Soap and Oil.—To soap leather work, apply a lather of yellow soap with a sponge, using as little water as possible, and work in well with a dry rag. If saddle soap is used, a fair polish may be attained, but no polish can be expected with yellow soap, although the leather can be kept in good serviceable condition.

The steel work should be cleaned and rubbed over with a slightly oily rag.

Polish.—The leather work is beeswaxed, and then, as a rule, a little composition is used.

The steel work is cleaned with silver sand and brickdust, and often burnished with a burnisher.

Polish means a lot of elbow grease and work, and from a purely practical point of view the leather is preserved much better by the use of soap.

CHAPTER XVIII.

PART I.

THE METHODS OF DEALING WITH OFFENCES IN A BATTALION.

By LIEUTENANT-COLONEL J. G. RAMSAY, Cameron Highlanders.

ABBREVIATIONS:—

M.M.L.,Ch. IV. (15),	abbreviation for	Manual of Military Law. Chapter IV, para. 15.
A.A. 46 (3)	,,	,, Army Act, section 46. sub-section 3.
A.A. 45 (Note 4)	,,	,, Army Act 45, footnote para. 4.
R.P. 5	,,	,, Rules of Procedure, Rule 5.
K.R. 469	,,	,, King's Regulations, para. 469.

The sequence of events is Arrest, Investigation, Award. These are dealt with in A.A. 45 and 46; R.P. 2—8; K.R. 463—513; and explained in M.M.L., Ch. IV.

See also F.S.R., Part II (106 and 107), and Field Service Pocket Book (reprinted 1916), page 216.

OFFICERS.

Arrest.

M.M.L., Ch. IV (2 & 3). Usually through medium of Adjutant or Second in Command. Inform him in writing whether arrest is "close" or "open." May be under the escort of an Officer; or in charge of a guard, under a sentry.

May be permitted to take exercise under escort.

M.M.L., Ch. IV (4).
K.R. 409.
A.A. 45 (Note 4).
If possible, a preliminary investigation should be made before the Officer is placed under arrest.

If he is placed under arrest a report should be sent to Brigade Headquarters.

M.M.L., Ch. IV (5).
A.A. 45 (3).
A Junior Officer may place his Senior under arrest if the Senior is engaged in a quarrel, fray or disorder, or commits a glaring impropriety.

K.R. 468.
Under normal circumstances the Officer should not be released without the sanction of the highest authority to whom his case has been referred.

Investigation.

M.M.L., Ch. IV (19).
R.P. 8.
Investigation may be by Commanding Officer or by a Court of Inquiry. He cannot demand a Court of Inquiry, but can demand that the evidence be taken down in writing in his presence.

The Commanding Officer may at his discretion dismiss the case. If the case is remanded for Court Martial, the Officer should receive a copy of the evidence.

NON-COMMISSIONED OFFICERS.

Arrest.

M.M.L., Ch. IV (10).
K.R. 471.
If a serious offence, the Non-Commissioned Officer should be placed under arrest at once.

If the offence is trivial, arrest need not be enforced until the investigation proves it necessary.

The rules as to "close" and "open" arrest laid down for Officers apply generally to Warrant Officers and Non-Commissioned Officers.

Investigation.

M.M.L., Ch. IV (20).
First investigation will be by Company Commanders.

Powers of Company Commanders are limited.

K.R. 484 & 499.
In the case of lance-sergeants or upwards, he may dismiss the case or remand for Commanding Officer.

A.A. 45 (Note 9).
Corporals or lance-corporals he may admonish or reprimand; he may not "severely reprimand" nor award any "C.B."

If the Company Commander remands the case, the Commanding Officer may :—

(a) Dismiss the case.

R.P 4.
(b) Deal with the case in accordance with his power of punishment.

(c) Remand to have the evidence reduced to writing.

(d) Apply to superior authority to deal with the case.

Awards.

M.M.L., Ch. IV (31).
K.R. 499.
Commanding Officer cannot award a summary or minor punishment, except that he may admonish, reprimand, or severely reprimand, or may deprive of acting or lance rank.

K.R. 302.
A.A. 46 (Note 3).
The "deductions" from ordinary pay applicable to privates apply also to non-commissioned officers.

A.A. 183 (2).
Commanding Officer may apply for summary reduction of a warrant officer or non-commissioned officer for other than disciplinary reasons. Corps Commander may sanction.

Commanding Officer may also apply to have a warrant officer or non-commissioned officer returned to England as being unsuitable for work in the field. Corps Commander may sanction.

PRIVATE SOLDIERS.

Arrest.

M.M.L., Ch. IV (11). — If the offence is trivial, the man will be placed under open arrest and will attend all parades.

K.R. 473, 475, 482. — If offence is serious, he should be confined at once; but under ordinary circumstances a private soldier will not be placed under close arrest for any offence unaccompanied by drunkenness, violence, or insubordination

K.R. 473, 475, 482. — When under close arrest he may be compelled to bear arms, or if the witnesses will not be available for some time, he may be released without prejudice to re-arrest when it becomes possible to deal with his case.

A man placed under close arrest should not be released without the sanction of the Commanding Officer.

K.R., 477. — A young non-commissioned officer should not as a rule place a soldier under arrest, but immediately report the case to his sergeant. A non-commissioned officer placing a soldier under arrest should avoid any altercation, and should not come in contact with the accused.

A.A. 45 (4). — The charge or "crime" should be handed into the Guard as soon as possible after the man has been confined; this should be at once entered up in the Guard Report.

K.R. 478
M.M.L., Ch. IV (21). — A soldier confined for drunkenness should be deprived of articles with which he might injure himself; he should be visited periodically; he should not be put through any drill or test; he should not be brought before his Officer until perfectly sober.

Investigation.

A.A 45 (5).
K.R. 484 — All offences should be investigated without unnecessary delay

K.R. 484.	The first investigation will be by the Officer Commanding Company. This applies also in the case of non-commissioned officers.
K.R. 481.	When the accused is brought before the Officer his cap will be removed.
	The Officer Commanding Company may dismiss the case, deal with it according to his powers of punishment, or remand the case for the Commanding Officer.
K.R. 485.	The investigation by Officer Commanding Company should take place at such an hour as to allow complete preparation of the case in time for Commanding Officer's Orderly Room.
R.P. 3. A.A. 46 (6). M M L., Ch. IV (22).	At the Commanding Officer's investigation the Officer Commanding Company will attend with the Conduct Sheet of accused; the charge will be read out in the presence of the accused and witnesses; the evidence will be given in the presence of the accused; at the request of the accused the evidence may be given on oath, if it is a case with which the Commanding Officer can deal; the accused may cross-examine the witnesses or make a statement.

The Commanding Officer will then decide on one of the following lines of procedure :—

A. Dismiss the case.

R.P. 4.

B. Deal with the case according to his powers of punishment.

M.M L. Ch. IV (23).

C. Adjourn the case to have the evidence reduced to writing.

D. Remand for trial by Court-Martial.

E. Apply to Brigade Headquarters for authority for permission to deal with the case.

A. Commanding Officer may dismiss the case under the following circumstances :—

    (a) Evidence doubtful.
    (b) Triviality of the case.
R.P. 4 (Note 2)   (c) Doubtful whether the act is to the prejudice of good order and military discipline.
    (d) Good character of the accused.
    (e) Matter of discretion for any reason.
    (f) Accused previously acquitted or convicted on the same charge (*i.e.*, the same instance of offence).

B. If the Commanding Officer does not dismiss the case, he will deal with it according to his powers of punishment, unless :—

    (a) The case is not clear to him.
R.P. 4 (Note 3).   (b) It is obviously a case for Court-Martial.
    (c) It is a case with which, under K.R. 487, he has not power to deal without reference to higher authority.

C. Where the case is adjourned to have the evidence reduced to writing, this should, if possible, be done the same day.

P.P. 4
M.M.L., Ch. IV (26 & 27).

It is compiled in the form of a Summary of Evidence in accordance with R.P. 4.

Great care should be taken in proper arranging of the evidence.

M.M.L., Ch. IV (28).
R.P. 4 (Note 3).
R.P. 5.
K.R. 488.

D. Because the evidence is reduced to writing, it does not follow that the case is remanded for Court-Martial. The Commanding Officer may re-hear the charge and then dismiss the case, deal with it himself, apply to higher authority to deal with the case himself, or remand the case for trial by

Court-Martial. If it appears doubtful whether the evidence will lead to a conviction, the case should not be remanded for Court-Martial.

K.R. 487.
E. The offences with which a Commanding Officer may deal are stated in K.R. 487, and the various sections of the Army Act mentioned therein. If he wishes to dispose of any other case instead of remanding for Court-Martial, he may apply to higher authority.

Awards.

The following are the summary punishments (maximum) which a Commanding Officer, or an Officer Commanding Detachment of field rank, may award :—

A.A. 46.
K.R. 493.
Detention   28 days (not in France).

Deductions from ordinary pay ... { to make good damage for loss of arms, equipment, etc., etc.

M.M.L., Ch. IV (31 & 38).
Fines (for drunkenness only) .. { according to scale stated in K.R. 512 (if field punishment is not awarded).

Field punishment... 28 days.

Deprivation of pay 28 days.

A.A. 46 (5).
M.M.L., Ch. IV (33).
If detention is awarded for absence without leave during a period longer than seven days, the number of days' detention must not exceed the number of days' absence.

A.A. 46 (Note 6).
K.R. 494.
Detention up to seven days is awarded in hours, over seven days in days.

A.A. 138 & 140.
K.R. 495 & 504.
A.A. 46 (Note 1).
Pay is forfeited automatically apart from the Commanding Officer's powers of punishment for every " day " of illegal absence ;

detention; field punishment; in custody on any charge resulting in conviction by Court-Martial; in custody on a charge of illegal absence for which the Commanding Officer awards detention or field punishment. These are not Commanding Officer's awards, but the accused should be informed as to how many days' pay he forfeits under these headings. This should be recorded in the column " Remarks."

A.A. 140 (2).
A.A. 138 (Note 3). A " day " consists of six or more hours; if more than twelve hours, pay is forfeited for each calendar day which the period of absence touches.

R. 194 (Note) An award of field punishment carries with it deprivation of pay; if the Commanding Officer wishes the accused to be deprived of fourteen days' pay in addition to undergoing ten days' field punishment, he should award " Ten days' field punishment and to be deprived of twenty-four days' pay."

Field punishment commences on the day of award, even if the accused is already undergoing sentence.

The consecutive awards of a Commanding Officer of field punishment should not aggregate more than 28 days consecutively.

" If field punishment were carried out more rigorously it would act as a far greater deterrent to crime than is often the case.

" A man under sentence, if not in the trenches or on duty or fatigue, should be treated as if he were undergoing imprisonment with hard labour, should be confined and deprived of tobacco, rum or beer."

With certain exceptions a Commanding Officer is compelled to dispose of cases of drunkenness; it is not implied that a Commanding Officer may not deal with these exceptions. The exceptions are :—

<small>A.A. 46 (3).
A.A 183 1).
A.A. 46 (Note 9).
K.R. 509 & 510.</small>

(a) If the accused is a non-commissioned officer.
(b) If committed on active service.
(c) If committed on duty.
(d) If committed after being warned for duty.
(e) If accused is rendered unfit for duty in consequence.
(f) If the accused has been convicted of drunkenness not less than four times during the preceding twelve months.

<small>K.R. 512.</small>

The fines for drunkenness (N.B. there are no other " fines ") are stated in K.R. 512. A Commanding Officer may not award a fine in addition to field punishment for drunkenness.

<small>R.M.L. Ch. IV (31).</small>

Apart from summary punishment, the Commanding Officer may award the following minor punishments :—

C.B. or C.C. ... ... up to 14 days.
Extra guards or piquets for offences connected with those duties.

<small>A.A. 46 (9).
K.R 494.</small>

A minor punishment may not be awarded in addition to detention, if detention exceeding 168 hours (7 days) is awarded. The whole period of consecutive punishment of detention and confinement to barracks may not exceed 42 days.

A.A. 46 (Note 16).
K.R. 507.

A Commanding Officer can at any time before the punishment has been completed remit or mitigate a minor or summary punishment. After the punishment has been completed, the Commanding Officer has no power to alter the record.

M.M L., Ch. IV (16).
A.A. 46 (Note 16).

A Commanding Officer cannot increase a punishment already awarded; the award is considered complete as soon as the man has left the Commanding Officer's presence.

K.R. 500.

No system of punishment other than that allowed by Regulations is to be introduced.

There is no appeal from a Commanding Officer's award, but under certain circumstances the accused may elect to be tried by "District" Court-Martial.

These circumstances are :—

M.M.L., Ch. IV (25).
A.A. 46 (8).
A.A. 46 (Note 12)

(a) When the Commanding Officer proposes to award other than a minor punishment.

(b) When the award or finding involves a forfeiture of pay.

A Company Commander may award minor punishments restricted to :—

M.M.L., Ch. V (37).
K.R. 501.

C.B. or C.C. ... ... 7 days.
Extra guards and piquets ... for offences connected with those duties.

In cases of absence without leave he may award up to 7 days' C.B., and inform the accused of the extent of forfeiture of pay.

The Commanding Officer may further restrict the powers of his Company Commanders if he considers it advisable.

The Commanding Officer may reduce the award of a Company Commander if he considers it excessive.

PART II.

FIELD GENERAL COURTS-MARTIAL IN FRANCE.

The majority of the points connected with Field General Courts-Martial will be found in A.A. 49; R.P. 105-123; M.M.L., Ch. V, 25 and 26.

ABBREVIATIONS :—

M.M.L., Ch. III. (17) means "Manual of Military Law," Chapter III., para. 17.

A.A. 6 (1.k) ,, Army Act, section 6, sub-section 1, para. k.

R.P. 45 (A) ,, Rules of Procedure, Rule 45, para. A.

Steps Leading to Assembly of a Field General Court-Martial.

(1) Investigation of case by Officer Commanding Company.

(2) Investigation of case by Officer Commanding Battalion.

(3) Evidence reduced to writing (Summary of Evidence).

(4) Reconsideration of case by Officer Commanding Battalion.

(5) Officer Commanding Battalion, unable to deal with case in any other way, remands "for Trial by Field General Court-Martial."

(6) Framing of charge.

(7) Application for assembly of a Field General Court-Martial.
(8) Field General Court-Martial convened, usually by Headquarters Brigade (in infantry).

How the Battalion Can Assist the Brigade.
(1) By not delaying any of the above stages.
(2) By compiling the summary of evidence on correct lines.
(3) By framing the charge correctly according to the evidence.

Summary of Evidence.
(1) R.P. 4, and Notes thereto, should be carefully studied.
(2) Compiled in the presence of the accused.
(3) Evidence as to facts should be taken in chronological order.
(4) Evidence of each witness should show his number, rank, initials, name, unit. It should then commence with a statement as to his appointment, followed by the time, date and place at which the incident occurred.
(5) If a witness cannot attend to give evidence when the summary is being compiled, a signed Statement may be accepted. The signed Statement will not be accepted as evidence at the trial if accused pleads " Not Guilty."
(6) The accused should receive a copy of the Summary or Statement of Evidence when being informed of the charge on which he will be tried.

Framing Charges.
Responsibility rests with Convening Officer, that is usually General Officer Commanding Infantry Brigade, to whom the Staff-Captain is responsible.

R.P. 108.   (1) A charge sheet is rarely necessary; the charge stated briefly in any wording sufficient to disclose an offence under the A.A. being entered on page 2, column 2, A.F. A 3.

425

- (2) A.A., 4—41, cover every offence that a soldier can commit.
- (3) Charge should be framed solely on the evidence in the summary.
- (4) Avoid multiplication of charges.
- (5) If charged with a serious offence, minor offences may be dropped.
- (6) If doubtful as to which charge to prefer, study the A.A. section concerned, the footnote to the section, the explanatory paragraphs in M.M.L., Ch. III, and the specimen charges shown on pages 650—676 of the M.M.L.
- (7) Alternative charges should be marked " ALTERNATIVE " on page 2, column 2, A.F. A 3. For specimen of alternative charges see M.M.L., page 670, example No. 59.
- (8) If the accused elected to be tried by Court-Martial, the words " Elects Trial " should be written prominently on A.F. A 3, and also on his charge sheet, if there is one.

Special Points Concerning Certain Charges.

The following points should be observed when compiling summaries of evidence or framing charges. Attention is directed to M.M.L., Ch. III, and the footnotes to the A.A. sections concerned.

Cowardice.

A.A. 4 (7).   Usually only under fire, unless evidence is exceptional; absence by itself does not constitute cowardice.

Offences by Sentries.

A.A. 6 (1 k).
Must be proved (a) what the post was; (b) that he had been properly posted; (c) that he was still on duty; (d) what rest he had had.

If given permission to leave his post for a short time, he cannot be charged with "leaving his post," even though he does not return.

If found asleep or drunk away from his post, cannot be charged with "sleeping on his post" or "being drunk on his post" (can be charged with "leaving his post").

A telephone operator is not a sentry.

If doubtful if offence comes under A.A. 6 (1), charge under A.A. 40.

Striking or Threatening Superior Officer.

A.A. 8.
Note difference between 8 (1) and 8 (2); accused should not be charged under 8 (1) unless his offence was committed under very grave circumstances, and unless it is intended that "Death" be awarded.

Disobedience.

A.A. 9.
Note difference between 9 (1) and 9 (2) explanation given in M.M.L., Ch. III, 7—12. Usually charged under 9 (2), unless the disobedience was with a view to intentionally showing "wilful" defiance, and unless it is intended that "Death" be awarded.

In the case of disobedience of a written order, the original order should be produced if possible.

The accused must have had sufficient opportunity of complying with the order.

Desertion.

A.A. 12.

Implies a special intention with knowledge to do one of the two following :—
- (A) Not to return to military duty at all.
- (B) To avoid some important military duty.

Under (B) two points must be proved :—
1. That the accused was absent, and thereby avoided the duty.
2. That the accused knew with reasonable certainty that he would be required for the special duty.

In order to prove (2) evidence must be given to show :—
- (a) That accused was warned; or
- (b) That the Company was warned while the accused was present; or
- (c) That according to the usual custom of reliefs the accused must have known that the turn of the Company was imminent; or
- (d) That the period of absence was so long that the accused must have known for certain that he would miss active operations in consequence.

Evidence should be produced to show when the absence commenced, also when and how it terminated. The certificate mentioned in A.A. 163 (j) will be accepted as evidence if accused surrenders himself. If he is arrested while absent, the witnesses of arrest will be required at the trial.

If the accused is arrested in England, A.F. O 1618 should be produced by a witness on oath.

Absence.

A.A. 15.

A charge under 15 (2) of "Failing to Appear at the Place of Parade" should not be preferred on active service. It should be laid under 15 (1), "Absence Without Leave."

Self-Inflicted Wounds.

A.A. 18.   Usually under A.A. 40, "Neglect to the Prejudice," as it is difficult to prove the "intention" necessary to support a charge of "maiming," under A.A. 18.

The object is to prevent the accused from being withdrawn further from the line or for a longer period than necessary. As soon as medically fit, the man returns to his unit, therefore advisable to award field punishment. Obtain medical evidence as to probable period of incapacity. Field General Court-Martial is usually held at Field Ambulance.

Drunkenness.

A.A. 19.   Whether committed on duty or not, the charge will be "Drunkenness"; the question of duty, etc., will be brought out in the particulars.

Reference to violence or insubordination in conjunction with drunkenness, see M.M.L., Ch. III, 30 and 31.

Designation of Accused.

If a private or non-commissioned officer holding acting rank, his permanent rank will be stated with the acting rank in brackets, e.g., private (acting corporal).

Sentence will be awarded in accordance with his permanent rank only. (See sentence 19.)

Reduction from acting rank must not be awarded by Field General Court-Martial. It may be dealt with by Commanding Officer.

The following information, with an explanation of the offences in question, should be given to reinforcements of all ranks received by a Battalion :—

Offences Punishable by Death.

Offences charged under the following sections of the Army Act are punishable by death, whether committed by Officers or other ranks :—

A.A., Sects. 4; 6 (1); 7; 8 (1); 9 (1).

Offences Punishable by Penal Servitude.

These sections apply to Officers and other ranks :—

A.A., Sects. 5; 8 (2) on active service; 9 (2) on active service; 17.

N.B.—Compare 8 (1) and 8 (2), also 9 (1) and 9 (2).

Offences with Higher Rate of Punishment on Active Service.

A.A., Sects. 6 (1) (A—K); 8 (2); 9 (2); 12.

Application for F.G.C.M.

The following documents should be forwarded by the unit making application :—

(a) Summary or Statement of Evidence.
(b) Proposed charges.
(c) Certified true copy of Conduct Sheet.

Other unnecessary documents should be removed before submitting the application.

Evidence.—(Read M.M.L., Ch. VI.)

(1) The accused is presumed to be innocent until it is proved that he is guilty.

(2) Irrelevant evidence should be disallowed. Nothing shall be admitted as evidence which does not tend to prove or disprove the charge. The defence is allowed greater latitude in this respect.

(3) The evidence produced must be the best obtainable under the circumstances, e.g., the verbal account of the contents of a document can never be received if the document itself is obtainable.

(4) Hearsay is not evidence; it may be defined as consisting of second-hand statements. Another definition is: "Any statement made in the absence of the accused, whether it was made by a third party or by the witness himself." The rule is: "No statements with reference to a person charged with an offence, relative to the charge, made in his absence can be received in evidence against him."

The written statement of a witness who does not appear before the Court on a plea of "Not Guilty" is classified as "hearsay" so far as that trial is concerned.

The originator of the statement should be called.

(5) Opinion or belief is not evidence.

The witness should state what he saw, heard, or otherwise observed, and the Court draws the inference. This rule does not apply to opinion of experts.

(6) Certain documents are accepted as evidence; these are enumerated in A.A., 163.

- (7) No document is admissible in evidence for the Prosecution unless it is produced by a witness on oath.
- (8) Documents produced should be distinctively marked, initialled by the President and attached in proper sequence.
- (9) If the case involves disobedience of " written orders," the original should be produced if possible, failing that a certified true copy.

Duties of President.

R.P. 59.

- (1) See that trial is properly conducted, and accused has a fair trial.
- (2) See that accused is not obstructed in his defence.
- (3) Will secure presence of witnesses whose evidence he thinks may be material, even though not called either by prosecution or defence.
- (4) Must not cross-examine the accused with a view to supplementing the evidence for the prosecution.
- (5) It is his duty to assist the accused throughout the trial.

Duties of Prosecutor.

R.P. 89 (Note).

- (1) Does not as a rule give evidence before the finding unless on some formal point, e.g., a date.
- (2) If prosecutor on more than one case, must be sworn for each separate case.
- (3) He must be quite impartial, and will bring out all evidence for or against the accused.
- (4) If applicable, he should produce evidence as to provocation or extenuating circumstances.

Composition of Field General Court-Martial.

R.P. 20 (Note 1).
R.P. 10d.
M.M.L., Ch. V.
(26).

(1) Consists of three Officers, if possible of different units.
(2) Field General Court-Martial of less than three members cannot award sentence of death or penal servitude.
(3) President, a Field Officer.
(4) Each member not less than one year's service.
(5) See R.P. 19 as to eligibility and qualifications of members.

If President receives papers before the Court assembles, he should study them carefully, and if any point appears doubtful, consult the Convening Officer.

In any case before the trial commences he should :—
(1) Compare charge with section of A.A.
(2) Read the section and its footnotes.
(3) Split up the charge into its component parts, and decide what separate points will have to be proved in the event of accused pleading not guilty.

Example : A.A. 6 (1 K), "When a soldier acting as a sentinel on active service sleeping on his post."
Following should be proved :—
(a) That accused had been posted as a sentry.
(b) What his post was.
(c) That accused was found asleep.
(d) That he was then on his post.
(e) That he was then still on duty.
(f) What previous rest he had had.

Procedure on Opening the Court.

M M.L., Ch. V.
(37—39).

(1) Check over the papers; see that all is correct.
(2) March in all the accused, prosecutors, witnesses, etc., and read over to them page 1 of A.F. A 3.

(3) The charge must not be altered in any way by the Court.

(4) Any alteration made to page 1, A.F. A 3, or on first or second column of the schedule, must be initialled by the Convening Officer.

R.P. 25.
R.P. 110.
M.M.L., Ch. V.
(44-45).

(5) Give each accused his right of challenge; if challenge is valid, refer to Convening Officer.

A.A. 52
R P. 111.
M M.L., Ch. V.
(46-48).

(6) Swear the members of the Court; members first, then the President.

(7) March out everyone except the accused, the escort, the prosecutor, the friend of accused.

R.P. 112.
M.M.L., Ch. V.
(54—56).

(8) Arraign the accused, and enter in column 3 of page 2, A.F. A3, his plea on each charge.

Choice of Plea.

(1) President will ascertain that accused understands meaning of charge in detail.

(2) The effect of a plea of " Guilty " will be explained and the difference in the procedure resulting.

(3) President will advise accused to withdraw plea of " Guilty," if it appears from the summary that he should plead " Not Guilty."

(4) Accused must not be allowed to plead " Guilty " to charge for which " Death " is likely to be awarded.

(5) If accused is charged with several offences and pleads " Guilty " to some and " Not Guilty " to others, the latter will be dealt with first.

(6) When an alternative charge is preferred, and the accused pleads " Guilty " to the more serious

charge, the Court, instead of trying him, may record a finding of "Not Guilty" on the lesser charge.

If accused pleads "Not Guilty" to the more serious charge, the Court may proceed as if accused had pleaded "Not Guilty" to both charges.

A plea of "Guilty" cannot be taken on both charges.

(7) At any time during the trial (e.g., statement in mitigation) the President may alter a plea of "Guilty" to "Not Guilty," and proceed with the trial in accordance with the new plea.

On Plea of Guilty.

R P. 37.
(1) Summary is attached; if not available, sufficient evidence on oath to be taken down for guidance of Convening Officer as to gravity of offence.

Plea of "Guilty" covers all defects in evidence, unless it is obvious that an injustice is being inflicted on the accused.

(2) Statement in mitigation, if offered, is taken down.

(3) Evidence as to character is taken down, or an entry to the effect that none is available. (See p. 3 on a finding of "Guilty.")

(4) Complete and sign A.F. A 3.

On Plea of Not Guilty.

R P. 114
(1) Summary is not used as evidence against accused.

(2) Evidence on oath by witnesses for prosecution will be taken down in *narrative* form. (See sample Summary of Evidence.)

(If possible avoid taking down in form of Question and Answer.)

R.P. 40.
(3) Evidence on oath for defence.
(4) Accused may give evidence on oath, or hand in a written statement on oath, and be liable to cross-examination; evidence not on oath, or a written statement not on oath, and not liable to cross-examination; or say nothing. The accused should be so informed by the President.
(5) Accused may call witnesses as to character *before* the finding; he is liable to cross-examination, or rebutting evidence may be obtained.
(6) If he urges a valid plea on medical grounds, a medical witness should be called to corroborate or rebut. If it is offered as a defence, this evidence should be taken before the finding. If in mitigation, then after the finding.
(7) Omit such phrases, " Witness withdraws," " Prosecution is closed," etc.

Finding (See R.P., 43 and 44).

(1) Finding on each separate charge must be entered on page 2, column 4, A.F. A 3; this applies also to alternative charges.
(2) If the plea is " Guilty," the finding of " Guilty " must also be entered, even though no evidence is taken.

A.A. 53 (8).
R.P. 117.
(3) In the event of an equality of votes the finding is entered as " Not Guilty."

(4) If in doubt on which alternative charge to convict accused, find "Guilty" on the lesser charge.

R.P. 45 (A).
(5) If the finding is "Not Guilty," the accused should be so informed and released. An acquittal does not require confirmation.

On a Finding of Guilty.

(1) Evidence as to good character and particulars of service should be taken down.
(2) If no evidence as to character is available, an entry to that effect should be made.
(3) Any evidence as to good character is admissible. A written statement, if handed in, will be accepted, although the writer is not present.
(4) Evidence as to BAD character should not be taken.
(5) It should be stated as to whether evidence as to character is taken before or after the finding.
(6) Certified true copy of A.F. B 122 (Field Conduct Sheet) should be attached to A.F. A 3. The Conduct Sheet should have written on it "Certified true copy," signed by an Officer, and dated. It should be produced by the Prosecutor on oath, compared by the Court with the original, initialled by the President, and attached to the proceedings.
(7) If accused is under a suspended sentence or a sentence of field punishment, the Court will be informed of this *after* the finding, and the fact will be recorded.

(8) When evidence as to character is taken, it should be stated whether it is taken *before* or *after* the finding.

Sentence.

(1) Before passing sentence (i.e., after the finding), accused will be asked if he has anything further to say in mitigation of punishment. If he declines to make a statement the fact should be recorded.

R.P. 48. (2) Only one sentence will be awarded, although convicted on more than one charge.

M.M.L., Ch. V. (80—88).
K.R. 583.
(3) Where authorised by A.A., sentence may consist of more than one punishment (e.g., reduction to the ranks plus stoppages).

(4) Sentence is entered on page 2, column 4, A.F. A 3, below all the findings.

(5) Should be stated briefly, e.g., " 3 months' F.P. No. 1," " 2 years' I.H.L.," " Death," etc.

(6) Maximum punishment is shown in the section of A.A. under which charge is laid.

(7) " Such less punishment " is shown in A.A. 44.

A.A. 49 (1d).
A.A. 49 (2).
(8) Sentence of " Death " cannot be awarded unless Court consists of not less than three members, and all are in agreement as to sentence.

A.A. 44. (9) Penal servitude cannot be awarded for *less* than three years. The Court must consist of not less than three members.

(10) Imprisonment, with or without hard labour, cannot be awarded for *more* than two years. (*N.B.*—Do not award imprisonment without hard labour.)

(11) Field punishment cannot be awarded for more than three months, including any sentence he may be already undergoing.
(12) Punishments up to three months should be awarded in field punishment and not in imprisonment with hard labour.
(13) Detention or discharge with ignominy should not be awarded in France.
(14) Forfeiture of pay up to three months may be awarded on active service, in addition to, or without, other punishment. (*N.B.*—Field punishment and forfeiture of pay run concurrently.)
(15) Forfeiture of seniority, reduction to a lower grade, reduction to the ranks (applies to non-commissioned officers, but not to temporary or acting appointments; acting and lance ranks can only be dealt with by the Commanding Officer).
(16) Fines, for drunkenness only, up to £1. (See A.A. 19.)
(17) Stoppages; the amount of damage must be stated in the charge and proved.
(18) No punishment other than that mentioned in A.A. 44 may be awarded; thus a Court cannot award confinement to barracks, nor reprimand, nor severe reprimand, of non-commissioned officers; it may reprimand an Officer.
(19) A non-commissioned officer reduced to the ranks may in addition be awarded any punishment applicable to a private soldier, the reduction being awarded first.

Any sentence involving loss of liberty, e.g., one day's field punishment or upwards, will automatically reduce any non-commissioned officer, "acting" or otherwise, to the ranks.

Deprivation of acting or lance rank can only be awarded by a Commanding Officer. It may not be awarded by Court-Martial.

N.B.—In deciding on both the finding and sentence, every member must give his opinion, beginning with the junior in rank.

A.A. 53 (8).

Finding.—In case of equality of votes, accused is acquitted.

Sentence.—In case of equality of votes, President has a second or deciding vote.

Order of Seriousness of Offences.

(1) With premeditation, without provocation.
(2) With premeditation, with provocation.
(3) Without premeditation, without provocation.
(4) Without premeditation, with provocation.

In cases of doubt as to the amount of punishment to be awarded, this classification is a useful guide.

Completion of A.F. A 3.

(1) Sentence having been entered, President must sign at the bottom of page 2, and also the certificate on page 3.
(2) Only documents used at the trial, and of them only those that are necessary, should be attached to A.F. A 3.

(3) The following only are required, and should be attached in the order named :—

(A) On a plea of " Guilty " :—
 (a) Summary of evidence.
 (b) Evidence of character.
 (c) Statement, if any, made by accused in mitigation of punishment.
 (d) Certified true copy of conduct sheet, which must be initialled by the President.

(B) On a plea of " Not Guilty " :—
 (a) Charge sheet (in complicated or special cases only).
 (b) Evidence taken at the trial.
 (c) Any exhibits produced.
 (d) Evidence of character taken after the finding.
 (e) Certified true copy of conduct sheet, which must be initialled.

The other numerous Army Forms and documents which are sometimes laid before the Court may be destroyed; they should not be forwarded with the proceedings.

Confirmation and Promulgation.

The Confirming Officer is usually the Officer who convened the Court.

An acquittal does not require confirmation.

If the finding and sentence are confirmed, the word " Confirmed " will be entered in the last column of page 2, A.F. A 3, and the Certificate C on page 3 signed by the Confirming Officer.

The proceedings are then returned to the unit; the Officer Commanding Unit promulgates the finding and sentence, publishes them in Battalion Orders, Part II, and enters the following certificate at the foot of page 3 :—

"Promulgated and extracts taken at......
.........this ....day of .... 1917."

Signature.

The proceedings are then returned without delay through the usual channels.

The following sentences should not, however, be promulgated until final approval has been received from higher authority.

Officers.—Death, Penal Servitude, Imprisonment, Cashiering, Dismissal.
Other ranks.—Death.

N.B.—Every effort should be made to expedite Court-Martial cases. The object of Field General Court-Martial is to bring an offender to justice without delay.

Notification to Base.

Officers Commanding Units are responsible that the following particulars are entered on A.F. B 2069 and forwarded to Deputy Adjutant-General, Base :—

Date and place of trial, charge, finding, sentence, confirmation and authority, remission (if any), time in confinement awaiting trial.

Death Sentence for "Constructive" Desertion.

Following information to be forwarded by the Confirming Officer with the proceedings if " Death " is awarded for "Constructive" Desertion :—

(1) Character—fighting as well as behaviour, previous conduct in action, period of service in Expeditionary Force.

(2) State of discipline of his unit.

(3) Commanding Officer's opinion, based on his personal knowledge (or that of his Officers) of the man's characteristics, as to whether the offence was *deliberately* committed with the sole object of avoiding the particular service specified.

(4) The reasons *why* the various authorities recommend that the extreme penalty be inflicted or otherwise.

Object :—To prevent a good fighting man from being shot for absence resulting from simple absence or a drunken spree.

CHAPTER XIX.

AN ADDRESS TO THE SENIOR OFFICERS
on
THE RÔLE AND THE RESPONSIBILITIES OF THE COMMANDING OFFICER IN A BATTALION MESS,
By BRIGADIER-GENERAL R. J. KENTISH, D.S.O.
August, 1917.

The general state and efficiency of a Regiment can be quickly gauged by the tone and bearing of its Officers when in their Mess. It is the duty of a Commanding Officer to first set the standard of life and then to insist on his Officers living up to that standard. The Commanding Officer who does so is correctly interpreting one of the many responsibilities that are his and his alone.

BEFORE THE WAR.

I think perhaps there is a tendency on the part of Commanding Officers, and a tendency that is not unnatural in these days, to overlook the traditions and customs of the Mess of the British Army and the importance generally that the Mess plays in the life of a Regiment. In the pre-war days the Soul of the Regiment, so to speak, could be found in the ante-room or dining-room of an Officers' Mess, and from the Officers gathered together in one or other of those rooms emanated the tone and standard of life of every individual of the Regiment. If their conversation or their actions generally were not all that could be desired, the effect was evident throughout the Regiment, the sergeants, then the corporals, and then the privates taking their standard and example from their Officers, and living well up to that standard and example, whether it was a high or low one.

A stranger in the old days walking into the ante-room of a Regiment in which were seated a number of Officers could at a glance gauge the standard of life and the tone generally of that Regiment. If they immediately got up from their seats and received him as one gentleman should receive another coming into his house for the first time; if their conversation revealed a proper tone and spirit; if their appearance generally was what the appearance of Officers should be—the stranger, without doubt, left the Mess with the impression that he had just left a Regiment in which the Officers were gentlemen, and who were all maintaining the best traditions of the Officer class of His Majesty's Army. And he would be perfectly justified in deciding off-hand that the tone and general standard of all ranks of that Regiment probably approached the same standard set by its Officers.

If, on the contrary, he had been coldly received; if the Officers remained seated with the exception, perhaps, of one young subaltern, who, being a gentleman himself, knew at any rate what his rôle was on such an occasion, and stood up and alone welcomed the visitor; if their conversation disclosed a bad tone and a bad spirit; if, in addition, they were standing each other drinks in their own Mess; and if their appearance was not at all in keeping with what the stranger—himself an Officer—was accustomed to in his own Regiment; and if, finally, the general appearance of the ante-room was more in keeping with that of the smoking-room of a second-class provincial club than with that of the ante-room of a British Regiment—the stranger would be equally justified in coming to the decision that he was in the Mess of a Regiment in which the tone and general standard was decidedly not in accordance with the best traditions of the British Officer, and he would be equally justified in assuming that a similar state of things, e.g., bad tone and a low standard of life and discipline, probably existed throughout the whole Regiment.

In a word, the Officers' Mess in the pre-war days set the standard of life for the Regiment, and its general state and efficiency varied, according as the tone was good or bad in that Mess. And this being the case before the Great War, it is interesting to turn to the situation to-day, and to see whether those sound principles and rules of Mess life, which meant so much to us all, and which were so highly prized by all the Officers of the Old Regular Army, still hold the same position and carry the same weight in the Battalions of not only the Old Regular Army, but of every Battalion, no matter to what Army, viz., New, Territorial, or Overseas, that Battalion may belong.

THE SITUATION TO-DAY.

The Notes, Lectures, and Addresses contained in this Book deal particularly with the present day situation, and it is therefore essential that we should here concentrate on the Mess question as it presents itself to us, and show how it bears on the tone and standard of each individual unit. As one who derives great pleasure in getting to know—really getting to know—the Officers of every branch and arm of the service, I can only tell you that in the course of my visits to the Messes of other Regiments—in all of which I am bent on making friends—I have found a very marked difference in the tone and standard of the various Officers' Messes I have chanced to visit. On entering the billet, in which perhaps the Headquarters Mess or a Company Mess may have been installed, I have been received in both the manners described above, and as a result of my reception I have been able to sum up very quickly the general state of the Regiment. It will, if I enumerate the essential factors in preserving in the Officers' Messes a proper tone, perhaps help me to make my points, and also help you whom I am addressing when you find yourselves in command of one or other of those splendid Battalions of our Army in France, to conduct your Messes in the manner which before the war was traditional of the best Regiments of our Army. I therefore do so.

MESS RULES.

In every Battalion there should be Mess Rules in print, a copy of which should be given to every Officer on joining. The nature of these Rules for a Battalion on service in the Field must vary according to the circumstances in which the Battalion finds itself placed, but the Mess Rules of this School which are attached to this paper are a sample of what is usual for a Battalion serving under peace conditions. It is impracticable for all these Rules to be observed on Service, but it is the duty of any Commanding Officer serving with a Battalion in the field to see that the spirit of such Rules are observed by his Officers as far as the conditions existing at the time permit. The mere drawing up and issuing of Orders, Rules, or Regulations is a waste of time if the matter is not pursued further. It is the duty and rôle of the Commanding Officer to see that his orders are observed, and this can only be provided he himself takes a live and active part in ensuring that they are. I now propose to take and discuss in detail each of the things that matter in the proper conduct of an Officers' Mess.

THE BEARING OF THE OFFICERS OF A REGIMENT TOWARDS STRANGERS.

First and foremost the Officers should realise the importance of knowing what their duties are, whether in a Battalion or a Company Mess, when a stranger enters their billet. Those who remain seated or silent create a bad impression, whereas those who immediately get up and say " Good-morning " or " Good-afternoon "—adding the word " sir " if the stranger, be he soldier or civilian, is senior in rank or years—and follow it up by asking the stranger if he will not sit down, or what they can do for him, and who, if a meal is just about to commence, invite him to stay and join them, create a very good impression. I have already told you that I have often entered Messes, both Battalion and Company, and found the two situations as described, and I have left with the impression that each created so firmly in my mind that I do not hesitate to emphasise to you the importance of giving your Officers very clear direction as to their duties in this respect, and to ask you to do all in your power to put them on the right lines.

The offering of hospitality, or, rather, the manner and method of offering hospitality, will reveal the tone of the Mess. There are certain Officers who are under the impression that if a stranger entered an Officers' Mess in the pre-war days he could not be permitted to leave it until at least two or three drinks had been ordered and drank; or if he accepted an invitation to dine he could not be said to have really dined unless he had drunk a great deal more than he really wished to. Certainly there were one or two isolated cases of Regiments in which the Officers drank a good deal more than was good either for themselves or for the reputation of the Service, and in which the standing of each other drinks was permitted and encouraged. A stranger dining in such a Mess probably had to fight hard to avoid drinking more than the two or three glasses of wine he wanted during dinner, and afterwards the mild fight at the dining table probably developed into a real battle against the whiskies and sodas in the billiard-room. It is not true hospitality to force it on your guests, and whenever I meet with an Officer who persists in trying to force me to take that which I neither require or desire, the opinion I form of him and of his Regiment is generally an adverse one. Make your Officers realise that in asking an Officer to dine and sending him away in a semi-drunken condition they are doing both their own Regiment and their guest a grave injury, the after effects of which are often at the moment not considered. No Regiment in which the Officers systematically conduct their Mess on these lines can ever be regarded as an efficient Regiment. Teach your Officers to receive strangers as they would receive them in their own homes, and this, I assure you, is all that we aim at in the Mess life of the British Army.

THE BEARING OF THE OFFICERS OF A REGIMENT TOWARDS EACH OTHER.

It is traditional of the old Regular Army that the Officers, when meeting each other in their own Mess, unbend, so to speak, and, with certain exceptions, treat each other more or less as equals. So it should be in the case of every Regiment to-day, and this address to you aims at effecting this. In my Regiment it is the custom for every Officer to address each other by their Christian or any nickname each may have, the only exception being the Commanding Officer, who, though applying the same principle to all his officers, is himself invariably addressed as " Sir " or " Colonel." Similarly the Second-in-Command is invariably addressed as " Sir " or " Major," but all other Majors are, so far as this point is concerned, addressed as Dick, Tom, or Harry, and the result of it all is we find in this the framework of a form of Mess life which suggests from the start the " happy family." Contrast this Mess with one in which the strictest formality is the order of the day; where the etiquette of the parade ground is carried right into the dining-room; where the Colonel is continually referring to his Officers as Mr. " So-and-So "; where it is nothing but Major " This " and Major " That "; where at dinner an Officer who wants perhaps the salt, says to his neighbour, " Mr. Jones, will you please pass the salt? " If you do contrast this Regiment with the other, I do not think that there is any doubt as to which is the most comfortable to live in, and when we are aiming to-day at keeping everybody merry and bright there is no doubt that every Commanding Officer should, and must, ensure that the Mess life of his Officers is conducted on the lines of the former rather than on those of the latter. But because I suggest to you the desirability of beating down all formality in the Mess, I do not for one moment suggest that the Senior Officers of a Regiment are not entitled to the respect their rank and years demand, and the younger Officers, when in the presence of their seniors, will do well not to assert themselves too much, either in their conversation or in their general attitude and bearing. For instance, it is not a good thing for the Junior Officers to possess themselves of all the comfortable chairs in a billet whilst their seniors stand, or to take possession of every paper in the Mess with their Commanding Officer standing by and waiting for something to read, or to take the only pack of cards and table available for a rubber of bridge, without asking, perhaps, the Second-in-Command or the Senior Officers present if they desire to play.

These are points of ordinary common politeness which will in good Regiments always be remembered, and which go hand in hand with the happy family type of Mess. My only other remark under this heading is the duty the Officers of a Mess (Regimental or Company) owe to each other in the matter of their personal cleanliness and appearance and behaviour in Mess. To sit down to table next to an Officer who has omitted to brush his hair, to wash—really wash—his hands, or, after the day's work, to change his clothes, is not pleasant, and does not make for harmony. I suggest to you that it is your duty, or the duty of your Second-in-Command, to see that your Officers comport themselves correctly in this respect, and I know that many of them will only do so provided you yourselves give them direction and friendly advice on the lines they should go. Again, to see an Officer who obviously does not know how to use his knife and fork, or what to do with his napkin if he has one, is not an inspiring spectacle, neither is this conducive to the good tone all of us desire to see throughout the Officers' Messes of our Imperial Army. Many Commanding Officers, however, permit these breaches of etiquette to go unchecked, and yet they are the first to cry out and bemoan the habits and general behaviour in Mess of the young Officer of to-day.

THE GENERAL STATE OF A MESS.

I do not think anyone will disagree with me when I say that to enter a room occupied as a Mess, and to find it in a very dirty and untidy state, depresses one at once and lowers the Moral. It is the old story of endeavouring to raise the tone of the working classes while condemning them at the same time to live in the worst surroundings and under the most adverse conditions. It cannot be done. To raise the tone of their conversation and their general standard of living, you must first of all get them to live under conditions more nearly approximating to our own conditions of life. So it is in the Army. If we would see a high standard of life and the best traditions of the Old British Army observed in this respect, we must first of all ensure that the Officers are living as gentlemen and in a manner befitting those who hold His Majesty's Commission. This will not be if you Commanding Officers permit your own Messes to be run on squalid lines and your young Officers to follow your example. Therefore I say to you, " See to the points that matter; see to it that your Mess appurtenances are sufficient in quantity, and of the right quality ; see to it that the tablecloths are clean, and that the knives, forks, spoons and plates are equally clean; do not permit your servants to lay a dirty and untidy table, or to appear themselves at your table in a dirty, unshaved, and untidy state; and, above all, see to it that your Mess-rooms in billets have at all times a bright and cheerful appearance." It makes such a difference to the temper, mood and Moral of the Officers of a Battalion when they are living in a well-appointed and well-kept Mess, as compared to when they are living in dirty, squalid and cheerless surroundings. Flowers are a great help. On me they have the same effect as music does; they raise my Moral, and all through my period of command in France, both in billets and in my headquarters in the front line, my Mess servants had orders to get flowers whenever possible for the Mess table. Remember that the example you set in your Headquarters Mess will be immediately imitated by your Company Commanders, and the Company Messes will be good or bad according to the standard set in the Headquarters Mess in this particular respect, and so I ask you to ensure that none of the points referred to under this heading are ever lost sight of.

THE MESS STAFF.

First and foremost comes the choice of a Mess President. I do not propose to lay down any hard and fast rule on this subject, because I have met Regiments in France in which the Mess President's duties have been filled, and filled well, by the Second-in-Command, the Padre, the Medical Officer, and the Transport Officer. All I do say is this : Whomever you do select, impress on him the importance you attach to the appointment, and make him realise that the successful and satisfactory performance of his duties will add much to the general happiness and comfort of the whole of your Officers, and very greatly assist them in the performance of their work. Make him realise this, and if at the same time you give him your ideas on what you consider should be the lines on which an Officers' Mess should be conducted, you will ensure success from the very commencement of his appointment. You will find that according to the importance which you attach to, and the interest you take in, the Mess President and his duties, so will you find your own Mess and the Company Messes conducted. Take an interest in him, and all will be well; disregard him, and nothing will go right.

Next to the Mess President comes the Mess Sergeant. This individual, who should be well chosen, is essential for the proper conduct of the Regimental Mess, and without him a Mess President will always find it difficult to carry on. I have known cases where the Mess President has endeavoured to carry on without one, and he has made good up to a certain point, but sooner or later the want of such an individual has been felt, and a good deal of inconvenience and discomfort caused in consequence. I therefore strongly urge you to keep this appointment and to select the most suitable man you have in your Battalion for the duties. If you yourself will take the same interest in him as you do in your Mess President, and will let him know and see the importance you attach to a correct standard of living, and to proper surroundings in an Officers' Mess, he will repeat your words to his staff, viz., the Cook, Kitchen Man, and Waiters, and all will strive with him to study your wishes, because they know what you think and feel regarding Messes generally and your own in particular. Above all, insist on the staff being adequate in numbers, and do not for a moment expect anything but dirt, discomfort, and general dissatisfaction if your Mess President, either because of economy of purse or men, attempts to run the Mess with an insufficient staff. A Mess Sergeant, a Cook, a Kitchen Man, and one good Waiter are absolutely essential in a Headquarters Mess, and do not let the number of your Mess staff go below this.

STANDARD OF LIVING.

Now let us discuss for a few moments what should be the proper standard of living in an Officers' Mess. There are a certain number of Officers who have their stomachs lined with the same material as the inside of the lady who was 60 cubits long and 30 cubits wide in Lieutenant-General Sir Henry Wilson's story,* viz., with tar and pitch, and no matter what you put in front of them they will pass it down and be perfectly satisfied with the situation. And as long as these officers themselves are perfectly satisfied with this fare, and confine their disregard of what goes into their stomachs to

---

* An amusing story told by Lieut.-General Sir H. H. Wilson, K.C.B., when addressing the Senior Officers on "Our Friends and Enemies in the War." August, 1917.

themselves, all is well. When, however, they presume to dictate to the rest of the Officers that their stomachs should be able to submit to the same hard usage as their own, and not only dictate but insist, then we at once find a most uncomfortable, unpleasant, and falsely economical Mess. By the expression "falsely economical," I mean that the Officer in question thinks that by ordering his Officers to live on their rations, and to put badly-cooked food into their stomachs, he is economising and making it simple and easy for his Officers to live. Well, he certainly is economising from the financial point of view, but in insisting on a standard of living that is well below that to which many of them are accustomed, he affects the health of some of his Officers, and because bad health leads to loss of Moral, he is really economising financially at the expense of Moral, and this is practising a very false economy. If our Officers are insufficiently fed and are living under depressing conditions, their health will certainly suffer, and with the loss of health comes irritation, loss of temper, and weak Moral, and when this state of things prevails we all know that the men frequently suffer. I have personally lived in many Messes, and have by design and on principle had many a meal in many other Messes (Army, Corps, Divisional, Brigade, Battalion, Battery, and Company), and I definitely state that in those Messes in which the Senior Officer has that peculiar stomach and those ideas of living, a general air of depression has been manifest throughout the meal. Listen to this:—Bully-Beef, Biscuit, Cheese, and Butter, washed down with Tea, as opposed to Soup, Saumon Mayonnaise, Filet de Bœuf aux Champignons, Pêche Melba, Sardines au Croût, washed down with Heidsiek (Triple sec), 1906, followed by a cup of Coffee, a glass of Old Brandy, and a "Bon Cigare." You can picture the two types of Messes, and you can almost scent the air of depression in the one, and hear the laughter in the other, with its Commanding Officer and his Officers all full of life and "bonnes histoires." Take my advice, gentlemen, and have nothing to do with the " Bully-Beef " set ! Live well yourselves and enjoy your food and make all your young Officers do likewise, and above all invite your General, not once, but frequently, to dinner, and see to it that you do him well. Should he be disposed to soda water rather than a glass of champagne, arrange that there is **by mere chance** nothing to drink except champagne ! When in close touch with big towns, like Amiens, Boulogne, Doullens, Ypres, etc., see that your Mess President does not forget the fact, and when out of touch then have a standing order with Fortnum and Mason, of Piccadilly, or other equally well-known firm of **" Moral-Raisers,"** to supply you with some of the good things that still come to these shores, in spite of the " Hun " and his " Hunnish " devices.

CONCLUSION.

I have nothing further to add, except this : I trust that I have not, in advocating a standard of living which may appear to some to be not quite in keeping with the times in which we are living, created the impression that I am of the opinion that unless an Officer is eating the richest of food and drinking champagne he cannot carry on his duties in a manner both satisfactory to himself and his Regiment. Nothing is further from my mind, and I hope that no Officer who reads this address will take that impression away with him. I am, however, desirous of drawing attention to the danger of Officers living in surroundings that are not in keeping with the surroundings of the Officer class of His Majesty's Army, and of accepting fare that is altogether different to that to which many of them have been accustomed, and I hope that I have succeeded. The Commanding Officer who, because his Regiment is on Active Service, thinks and lays down that everybody must live on his rations and in discomfort is a dangerous type, and although, I will admit, he is ignorant of the fact, still **he does an immense amount of harm to the Moral of his Regiment.**

The British Officer will live on anything—even down to acorns and black beetles—should the occasion demand it. But, gentlemen, the occasion has not yet called for such sacrifice on our part, and until it does I say live well, and in the Mess Regulations of your Regiment let the following formulæ occupy a very prominent position :—

Bully Beef Hard Biscuit Plum and Apple Jam Tea and Virginia Cigarettes	Produce (partaken in silence)	Stomach Ache. Indigestion Irritation of Mind. Depression. Pessimism and Weak Moral.

and

A BAD SHOW.

Whereas—

*Consômmé
Saumon Mayonnaise
Filet de Bœuf aux
   Champignons
Pêche Melba
Sardines au Croûte
Heidsick, 1906
A Glass of Old
   Brandy and
A Corona
	Produce
	(to the
	strains of the
	Battalion
	Orchestra)
		Contentment of
		   Mind.
		Peace with all Men
		   except the Hun.
		Bonnes Histoires.
		Mirth.
		Laughter.
		Optimism and
		   Strong Moral.

and

A GOOD SHOW.

---

*The above is a simple dinner that any Mess President should be able to produce for his officers, and it is a menu that I have enjoyed during the hardest times in France, both as a Battalion and as a Company Commander : what time my men were getting all that human power could get them, e.g., their rations, plenty of beer, a good Regimental Supper Bar, and every drop of RUM obtainable, and everyone—officers and men—were in good heart and merry and bright in consequence, even during the hardest days of the Second Battle of YPRES.

MESS RULES FOR THE SENIOR OFFICERS' SCHOOL AND INSTRUCTORS' SCHOOL, ALDERSHOT.

1. Committee.

A Committee will be formed in each Mess, consisting of three Dining Members, the Senior of whom will be President. One member to be responsible for the messing, wine, etc., the other for the ante-rooms.

2. Guest Nights.

(a) There will be one Guest Night every week. On this night the health of His Majesty the King will invariably be proposed and drunk.

(b) Should a band be playing, the Bandmaster will be invited to drink wine with the Officers.

3. Etiquette.

(a) The Senior Officer in Mess is responsible for the tone and behaviour of the Officers, and for the observance of all rules of the Mess.

(b) At Mess all Members are equal, at the same time Junior Officers must not forget the respect due to their seniors in rank, age, and service.

(c) All Officers present will stand up when a stranger enters the Mess.

(d) When the Senior Officer dining enters the ante-room he is to be addressed " Good-evening, Sir."

(e) No Officer will leave the Mess table at dinner—

    (i.) When a Mess guest is dining until the guest has left the table.

    (ii.) At any other time until the wine has passed round once.

If for urgent reasons a Member wishes to leave before the wine has passed, he must ask permission either from the President or the Vice-President.

(f) No letters or telegrams are to be opened at the table without first asking the permission of the President or Vice-President to do so.

(g) No member will start smoking before the wine has passed round once, nor will anyone smoke in the ante-rooms or halls half an hour before dinner.

(h) Between meal hours no drinks will be served anywhere except in the ante-rooms. Drinks are not allowed to be served in Officers' bedrooms.

(i) Standing of drinks by Members of the same Mess to each other is not in keeping with the traditions of the Mess life in the Army, and is strictly prohibited.

(j) Ladies' names will never be mentioned in Mess.

(k) A Member coming in late to Mess must invariably apologise to the President or to the Vice-President.

4. Cards.

Mess points will be 1/- a hundred.
Gambling is prohibited in Officers' bedrooms.

5. Dress.

Officers will change into trousers or other suitable kit after the day's work.

6. Papers.

The Mess Papers are to be folded up and replaced on the table, and not left lying about on the floor.

7. Complaints.

Any Officer who wishes to make a complaint must do so to the Mess President. On no account will any rebuke or complaint be made to any of the Mess servants.

8. Registered Letters and Parcels.

Registered letters and parcels will not be left about. The Mess President will make special arrangements for the issue of registered letters and parcels, and see that a receipt book is kept and duly signed

9. Closing of Mess.

The Mess will be closed at 11 p.m., except on recognised Guest Nights.

10. Daily Messing Book.

This book will be placed in the Mess every day, and members are responsible that their accounts are correct.

11. Mess Bills.

Mess bills must be paid by the 3rd of each month, and the final one settled before leaving the School.

NOTES ON THE ABOVE.

1. The Brigadier enters the various Messes so frequently that he does not wish Officers as he enters to stand up. If the Brigadier, when standing himself, addresses himself to an Officer who is sitting, that Officer should at once stand up.

2. With regard to 2 (*a*) and 2 (*b*) on p. 456—
   (*a*) The King's health will be proposed by the President, responded to by the Vice-President, and drunk standing by all Members present.
   (*b*) The toast will be delivered in the following manner :—
   The President, " Mr. Vice, the King."
   The Vice-President, " Gentlemen, the King."
   The band, if present, will play the National Anthem, and then
   The Dining Members, " The King, God bless him."

3. With regard to 3 (*c*): When speaking to the Officers with regard to Mess Etiquette, the Commandant wishes the Syndicate Commanders to emphasise the importance of Officers immediately rising if a stranger enters their Mess, and of Commanding Officers giving their younger Officers instruction in this point

when they first join their Regiments in France or elsewhere. (*N.B.*—The definition of a " stranger " is an Officer who is neither a Member nor an Honorary Member of the Mess.)

4. With regard to 5 (dress) : Syndicate Commanders will, when discussing Mess Etiquette with their Syndicates, emphasise the importance of Commanding Officers insisting on their Officers always, in France and elsewhere, changing their clothes for dinner, and of setting the best possible example in this respect themselves.

www.ingramcontent.com/pod-product-compliance
Lightning Source LLC
Chambersburg PA
CBHW070945160426
43193CB00012B/1809